# 1809: BETWEEN HOPE AND HISTORY

The Impetus to Reform
in the years between Pitt and Liverpool
1806 - 1812

# 1809: BETWEEN HOPE AND HISTORY

*The Impetus to Reform in the years between Pitt and Liverpool*
*1806 - 1812*

## Hugh Gault

**Gretton Books**

Cambridge

First published in 2009 by Gretton Books, Cambridge,
Cambridgeshire, England

A CIP catalogue record for this title is available from the British
Library.

ISBN
978-0-9562041-0-3

Set in 9/11 pt Arial

Printed and bound by MPG Books Group in the UK

# 1809: BETWEEN HOPE AND HISTORY

| CONTENTS | Page |
|---|---|

| CONTENTS | Page |
|---|---|

# FOREWORD

*"... people with long-term stakes don't always act wisely. Often they still prefer short-term goals, and often again they do things that are foolish in both the short term and the long term. That's what makes biography and history infinitely more complicated and less predictable ..."*

Jared Diamond, 2005

*"... it at least avoids the mistake of taking off or landing in 1815, a date which was of no more than military significance."*

Boyd Hilton, 2006

Change is not necessarily the same as improvement. Change simply means that the future is different to the past. Some change can represent a step backwards and progress is not necessarily linear and predictable. Diamond introduces the concept of "lurching" from one extreme to the other as people and generations reject what has gone before. Even if the goal is agreed, the best route for getting there may not be. Even if the means is accepted, there may well be diversions along the route as unforeseen obstacles are negotiated and individual interests overcome.

The psychologist Jean Piaget described development and growth for individuals in terms of the twin processes of assimilation and accommodation. Change for society results from the same forces. Ideally, society will find a common ground that feels like, and is, progress that lasts. Some people will embrace the unknown and take a chance on the future. Others prefer, and may cling to, the certainties of the past. Diagrammatically, this can be represented as

**revolution ⟶ reform ⟵ reaction**

where political change is concerned.

**Between hope and history** is another way of putting it.

1809 was a key transition year in the transformation of Britain from an eighteenth century society to the world that was apparent by the Reform Act of 1832. These changes were political, industrial and economic. In other words, they were primarily social - with collective action and co-operation growing, awareness expanding and consciousness embracing national as well as local levels.

I first had the idea for this book in 2006 with the 200th anniversary of 1809 fast approaching. (I was also curious that Darwin, Lincoln and Gladstone had all been born in 1809. There was obviously something about the year!) When I began to look in more detail in mid-2007, I was struck by several things:

- A lot did happen in 1809 and, while this was not necessarily more than in the surrounding years, the events were qualitatively more interesting and seemed more significant for the future.
- Despite this, of course, 1809 could best be understood, and needed to be placed and seen, in the context of the years around it.
- I knew relatively little about this period. The same was true of others with whom I checked. Most disconcertingly, history courses and examinations seemed to leap from Pitt to Liverpool as if the years 1806 to 1812 had never happened (other than in the Peninsular War).
- Spencer Perceval had become Prime Minister in 1809 and been assassinated in 1812. This is a unique event in this country, but he has been largely forgotten nevertheless - as have his contributions in this and other roles.
- I was encouraged by the view of historians such as Colley and Briggs, among others, that the fifty years after 1776 were critically significant to Britain's future. While the industrial revolution and the development of another empire were key parts of this, the years around 1809 were at the heart of it. This reinforced my belief that this was a crucial stage in the transition.
- I came across a number of publications in the 1970s that took a similar line. For example, AD Harvey had chosen to focus on the twelve years to 1812, but saw the events of 1809 as a seminal part of this change. John Cannon rightly said that the parliamentary session in 1809 was dominated by the issue of reform. A generation later these publications and their conclusions are rarely recalled. Different (perhaps improved) production values now don't reduce their importance or relevance. (And, without labouring the point, one can share Diamond's concern that each generation of historians rejects the conclusions of the preceding one. RF Foster says in 'The

Irish Story' that this is bound to be the case while historians require jobs.)

- Boyd Hilton says that "Back in the days when so many histories began or ended in 1815, there was widespread neglect of the previous fifteen years, as though they did not belong properly to either century." [2006, p707] This is correct, but these years are often relatively neglected as well in more recent histories that choose to start or finish on other dates.

All of these discoveries reinforced my initial view that I had stumbled across a story worth telling. Either that, or recent historians had discounted these years for good reason. In their view, the past could be recreated, and the future foretold, without them. I'm afraid I didn't believe this; and the more I looked into the period the less I accepted it.

Professional historians can tell the same story very differently. For example, Perceval's biographer Gray and Canning's biographer Hinde make diametrically opposed points in favour of their subject. Neither is necessarily incorrect, but perhaps inevitably they are displaying their prejudices (or perhaps simply their understanding). This is as obvious a point in history as it is in psychology or physics: events do not exist independently of how they are reported; the observer has an impact. But it did make me more certain there was a new story amongst the different presentations and perspectives.

I was also aware that historians could even disagree over dates. John O'Farrell makes a similar point in the introduction to his book 'An Utterly Impartial History of Britain or 2000 Years of Upper-class Idiots in Charge' (2007) and has got round it by the customary formulations of generalisation. This is fine for a humorist, but should raise questions in a historian.

To nobody's great surprise, least of all mine, I became increasingly concerned that the internet is riddled with errors. Because many websites have a veneer of authenticity and respectability, these errors are rapidly multiplied. Others are perpetuated. I determined early on that I would not use any website as a source unless verification also existed elsewhere. As the internet expands, it might become more useful to the researcher; as the errors increase, however, it becomes less so.

Christian Wolmar is just one of those who points out (in 'Fire and Steam', page 339) that books can contain errors too. The difference though is that the internet is much more pervasive for being widely available. The important thing in both cases is that information is not accepted uncritically, whatever its source, and that its veracity is challenged (or "triangulated" in the vernacular).

I hope this book corrects some of the grosser errors and does not add others. I have no illusions though that it can do more than scrape the surface. I recognise my good fortune in having access to an outstanding university library nearby. I have also benefited from the support, advice and guidance of others whose historical expertise and experience was considerably greater. They were generous with their time in helping a novice. They know who they are and I thank them. By maintaining their anonymity I can claim more than my share of the credit, but unfortunately the errors remain mine.

Finally, thanks to all those who made this possible.

For these and other reasons, I was determined to make sure the book saw the light of day.

Hugh Gault
Cambridge, March 2009

# INTRODUCTION

*"The [reform] flame of 1809 burned lower and lower ..."*

John Cannon, 1972

*"In fact, Britain was much nearer to revolution in 1809-1812 [than in 1780]."*

AD Harvey, 1978

*"... the government's view [was] that the radical leaders sought revolution rather than reform."*

Frank Prochaska, 2000

The events of 24th February and 14th December 1809 encapsulate the year.

On 24th February 1809 the House of Commons was engaged in an acrimonious debate on the disastrous course of the war in Spain. The ignominious retreat to Corunna had taken place a month earlier and General Sir John Moore (1761-1809)[1] had been killed as the defeated troops embarked for England. The leader of the opposition Whigs George Ponsonby (1755-1817) had opened the debate, calling for an inquiry into the "causes, consequences and events of the Spanish campaign"[2]. The government's competence to conduct the war was once again in question.

The leaders of the administration were much in evidence in the House of Commons that evening. In current parlance, they might be described as the "big beasts", but the word "leaders" is apt given that the nominal Prime Minister Portland was in the Lords and in any case was a figurehead. The Chancellor of the Exchequer Spencer Perceval had already spoken several times, most notably in relation to the Duke of York inquiry. Lord Castlereagh, the Secretary for War, was the first to respond to the Whig motion by denying the necessity for an inquiry. In his view the administration deserved the confidence of the House. Meanwhile, the Foreign Secretary George Canning could be seen biding his time. Not unusually, the House anticipated both his anger and "vehement

---

[1] Dates are included here when people are first mentioned unless they are also included in the chart of Key People on pages 18-19. In this case they appear frequently in the book in most cases and the chart incorporates their dates.
[2] *The Times*, Saturday 25th February 1809

1

bursts of eloquence"[3]. As was frequently the case, Canning gave way to several other speakers, allegedly because he wished to hear their views. When he did get up to speak, he accused Ponsonby of mis-representation: innuendo and rumour had been confused with facts. The commanders in Spain had decided how to proceed; they had not been coerced by the government at home. But French despotism could only be checked by British support for Spain. The administration of the war should not be taken out of the government's hands.

While Canning was speaking, the Theatre Royal, Drury Lane went up in flames. According to *The Times*, "The latter part of [Canning's] speech was occasionally interrupted by the eagerness of Members to look through the windows at the dreadful conflagration ..." The owner of the theatre, Richard Brinsley Sheridan (1751-1816), was also an MP and was on the Whig benches during the debate. Other Members offered to adjourn the sitting, but Sheridan refused, saying that "individual loss" was of little consequence beside the importance of the "business before the House".

Ponsonby's call for an inquiry into the war was eventually defeated and the House adjourned at almost four on the Saturday morning. By now Sheridan had gone to the Piazza coffee house close to the theatre in Covent Garden. As he watched its final destruction in the flames, he is famously said to have observed "A man may surely take a glass of wine by his own fireside"[4].

The other patent theatre[5] in London at the Theatre Royal, Covent Garden had been destroyed by fire the previous September. It was rapidly re-built and re-opened on 18th September 1809 with John Kemble (1757-1823) and Sarah Siddons (1755-1831) in 'Macbeth'. In the meantime, however, the number of boxes had been increased, as had the prices for the remaining seats - in part, perhaps, because the competition had disappeared. The audiences were incensed and, as the days went by, increasingly demonstrated

---

[3] Ibid
[4] Fintan O'Toole, 'A Traitor's Kiss: The Life of Richard Brinsley Sheridan, 1751-1816', New York, Farrar, Strauss & Giroux, 1998, p434
[5] There were other theatres in London - for example, the Lyceum, Royalty, Her Majesty's, Sans Pareil, Olympic - but these were the only two licensed for "legitimate drama" in the capital.

their anger by drowning out the play and behaving in whatever ways might most obviously disrupt it. The actor-manager Kemble was eventually forced to accede to their demands and reduce prices. The "Old Price riots", as they are known, came to an end after a meeting on the 14th December at the Crown and Anchor tavern.

These events at the end of the year were significant in a number of respects. Notably the riots were effective. As far as the public were concerned, increased prices would reduce their opportunity to attend the theatre. Kemble might be trying to make more money rather than necessarily take Covent Garden up-market, but they were being denied access. This struck at what they considered their entitlement and they refused to be excluded in this way. Nor were they to be diverted from this course by the most famous actress of the day in the part she had made her own. In this regard, their determination and sense of purpose is worth noting.

Additionally, the Crown and Anchor tavern itself was to host many prominent meetings. Often these were of a radical nature, such as on the 1st May 1809 (a significant date) when Francis Burdett and others called for parliamentary reform. It was one of the most substantial venues in central London, capable of hosting a large and agitated crowd.

Less obviously, though, it was significant that only two theatres were licensed for serious drama. The other theatres offered more down-market fare and this was thought more than adequate for most people; the mob were expected to be happy with it. This reflected an era of privilege and control - throughout society as well as in the theatre, where patent rights holders such as Sheridan (a radical on many other issues) protected their position. But this monopoly could not last. Theatre managers were increasingly interested in making money and popular expectations were changing. As Roy says, the "struggle to free the stage in London intensified in the period after 1808"[6], sparked in part by the fires.

And, finally, theatres are about performance, about acts. That several should go up in flames in a short space of time might be

---

[6] See Donald Roy (ed.), 'Romantic and Revolutionary Theatre, 1789-1860', Cambridge, Cambridge University Press, 2003, p5

due to their timber construction, but it might also symbolise a world where the existing appearance was to be overtaken by a new reality. It was to prove an inflammatory year.

## The Approach

Any attempt to divide up history must of necessity be artificial, artful and, as Asa Briggs said, "arbitrary". For the purposes of analysis and explanation, however, breaking the flow to focus on a particular period is inevitable. In this sense 1809 is no more arbitrary or artificial a choice than any other. And ultimately 1809, and the years surrounding it, have been chosen for particular and positive reasons. This is a period characterised by major changes in Britain. These were political, economic, social and military in nature. The changes were in response to opportunities and challenges that came both from inside and outside the country. Often they were generated by wars and the other upheavals of this time. These included revolutions in France and America, rebellion in Ireland, the rise of Napoleon and war with France. Instability in Britain reflected and added to this explosive mixture.

Compared to some other dates in British history, 1809 might appear an in-between year at first sight. But it turned out to be in-between rather a lot and, in many ways, it became a turning-point in its own right. In this respect it is appropriate to say that 1809 was **between hope and history**. It proved to be both significant and eventful, and to have an impact on the future.

Claims have been made both for individual years, as well as for periods in history, as points when the world changed for Britain and its people. 1688 is an obvious example of the former, while Frank McLynn sees 1759 as the starting-point for empire and Edward Pearce would no doubt vote for 1832 and the Reform Act. Roy Porter sets out his stall for the late 18th century as a period characterised by ferment and change. Many historians have written similarly of the Victorian era and the Industrial Revolution. All periods have played their parts of course. The key questions as far as 1809 is concerned are "did the world change enough?" and "did later changes depend on what happened then?" This book demonstrates that the answer to both questions is affirmative.

4

According to Thomas Carlyle, the world is always changing.[7] As Harold Macmillan said, it is unforeseen events that can throw political objectives off course. 1809 was full of such unanticipated events. Recognising that change was an inevitable and recurrent feature, a search for stability came to be replaced thereafter by a preference for predictability, for evolution rather than revolution. 1809 was a key part of the route to a realistic approach to the future. It was based on direct knowledge and experience of the alternatives and their consequences.

Many authors have referred to Britain's revolution being economic and industrial rather than political. It appeared more gradual than elsewhere and, to some observers in the late eighteenth and early nineteenth centuries, may not have looked "revolutionary" at all. The period covered in this book included many of those changes; the conditions for others were set then.

Consequently, the arguments pursued in the following Chapters include:
- Changing expectations as the search for stability was replaced by a recognition that change and uncertainty were here to stay.
- Preference for predictability and continuity through evolution; for reform rather than revolution.
- An industrial rather than political revolution. The yardstick for progress was social and economic development rather than liberty or a thirst for equality.

In addition, the book sets out to demonstrate that political growth proved feasible largely because of the unstable tenor of the times, an instability compounded by war, and that, while people had drawn some lessons from the past, they were still in the process of adapting to the future.

It poses two fundamental questions:
- Did people in Britain swap the aspiration for liberty with an acceptance of gradual social reform?
- Why did British disorder and riots not become French or Irish rebellions?

---

[7] "All things are in revolution; in change from moment to moment ..." in 'The French Revolution', 1837. Richard L Stein includes a longer version of this quotation in his frontispiece to 'Victoria's Year: English Literature and Culture 1837-1838', Oxford, Oxford University Press, 1987.

Various contemporary illustrations are included in the text - particularly the drawings of James Gillray (1756-1815). Gillray[8] was the foremost political cartoonist and caricaturist of the day - certainly up to 1809 before others became more popular as his abilities and health declined. He was well-known for lampooning many of the key people who feature in the book, and for satirising Britain's relationship with other countries, France and Ireland in particular.

This introduction, like the book[9] as a whole, approaches the year in the context of its time, and with a view to the consequences for later years. It identifies and concentrates on those events in 1809 that show it to be a key transition year within a larger transformation of society. These events encompass political, social, economic and military developments.

**The Context Before 1809**

The opening Chapter addresses the international context in the immediate run-up to 1809. It tackles the political and geographical implications of Britain between the French empire and a neutral America, and the military defences and economic initiatives with which Britain protected itself. Other parts of Europe were still accommodating themselves to Napoleon's intentions, while Bolivar and South America began to campaign against what they saw as his betrayal. Given that invasion was out of the question after Trafalgar, Napoleon was waging economic warfare against Britain (with cash payments having been suspended since Pitt's Restriction Act of 1797).

---

[8] The National Portrait Gallery website includes almost 900 examples of Gillray's work. (See
http://www.npg.org.uk/live/search/person.asp?LinkID=mp01777&role=art )
However, it is rare for it to be on display. Some can be seen in recent books by Kenneth Baker on George III (2007) and in the British Museum's 'Caricatures of the People of the British Isles' (edited by Tim Clayton, 2007), as well as in Vic Gatrell, 'City of Laughter: Sex and Satire in Eighteenth-Century London', London, Atlantic Books, 2006.
[9] In keeping with current use and convention, the term Prime Minister is generally used rather than First Minister, even though this or First Lord of the Treasury might have been the term by which the leader of a government was known at the time. Similarly, each person is referred to by the name by which they are now usually recognised (e.g., Wellington rather than Wellesley), even though this may represent an honorific that came later in their career than the period referred to.

The thirty years between 1776 and 1806 saw the granting of American independence, the French revolution, an uprising in Ireland and the emergence of Napoleon. Chapter 1 considers the implications. While William Pitt (1759-1806) provided Britain with stability and leadership, there was otherwise uncertainty that revolutionary change might take place there as well. The subsequent impact was to ensure an increasing search for stability, and a preference for change to evolve gradually.

Chapter 2 focusses on the domestic context in the three years up to 1809. It opens with Grenville's so-called 'Ministry of All the Talents' and its replacement a year later by the Duke of Portland's administration. The former included Fox (1749-1806), hence its name, but excluded several former Pitt supporters. They returned to government with Portland. Portland fought the 1807 election on a platform of 'no popery' to distinguish his stance from that of his immediate predecessors, including Pitt. Canning was influential in the Portland "government" both at home and abroad, not least as the abhorrent implications of the Convention of Cintra became clear. Meanwhile, Wellington and Castlereagh formed a strategy for the number of troops that would be required in Portugal.

**Key Events in 1809**

On Monday 2$^{nd}$ January 1809 'Romeo and Juliet' was followed by Sheridan's 'Robinson Crusoe' at the Theatre Royal, Drury Lane. On the Tuesday 'Robinson Crusoe' was preceded by a performance of the 'School for Scandal'. These plays could be said to sum up the year to come: duels and scandals, misunderstandings, unforeseen consequences, the perils of isolation, and – eventually – new, and possibly better, times ahead.

On 22$^{nd}$ December 1808 (according to the *Edinburgh Annual Register*, though it was not reported in *The Times* for another week), the Board of Inquiry set out its conclusions on the temporary armistice in the Peninsular War and the terms that had been agreed under the Convention of Cintra following the battle of Vimeiro. The Convention had caused such a furore that it had been widely disbelieved the preceding September. While the armistice was supported, the Board's views of the terms were mixed, with three out of the seven members indicating that they were against them. This was the second version of the report, George III having been

7

dissatisfied with the lack of clarity in the first, and although no further military proceedings followed, the two senior generals involved in the negotiations were never deployed on active service again. The third general, Wellington, or Wellesley as he then was, was left unscathed. The national mood of despair and disbelief three months earlier had been justified by the inquiry outcomes. The date on which the report was delivered, its effect on the future of the Peninsular War and its impact on the careers of Wellington and Napoleon, as well as those of Canning and Castlereagh, signalled a break with the past. Few people will have read about the report at the time[10], or necessarily realised its significance, but its conclusions and date of release remain symbolically important.

Not surprisingly, dispatches from Spain accounted for one page out of four in *The Times* at this point. The paper was also concerned with the embargo by which America was trying to maintain its neutrality. Britain was clearly on a war footing, though this was not total war and it had positive connotations for the country as well as negative ones.

Chapters 3 to 6 focus on 1809. They open with an analysis of the country's demography and what people were doing as the effects of the first industrial revolution began to be felt. Some of the key events of the year are considered below under the five categories of:
- political growth and development
- political instability
- military change
- economic pressures
- social change and social trends.

**Political growth and development**

The House of Commons conducted a number of corruption inquiries and examinations in 1809 that were to have long-lasting effects. These concerned both individuals and the organisation and reform of parliament itself. They are primarily covered in Chapters 5 and 6.

---

[10] Although the circulation of *The Times* reached 50,000 by the 1850s, it was restricted to about 5,000 copies at this stage. Even allowing for multiple readership of each copy, perhaps 50,000 people, or 0.4% of the country's population of 12m, mostly in London, will have seen the report of the inquiry in *The Times*.

The most prominent inquiry directed at an individual was that involving the Duke of York as army commander in chief. The inquiry focussed on the sale of army commissions by one of his mistresses. Even if Mrs Clarke (1776-1852) did not get the information from the Duke of York, it was clear that she had taken money and knew more than might be expected of army business. The House of Commons acquitted the Duke of York of corruption, despite evidence that he had known of the corruption even if he was not directly involved in it. He resigned as commander in chief anyway, and was not re-instated to this post until May 1811 as a result of pressure from his brother the Prince Regent. This inquiry encouraged radicals such as Cobbett and Burdett to press harder for political and economic reform. They felt they had no option as people's views hardened about the impact on their lives of corrupt behaviour by the aristocracy. Cobbett described it as robbery in the *Political Register*.

Equally significant to the overall reform of parliament were other measures, such as the committee of inquiry that found 76 members of parliament being paid for holding grace and favour offices. These sinecures, as they were known, eventually came to an end – but not immediately. The Finance Committee, with Henry Bankes (1757-1834) as Chair, reported several times, while MPs such as Henry Martin (1763-1839) moved for their abolition.

1809 also saw the Curwen Bribery Act that aimed to prevent the sale of parliamentary seats. The importance of this in the long-term to the House of Commons is illustrated by Edward Pearce referring to it as the "1809 Reform Act". It was a significant step on the path to reform - even if the Bill was emasculated in Committee. The eventual impact of this and other measures was to substantially enhance the credibility and accountability of members of parliament as the political appetite for change increased.

**Political instability**

Alongside this growth and development, however, 1809 was also characterised by political instability. For example, Canning had blamed Castlereagh for allowing a defeated French army to be repatriated under the terms of the Convention of Cintra. That their enmity increased in 1809 was perhaps inevitable given that Britain was at war and both were responsible for progress – Canning as

Foreign Secretary, Castlereagh at the War Office. Events in 1809 led Canning to seek Castlereagh's replacement in the government. However, Castlereagh was not informed of this by Portland or anyone else as intended. When he found out, it looked like Canning had been seeking to remove him in an underhand way. He challenged Canning to a duel, and Canning was slightly injured. Both resigned from the government.

The Duke of Portland had become Prime Minister in March 1807. He was already nearly 70 and in poor health. He provided little leadership and other members of the government operated their departments as they saw fit. Portland resigned in September, worn down by the challenges of government, and was replaced by Spencer Perceval in early October 1809. Perceval had been Chancellor of the Exchequer previously, and with Canning and Castlereagh out of the running, was one of the prime candidates for Prime Minister. However, his unassuming and self-deprecating manner was such that he only got the post because George III saw him as straightforward and reliable. (There is some suggestion too that the King's initial approaches had been turned down by Charles Grey (1764-1845) and William Wyndham Grenville (1759-1834), the leaders of the Whig faction, who had misunderstood their nature. That George III approached the Whigs at all shows his desperation.) Perceval's government did not start promisingly and was viewed as mediocre. It improved.

Catholic emancipation was the key issue alongside reform. It was to prove even more resistant to change - especially in Ireland. In the ten years before 1809 it had been an overt issue. This included, for example, the Irish rebellion led by Wolfe Tone (1763-1798) in 1798, Pitt's Act of Union between Britain and Ireland in 1800, Robert Emmet's attempted uprising in 1803, George III's dismissal of Grenville in 1806 over army commissions for Catholics and Portland's subsequent general election slogan in 1807 of 'no popery'.

Even in 1809 the significance of the issue continued to rumble on. Daniel O'Connell was beginning to lead on Catholic emancipation. Like Portland, Spencer Perceval was against it. Wellington was the Chief Secretary for Ireland before he resigned as an MP to return to

Portugal in April 1809[11]. Robert Peel's father bought him into the House of Commons for the first time, representing Cashel in Tipperary[12]. (Three years later he was Chief Secretary for Ireland. His continuing opposition to Catholic emancipation led O'Connell to call him "Orange Peel".) The influential 'Impartial History of Ireland' by Dennis Taaffe was published. This argued against the 1800 Act of Union and Pitt's "insidious" policy against Ireland.[13]

Such was the importance of these two issues that the following matrix provides one way of distinguishing people's affiliations and those of the main factions in 1809 (though not necessarily parties).

|  |  | Political reform | |
|  |  | For | Against |
| **Catholic emancipation** | For | Cobbett, Burdett All radicals and most Whigs | Canning and other moderate Tories Individuals such as Windham |
|  | Against | Southey → | Perceval |

This ignores of course the complexities of economic reform[14] (which Robert Southey continued to champion throughout his life, whereas he became disillusioned with political reform). It also ignores people such as Liverpool whose philosophy was to "wait and see", or *laissez-faire*[15], and who opposed general systems as a matter of

[11] Curiously, given his conservative outlook, the Catholic Emancipation Act was finally passed in 1829 when Wellington was Prime Minister. This permitted Catholics to sit in parliament and recognised virtually full civil rights for catholic citizens in Britain. Another Catholic Relief Act was passed the same year.
[12] Replacing Quintin Dick who had resigned rather than vote with the government in the Duke of York affair. Madocks believed Dick had been forced to take this action and, as a result, accused Castlereagh of corruption and Perceval of colluding with it. Peel's purchase of Cashel took place before the Curwen Bribery Act seeking to outlaw the sale of seats.
[13] Dennis Taaffe, 'Impartial History of Ireland', Dublin, J Christie, 1809, p491
[14] It has been suggested that Catholic emancipation should be included in the political polarity, allowing the other axis of the matrix to distinguish economic perspectives.
[15] In other words, as little intervention and interference as possible, whether this is minimum government intervention in the economic and political affairs of individuals and society (its usual meaning) or the hands-off management Liverpool was to practise as Prime Minister, where competent people were allowed to tackle

course, only responding to each case when there was no other option.

## Military change

1808 had closed with the Board of Inquiry reporting into apparent military humiliation at Cintra.  1809 ended with reports on other military debacles, not least Britain's belated attempt to support Austria through the Walcheren adventure.  This had provided some of the backdrop and much of the unfortunate colour to the second half of the year from July.  On 29th December 1809 *The Times* confirmed that Holland had been incorporated into the French empire.  It also reported briefly on the return that week of the final men and transports from Walcheren.  This is described in Chapter 5.  The enemy had not attempted to intervene when the final evacuation ships sailed.  A letter in *The Times* on 30th December referred to the "losses and disgrace" of Walcheren, and the "injuries" suffered by the country as a result.  It expressed surprise that no inquiry was to be held and said this was because Ministers had misled George III.  The government eventually, and reluctantly, agreed to an inquiry.

Wellington had proved more successful in the Peninsular War since his arrival in Lisbon in April 1809, with victories at Oporto in May and Talavera in July, the last fighting Wellington's army saw that year.  The latter in particular was thought to avenge Corunna.  British morale improved and Spain now had evidence that Britain would support them.  Although Wellington had seen Castlereagh replaced by Liverpool, his views continued to be sought and acted on.  This ministerial support was important to overall success in the war in the long-term, and ensured that Liverpool soon secured the trust and confidence that Wellington had previously placed in Castlereagh.

---

issues as they saw fit.  In due course *laissez-faire* was to acquire a specific meaning in relation to free trade and protectionism, but, even for social market liberals in 1847, there could be different administrative and social connotations, and sometimes apparently anomalous consequences.  See Boyd Hilton, 'A Mad, Bad and Dangerous People?: England 1783-1846', Oxford, Clarendon Press, 2006, pp590-591.

## Economic pressures

Like most wars, the Napoleonic wars were no different in being a mixture of boom and bust. The early years of the war encouraged increased production and consumption, only for demand to reduce when it could not be satisfied or confidence was eroded. 1809 proved to be on the cusp between the boom years before and the relative decline subsequently. But this decline was "relative". The overall wealth of Britain was increasing. It did so more rapidly once the full effects of the Industrial Revolution began to be felt and expenditure on the war reduced. The economic impact along the way included inflation and wage reductions for those groups whose skills were no longer in demand.

Grenville had responded to the Napoleonic blockade by introducing "Orders in Council". These sought to block all French and enemy ports and give Britain control of all neutral trade. They were tightened by the subsequent government. In effect, both sides were waging economic warfare on the other. By 1809 this was having an adverse impact on the trade and national debt of both Britain and France (see Chapter 6). Britain allowed some merchants to evade the Orders by issuing licences, while Napoleon changed the Continental System by permitting the exchange of goods so long as French exports exceeded imports. In 1809 Jefferson prevented both British and French ships using American harbours by introducing the Non-Intercourse Act. All sides continued to suffer.

One of the most prominent economists of the time, David Ricardo, criticised the rising costs of the war and the inflationary policy of the government. On 30th December 1809 he published 'The high price of bullion, a proof of the depreciation of bank notes'. Ricardo's criticisms were supported by a House of Commons committee report two years later. He was subsequently to tangle with the government over the Corn Laws. There was a loss of trade in 1809, presaging the imminent trade crisis that was to follow. Napoleon tried, but failed, to exploit this weakness. Matters improved for Britain inadvertently when the government took out more loans.

Chapter 4 refers to these issues, while Chapters 6 and 7 cover them in more detail.

## Social change and social trends

1809 saw the continuation of social trends that had begun earlier. They included aspects of life as disparate as enclosures, riots and reducing journey times as roads improved. These trends were apparent at the time, as was the development of canals. Others were not so obvious until some time later, such as the growth in the professions, increasing urbanisation and the growing gap between rich and poor. Jeremy Bentham was writing on parliamentary reform, while Francis Burdett was advocating it in parliament. Both received negligible support at this stage. In several ways their arguments harked back to those made by John Wilkes and others thirty years before.

Some social change was initiated in 1809. This included the introduction of the *Quarterly Review* to counter the Whig influence of the *Edinburgh Review* founded seven years earlier. Walter Scott, George Canning (after he had left the government) and Robert Southey were among those actively involved, as was John Murray as publisher and William Gifford as editor. This gave the Tory government a political platform for their views and provided support for the war, particularly in Spain. This was welcomed in January 1810 when Perceval's administration was severely criticised again.

Robert Owen improved living conditions at New Lanark in 1809. He was of the view that cooperation was preferable to competition, and that education and environment were critical to future potential. Unusually for his time, he also took the view that employers would benefit from improving the welfare of their employees. Chapter 7 assesses his contributions more fully, particularly in subsequent years to the trade union movement and cooperative societies, and to the development of socialism.

George III started his fiftieth year as monarch in 1809. The royal jubilee took place on Wednesday 25th October. *The Times* reported the following day on the celebrations in London. These included church services in the morning and illumination of all public buildings from early afternoon. According to *The Times*, the jubilee "was celebrated by all ranks of people ... in a manner worthy of an aged and venerable King, and a loyal and enlightened nation". *The Times* said that people's good wishes for the King on his jubilee had only been matched by their delight when he had previously recovered his health. However, this soon deteriorated again, with his last public appearance a year later on his fiftieth anniversary as King. The Regency was re-activated from December 1810, initially for twelve months on a limited basis, when Perceval re-introduced Pitt's Regency Bill.

Jane Austen, Walter Scott (at this stage as a poet) and William Blake were among those active in 1809. (For example, Jane Austen was then revising 'Pride and Prejudice' and 'Sense and Sensibility' at Chawton for later publication.) While Jane Austen is often described as an anti-Romantic along with George Crabbe, many of their contemporaries, including exponents in other arts such as painting, and other writers and poets, notably Byron and Wordsworth, were to become identified collectively as the Romantic Movement. The name itself suggests that 1809 was a critical part of the transition **from history to hope**.

**The Context After 1809**

The final Chapter considers some of the major changes after 1809, which in many cases were set in motion by the events that took place in that year. The opening section focusses on the three years to 1812. The main developments include in 1810 riots over Burdett's imprisonment and the start of the Regency, the trade crisis in 1811 and the peak of the Luddite riots in 1812. The Prince Regent did not replace Perceval as expected, but indicated his confidence in him by maintaining him as Prime Minister in preference to the Whigs. The remaining years of Perceval's administration are considered, as is his assassination and the consequences of Liverpool becoming Prime Minister.

The Chapter then looks at the changes initiated by Robert Owen. These start with the developments at New Lanark referred to in Chapter 4 and others such as 'A New View of Society'. Although the initiatives were sometimes short-lived at the time, a number of the plans instigated by Robert Owen have often shown themselves to have benefits for people in the longer term. Overall, they have made a significant difference to the quality of life. It is argued that this makes his example "a case in point".

The final section looks at the period after 1812. It addresses the impact of the stable Liverpool government and the removal of the threat from France. Changing expectations and the mismatch with experience saw the Luddite riots continue to 1817 and the Peterloo massacre take place in 1819. George IV became monarch in his own right in 1820. Poor Law, education and social change is addressed, and reform after 1820 and before 1832 is referred to.

## Conclusion

Until very recently (perhaps the 1950s), most people in Britain have had to concentrate on getting themselves and their families from one day to the next. In many parts of the world they still do. Most people in this country were no different in 1809, and many were beset with real concerns. They may have had broader aspirations, but they rarely had the opportunity to exercise them. For those people able to think beyond their daily existence there were hopes of a better future for themselves and their families, but even they were aware of the consequences of history. Their optimism was tempered by recent revolutions in America and France, by war in Ireland, by continuing concerns over Napoleon's intentions, and by growing upheaval at home as the Industrial Revolution took hold. Their expectations had changed, but would they be fulfilled?

It is a period that still challenges us today. This book takes up those challenges, identifying the most significant events and people, and seeking to explain the implications. It aims to draw conclusions from these. It takes the view that, while people had drawn some lessons from the past, they were still adapting, and learning to adapt, to the future.

Virginia Rounding quotes Robert Southey's conclusion some years later that "Britain was poised in the first decades of the 19th century between the old and the new. As the country recovered from war and fear of revolution, there was an optimism in the air, fostered by unprecedented material prosperity (for some) and a firm belief in scientific and intellectual progress."[16]

But this point had first to be reached. 1809 was one of the key years in that journey.

---

[16] Virginia Rounding review of Ben Wilson's 'Decency and Disorder' in *The Guardian*, June 2007

# SOME KEY PEOPLE IN 1809

1740 1745 1750 1755 1760 1765 1770 1775 1780 1785 1790 1795 1800 1805 1810 1815 1820 1825 1830 1835 1840 1845 1850 1855 1860 1865

**Monarchs**
George III (1738 – 1820) ----------------------------------→
George IV (1762 – 1830) -------------------------------→

**Politicians**
Francis Burdett (1770-1844) ------------------------------→
George Canning (1770 – 1827) ------------------→
Viscount Castlereagh (1769 – 1822) ---------------→
Earl of Liverpool (1770 – 1828) ------------------→
Daniel O'Connell (1775 – 1847) ------------------------------→
Spencer Perceval (1762 – 1812) -------→
Duke of Portland (1738 – 1809) →
Viscount Sidmouth (1757 – 1844) ---------------------------→
Thomas Jefferson (1743 – 1826) -------------------------→
Simon Bolivar (1783 – 1830) -------------------------→

**Soldiers**
Frederick, Duke of York (1763 – 1827) ------------------→
Wellington (1769 – 1852) --------------------------------→
Napoleon (1769 – 1821) ------------------→

**Economists**
Robert Malthus (1766 – 1834) ------------------→
David Ricardo (1772 – 1823) ---------------→

**Industrialists**
Matthew Boulton (1728 – 1809) -----------------------→
Robert Owen (1771 – 1858) --------------------------------→

1740 1745 1750 1755 1760 1765 1770 1775 1780 1785 1790 1795 1800 1805 1810 1815 1820 1825 1830 1835 1840 1845 1850 1855 1860 1865

| 1740 | 1745 | 1750 | 1755 | 1760 | 1765 | 1770 | 1775 | 1780 | 1785 | 1790 | 1795 | 1800 | 1805 | 1810 | 1815 | 1820 | 1825 | 1830 | 1835 | 1840 | 1845 | 1850 | 1855 | 1860 | 1865 |
|---|---|---|---|---|---|---|---|---|---|---|---|---|---|---|---|---|---|---|---|---|---|---|---|---|---|

**Journalists/Essayists**

William Cobbett (1763 – 1835) →

William Hazlitt (1778 – 1830) →

Charles Lamb (1775 – 1834) →

**Philosophers**

Jeremy Bentham (1748 – 1832) →

James Mill (1773 – 1836) →

Tom Paine (1737 – 1809) →

**Writers**

Jane Austen (1775 – 1817) →

Maria Edgeworth (1768 - 1849) →

Walter Scott (1771 – 1832) →

**Poets**

William Blake (1757 – 1827) →

George Byron (1788 – 1824) →

Samuel Taylor Coleridge (1772 – 1834) →

George Crabbe (1754 – 1832) →

Shelley (1792 – 1822) →

Robert Southey (1774 – 1843) →

William Wordsworth (1770 – 1850) →

**Artists**

John Constable (1776 – 1837) →

JMW Turner (1775 – 1851) →

**Architects/Engineers**

John Nash (1752 – 1835) →

John Soane (1753 – 1837) →

Thomas Telford (1757 – 1834) →

| 1740 | 1745 | 1750 | 1755 | 1760 | 1765 | 1770 | 1775 | 1780 | 1785 | 1790 | 1795 | 1800 | 1805 | 1810 | 1815 | 1820 | 1825 | 1830 | 1835 | 1840 | 1845 | 1850 | 1855 | 1860 | 1865 |
|---|---|---|---|---|---|---|---|---|---|---|---|---|---|---|---|---|---|---|---|---|---|---|---|---|---|

# 1. FROM LEFT AND RIGHT: BRITAIN AND ITS INTERNATIONAL POSITION

'From left and right' refers to the political, as well as geographical, implications for Britain at the start of the nineteenth century between the very different republics of France and America. The first was overtly hostile in every sense (not just militarily), while the ex-colonies were keen to demonstrate their independence. Britain faced both. This Chapter concentrates on the international run-up to 1809 and, although looking outwards, is nevertheless concerned with the military and economic steps that were taken to safeguard Britain from invasion and ensure its people could remain productive and continue to trade. By contrast, Chapter 2 focusses on the domestic situation and internal developments.

It was not unusual for Britain and France to be at war. This had happened often over the years and was unsurprising given their proximity, as well as their frequent clash of interests. This clash was both in the sense that their interests were often opposed, and sometimes that they chose conflict in order to exert influence and shape outcomes to their purposes. France represented a mainland and catholic Europe, while Britain had an island's interests in independence and was protestant. It had invited in Dutch and Hanoverian protestant monarchies to ensure this position was maintained, and regularised the exclusion of Catholics through the Act of Settlement in 1701. Britain's pre-eminence at sea after Pepys had developed the navy was countered by France's predominance on land through its army. Each provided the other with the nearest and most readily available opportunity to replace any concern over internal disorder by a focus on the external enemy. In other words, they could be relied on to provide an out-group almost immediately. Nationalism would increase while the anxiety and wrangling over internal difficulties correspondingly decreased. To this extent they were dependent on each other. In the eighteenth century alone they were at war for 42 years in total.[17]

---

[17] For example, Linda Colley in 'Britons – Forging the Nation 1707-1837', Yale, Yale University Press, 1992, pp1-4 identifies these years as 1702-1713 (War of Spanish Succession), 1743-1748 (War of Austrian Succession), 1756-1763 (Seven Years War), 1778-1783 (American War of Independence) and 1793-1802 (French Revolutionary War). These are the years in which France was at war with Britain, not necessarily the years of the wars themselves.

What was different at the end of this century was that France had become a republic and Britain had lost its first empire in America partly because of France. Britain was still coming to terms with the commercial impact at the start of the nineteenth century as it tried to open up new markets. Although Colley says that the American market remained dependent on British manufactured goods long after 1776[18], the writing was already on the wall. Continental Europe was inevitably much more difficult as well.

## The Legacy of Previous Political Generations

'Quixote and Sancho, or the Harlequin Warrior' was the pantomime at the Olympic Pavilion at the start of 1809. The story of Don Quixote provides an appropriate introduction, though not a parallel, to the thirty years from 1776 to 1807. In part because of his romantic and chivalrous nature, Quixote kept picking battles with imaginary foes; battles that, inevitably, he could never win. He depended on the loyalty and bravery of his squire Sancho Panza to extricate him from these situations.

In this thirty year period, Britain fought a war over American independence, the French revolution erupted, its success encouraged Irish Catholics[19] to seize the moment, rebelling against their protestant British rulers (most notably in 1798, but also in 1803) and Napoleon emerged as first consul in France before the end of the century. The American colonists, the French revolutionaries and the Irish Catholics were motivated by idealism, like Quixote, as well as by deep-seated and widely-felt grievances. Their foes were real enough (in contrast to the imaginary ones of Quixote), but the outcomes appear inevitable with the benefit of hindsight. There was little hope of victory for the vanquished at any point.[20]

---

[18] Ibid, p70

[19] Strictly speaking, the rebellion was to involve other radicals, such as Presbyterians, who were not catholic.

[20] A caricature 'The Knight of the Woeful Countenance Going to Extirpate the National Assembly' was published by William Holland in 1790. It shows Edmund Burke as Quixote, mounted on a donkey and holding the "shield of aristocracy and despotism". It is included as Plate 86 in M Dorothy George, 'English Political Caricature to 1792', Oxford, Clarendon Press, 1959. Her second volume covers the period 1793 to 1832.

This lack of stability abroad was also evident at home. Governments could frequently be distinguished by their position on press and democratic rights for their citizens (which often meant their attitude to John Wilkes), and by how well they matched the views of George III. The latter usually determined their longevity.

## America

Frederick North (1732-1792) had become Prime Minister in January 1770 after George III's entreaties overcame his initial reluctance. North's predecessor, the Duke of Grafton, had been brought down by the campaign in support of John Wilkes who had been expelled from parliament despite his continued election and re-election as MP for Middlesex. Wilkes' treatment by the government over several years invigorated many of his fellow countrymen to action, most notably in the national petitions organised on his behalf by the Bill of Rights Society in 1769. It was ironic that North should become Prime Minister as a result, given that he had first risen to prominence for his prosecution of Wilkes for libel in the earlier North Briton case.

As Prime Minister, North had first to survive the ensuing debate on the Middlesex election and a vote of confidence. He then saw off an opposition challenge over government corruption. The immediate crisis had been averted by Easter 1770, but it was soon replaced by the dispute with America.[21] North was not responsible for the conduct of the war, but he is irrevocably associated with it. Recent views are that the geographical and logistical problems would have proved too much in any case, especially after France

---

[21] Ostensibly, the American war was about 'taxation without representation', the Boston tea party. In reality it was about power and control – both parliament's sovereign authority and the King's ultimate jurisdiction. The Massachusetts colony had been the most antagonistic to British views for some time and was determined to take a stand. Equally, Britain was clear that it could deal with its colonies as it chose. Exporting East India tea to America was simply a tangible demonstration of this principle with regard to trade. Britain felt that it had the right to legislate for its colonies; the American congress disagreed. America concluded that Britain did not have its interests at heart and was not to be trusted.

Tom Paine's popular pamphlet 'Common Sense' appeared in the same year as George III rejected colonial demands and American independence was declared, and effectively gained, in 1776.

and Spain entered the war on the American side in 1778 and 1779 respectively.

North survived as Prime Minister until March 1782 after the surrender of Cornwallis at Yorktown the previous October. It might be thought he lasted this long because he deflected much of the responsibility for American independence from George III. North had been attempting to resign for some time before this was finally permitted by George III; even then the King accused him of "desertion".[22]

One of the consequences was that Irish Catholics drew conclusions about self-rule from Britain's failure to prevent American independence. The protracted nature of that failure and the lengthy war increased the attractions of self-rule for the Irish and helped foster their determination to realise it.

North is also condemned for according George III too much power. On the face of it, the latter view might appear to contradict Cabinet responsibility for policy. However, the division between the sovereign and parliament was not as marked at this stage as it was later to become, and in any case George III had exceptionally strong opinions and a determination to ensure his authority, and therefore his views, carried weight. He had shifted the balance of the constitution in his favour.[23]

---

[22] North is often condemned for the loss of the American colonies, but he was the victim of policy towards America as well as the author of it. Britain had sought and pursued an isolationist policy prior to 1770, relying on its naval power as much as on allies. The upshot with regard to America was that problems had lain dormant, but began to prove problematic from 1770 on. North had become Prime Minister by the time parliament voted on the previous government's policy that, while the other taxes on America would be removed, the tea duty would remain. North argued that this was appropriate because Britain was only the intermediary in this case rather than the manufacturer. Retaining this tax could not have an adverse effect on the economy, with the money raised used to pay colonial salaries. When Saratoga fell in 1777, North had sought peace by effectively offering America home rule under a British flag. America, however, was determined on nothing less than full independence. North saw that Britain could not win the war except at great financial cost and suffering, yet George III would not accept his view that the price of victory might be too great. From this point on the war became one of attrition with Britain seeking to avoid defeat in the south. The war came to an end when the British were defeated at Yorktown in 1781.

[23] He exercised the ultimate authority and executive control. According to William Cobbett in 1807, "... it is the King's prerogative; a prerogative which he possesses, and which he ought to possess, to change his ministers whensoever he pleases,

North's motivation to manage his monarch must have been clouded anyway by the personal responsibility he owed George III for clearing his debts in 1777 and for putting him on a better financial footing thereafter. George III had also demonstrated his support by awarding North the Garter. This was an exceptional honour for a Commoner (the second of the century). Since this award was, and still remains, in the monarch's personal gift as a recognition of allegiance and individual contribution, it reflects the King's esteem for North. North's government was followed by three very brief Whig administrations of Rockingham, Shelburne and Portland that lasted less than two years in total.[24]

## France

The French Revolution was very popular in Britain to begin with. The immediate cause of unrest in 1789 may have been a poor harvest, but the growing gap between rich and poor, the unearned (and undeserved) privileges of the rich, the bankrupt government and the recent American example were prominent considerations for many participants. Stability in Britain was therefore vital given the uncertainty across the Channel.[25] Two future British Prime Ministers George Canning and Charles Grey[26] took a positive view at first. As far as George Canning was concerned, it was up to each country to decide the form of government that suited them best. If America and France chose republicanism, then so be it. Britain should aim to learn from this.

---

and without being liable to be questioned or taunted respecting it by any power on earth." *Political Register*, volume XI, 4th April 1807, p532. This is referred to again in its original context in Chapter 2.

[24] See Appendix

[25] However, the "class war" analysis soon showed that patronage and influence remained as much a feature of the impact of the aristocratic and wealthy on British institutions, despite the constitutional changes of 1688, as it did in France. If one of the original causes of the revolution was political ideals in conflict with an aristocracy that was seen as despotic and not to be trusted, there were similarities in Britain. To reduce such inequalities, let alone remove them, Britain would have to become a more open and transparent society. Public opinion would have to be sought and listened to, with the press allowed to report freely and all citizens accorded full rights to democratic participation and representation. The options were reform or revolution.

[26] George Canning was aged 19 in 1789, and therefore of an age when such pronouncements might be expected; Charles Grey was 25 years of age.

Although Edmund Burke had sounded the alarm in 1790 with his 'Reflections on the Revolution in France', most people in Britain sustained an optimistic view until 1792. Within the Whig party, Burke's warnings were diametrically opposed to Fox's enthusiastic support. Burke foresaw the risk the Revolution posed to Britain and predicted its course. However, his views threatened the recovery of the Whigs under Portland and Fox, and Portland refused to support him. Meanwhile, William Pitt had been watching the revolution with interest, but as a by-stander determined not to interfere in French affairs. Indeed, he saw it as positive for Britain, promising "fifteen years of peace" in Europe, as he said in his budget speech of 1792.

At this point Thomas Paine's 'Rights of Man'[27] began to have more of an influence in Britain. Societies sprang up in support of his arguments that everybody should have equal rights and that democratic government was the only legitimate form. The societies also sought to promote these views widely to working people. This alarmed the government and those in power, an alarm compounded when Charles Grey then helped found the Society of the Friends of the People in the cause of parliamentary reform. Given that the name echoed events in France, it was seen as insensitive and poorly-timed.[28]

The country as a whole became alarmed at this point by the growing violence of the revolution.

---

[27] Thomas Paine wrote 'The Rights of Man' in 1791 and 1792. Part 1 covered "political rights for all men because of their natural equality in the sight of God". It condemned "all forms of hereditary government, including the British ... Only a democratic republic could be trusted to protect the equal political rights of all men". Part 2 set out to tackle the condition of the poor through "a ... program of social legislation". Inevitably, this raised the concerns of the authorities and, coupled with Paine's popularity, meant that he was forced to leave Britain in September 1792. He was outlawed in his absence.
He then left France for America in 1802 and was well-received by Thomas Jefferson initially, but was to die in poverty in New York in 1809. Paine's political influence was significant in Britain, but in France he was seen as a moderate who didn't really "understand" the Revolution. He had little practical influence anywhere. See Craig Nelson, 'Thomas Paine: Enlightenment, Revolution and the Birth of Modern Nations', London, Profile, 2007.
[28] Grey's initiative also helped put Fox and Portland at odds with each other. Fox continued to take the Rockingham line that parliamentary reform should be debated openly. Portland argued that this was not the time to consider the issue and that Fox's reaction was inappropriate. They were similarly divided in response to Paine's radical views.

Pitt became even more concerned later in 1792 when France defeated Austria and began to threaten the Dutch with their "fraternal decree" promising support for foreign revolutionaries – and, by implication, for revolutions in other countries. During December Pitt became worried about the growing threat to British interests and security. The French envoy was expelled from Britain in January 1793 after Louis XVI's execution.[29] The French then declared war on both Britain and Holland. An exhibition[30] at the Fitzwilliam Museum[31] in Cambridge explains in the catalogue that "After the execution of Louis XVI the stereotype of the Frenchman was no longer a laughing matter. They were no longer portrayed as foppish and generally harmless fools, but as dangerous sans-culottes, appearing in swarms as a grotesque, undifferentiated mass, or becoming diabolical or mad, devoid of humanity and behaving like wild beasts."

James Gillray's caricatures of the French Revolution convey this danger, and often seek to defuse it with humour. A particularly well-known example is 'French liberty, British slavery' published in 1792, where "the Frenchman thanks his country for his freedom while munching on raw onions, while his English counterpart gorges on a table of food as he curses his taxes"[32]. In 'The Zenith of French Glory: the Pinnacle of Liberty' from 1793 a bishop is hanged from a lamp-post while the "scene the revolutionary fiddler is watching is the guillotining of Louis XVI. The execution platform is surrounded

---

[29] Christopher Winn, 'I Never Knew That About Ireland', London, Ebury Press, 2006 says on pp91-2 that Louis XVI's attendant at his execution was the Abbe de Firmont. This was an Irishman Henry Essex Edgeworth (1745-1807) who had moved to Toulouse when his father converted to Catholicism. The Abbe was "drenched in the French King's blood. In the ensuing frenzy de Firmont was able to escape through the mob to Poland, where he died in 1807."
Marilyn Butler, 'Maria Edgeworth: A Literary Biography', Oxford, Clarendon Press, 1972, p196 refers to the Abbe's "subsequent loyalty to the French royal family in exile". He was a distant relative of Maria Edgeworth and her brother Sneyd was to write a Memoir of the Abbe with Maria's help in 1815.
[30] 'Vive la différence! The English and French stereotype in satirical prints, 1720-1815', 2007
[31] This museum was founded in 1816 by Richard Fitzwilliam 7th Viscount of Merrion (1745-1816), not the William Fitzwilliam (1748-1833) who was sent by Pitt as Lord Lieutenant of Ireland in 1794 (see below). They both held extensive lands in Ireland but were not related.
[32] Vive la différence! exhibition catalogue

by a swarm of fellow revolutionaries..."[33]  British attitudes to the Revolution had changed rapidly from one year to the next.

Gillray's cartoon 'Old England, New France, The Contrast' produced in 1796 illustrates the gulf between the countries by this stage.  The threat from France is stark, with British stability at risk from the violent and haphazard terror across the Channel.  Equally, though, France might be stifled by the British status quo of monarchy and patronage.

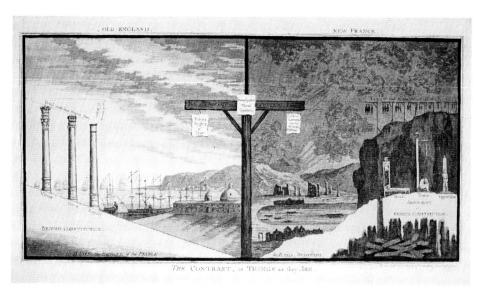

**Figure 1: 'Old England, New France, The Contrast',** James Gillray, 1796 © Courtesy of the Warden and Scholars of New College, Oxford/ The Bridgeman Art Library

France opened up the Scheldt river[34] to all in defiance of their previous assurances, and indeed treaties, that had guaranteed navigation rights on the waterway to Holland.  This would find its echo in 1809 when the British attempted to support Austria by sending the Walcheren expedition to the Scheldt.  Given the French

---

[33] Ibid
[34] The Scheldt river crosses the boundaries of modern Belgium and Holland, flowing through Ghent to join the North Sea close to Flushing and more or less directly across from London - hence its strategic significance to Britain as well as its symbolic importance.

disregard of their recent treaty agreements, and the consequent threat to Britain's trade, Pitt saw no alternative to war.

From 1794 there was a coalition government in Britain with Portland's Whigs supporting Pitt and the war. Fox continued to be on the side of the French. This was not a war that Britain would have chosen and the country was ill-prepared strategically and militarily. Nor was Pitt necessarily a war leader. He relied heavily on William Grenville, who had become his foreign secretary in 1791, and on his "continental policy". When this failed to produce results, Pitt had no fall-back position of his own and found himself at odds with, and not completely convinced by, the alternative proposals. Initially, Britain's stance was defensive rather than offensive. The war only came to be seen as a patriotic cause at a later stage, as the growing alarm translated into increasing popular loyalism. Britain's naval and economic strengths put the French off direct invasion, but they were not averse to backdoor methods and support for rebellion in Ireland.

Pitt had agreed the triple alliance with Prussia and the (United Provinces of the) Netherlands in 1788. This was seen as both a personal triumph and a model for diplomacy. It protected all parties against other aggressors, particularly the French, to 1791. In practice, however, Pitt did not allow these treaties to interfere with British support for Austria. He had to contend with both Prussian disputes and an attempt within the Austrian Netherlands to secede from Austria. The protection was temporary, however. By 1795 both Prussia and Holland had allied themselves with France. From the end of 1795 Britain was isolated, except for Austria which was prepared to continue the war so long as this was funded by Britain. Pitt and his administration began to think of peace, though achieving this would depend on what the French terms were.

1796 and most of 1797 were bleak years for Pitt, with cash payments being suspended from 1797.[35] The national debt

---

[35] The French price for peace was too heavy in 1796, and would have necessitated Britain giving up its gains and recognising France's frontiers. The French continued their campaign in Italy, weakening Pitt's hand further, and in August reached an offensive alliance with Spain. Pitt secured Austria's continued involvement in the war, and prevented them reaching a separate agreement with France, only by further loans. By the time peace negotiations opened in Paris in October 1796, Britain was seeking firmer terms than a month previously. The

increased substantially, with the French invasion in Pembrokeshire in early 1797, though easily repulsed, requiring Pitt to respond swiftly in order to avoid a run on the pound. Pitt's Restriction Act was important in itself and provides some of the background to the economic situation in 1809 and the resulting Bullion Report.[36] There were naval mutinies over pay in 1797. These raised questions about Pitt's competence and his leadership was challenged in the House of Commons. This made him more determined to restore confidence and reach a peace settlement on acceptable terms.[37] The war began to be seen as a patriotic cause. Pitt introduced "triple assessment" for the 1798/99 tax year and additional voluntary contributions from the most wealthy. However, when this did not raise as much as had been expected, Pitt introduced the graduated income tax from the following year. There were unrest and riots in 1799 and 1800 as crops failed and Pitt's government implemented a number of repressive policies.

The British government had lost any sense of strategy with the defeat of Grenville's continental coalition. While Pitt was prepared to fight on alone[38] to ensure Britain's security and guarantee

---

loans to Austria were beginning to produce some military success and Portugal had asked for British help against Spain's belligerence. Pitt was in close touch with the discussions, supported by the briefings he received from his envoy Lord Malmesbury (1746-1820) and from George Canning as Under-Secretary at the Foreign Office. Canning valued this friendship and Pitt's reliance on his advice was developing. (See Wendy Hinde, 'George Canning', London, Collins, 1973.) France called off the negotiations in December.

[36] See Chapter 4 below.

[37] The failure in the negotiations in December was a setback for Pitt and he considered standing down in favour of Addington who he thought had a better chance of concluding them. Austria did not sustain its military success and Britain made a further attempt to settle on reduced terms from May 1797. By this stage the Austrians had reached a separate in principle agreement with France. However, Britain was unaware of this and the Cabinet was divided as to whether to talk separately to the French. Pitt's view only just prevailed on the basis that they would ensure Portugal's interests were protected in the discussions. Once again the French demanded that Britain give up all its gains. Britain was prepared to concede some of these, but not all of them. The talks were rapidly called off as a result of the coup in France that September that saw the rise of Bonaparte and the "second Directory".

[38] From 1798 Britain had stepped up its search for strategic alliances (with similar limited success, in this case Russia, to its pursuit of commercial alliances between 1783 and 1792). Russian troops were sent to the Netherlands in return for some financial aid from Britain, while the Austrians re-opened hostilities with France in March 1799. Britain sought to help Russia in the Netherlands, though without the Prussian and Swedish assistance that had been hoped for, or any overarching or

stability, he saw Napoleon's ascension to the post of first consul from November 1799 as effectively reinstating a monarchy in France. He was prepared to agree peace terms but, when Napoleon's proposals reached George III on 31st December 1799, Pitt did not consider that they justified serious consideration. He was supported by the King, the Cabinet and, eventually, by the House of Commons.

However, Pitt had no clear alternatives to propose and his secretary for war Henry Dundas (1742-1811) was at loggerheads with the foreign secretary Grenville. The Austrians were roundly defeated at Marengo in June 1800 and reached a separate peace with France in February 1801. George III became increasingly dissatisfied with Pitt's handling of the war and began to dispute a number of decisions. In December 1800 Russia, Prussia and others began to challenge Britain's rights over neutral shipping. Although it was to be Ireland that led to the end of Pitt's tenure as Prime Minister, it would perhaps only have been a matter of time before he and George III disagreed decisively over the war with France. In this instance, however, there would have to be a better alternative for the King to choose as Prime Minister since there was no issue of over-riding principle at stake.

This phase ended with the Peace of Amiens in 1802 negotiated by Addington's government. From 1803 Britain (with the help of Austria and Russia) was at war with France again. Once Napoleon became emperor in 1804 the threat to Britain's interests became more direct. While Trafalgar in 1805 curtailed Napoleon's invasion plans, the pressure on Britain otherwise intensified. The repercussions would be felt to 1809 and beyond.

## Ireland

Ireland was a significant factor in several respects. It was over this issue, and specifically Catholic emancipation, that Pitt and George III would part company at the beginning of 1801. Before then, however, Irish nationalists attempted revolution in 1798, with France's help. Ireland was seen as critical to national defence, it

---

co-ordinated policy with their Austrian and Russian partners. Russia and Austria enjoyed some early successes, but these did not last. October 1799 brought news of decisive defeat for Russia in Switzerland and of British withdrawal from the Netherlands.

was to prove the cause of governmental change in 1807 and provide the Tories with their slogan in the ensuing general election, and demonstrate Perceval at his most bigoted. It would continue to reverberate as an issue well beyond 1809.[39]

Pitt understood from an early stage that the status quo in Ireland was unsustainable.[40] It demanded excessive British resources to maintain Protestant power, neither Britain nor Ireland as a whole were deriving much benefit from the connection, and Catholics in particular were often being tyrannised. He sought a political solution that would improve the position for all parties. The first step might have to be a positive association that provided improved strategic control for Britain, with resources then being re-directed more usefully. Ultimately, however, the Catholics would have to enjoy the same democratic and civil rights as their fellow countrymen.

Portland became Home Secretary in Pitt's coalition government from July 1794. The agreement had included Portland's insistence on his friend Earl Fitzwilliam as Lord Lieutenant of Ireland. When Fitzwilliam eventually reached Ireland in January 1795, he began to press for Catholic emancipation. His public support for this had not been authorised and had not been agreed by Portland or discussed with the Cabinet. Fitzwilliam had greatly exceeded his brief and had to be recalled from the post within a month. There was political alarm in Dublin and crisis in London, with the King ensuring Pitt was alerted to the impact. This erosion of trust and confidence resulted in long-lasting ruptures to the friendship between Portland and Fitzwilliam, with Pitt seeing the latter's actions as a breach of faith.

---

[39] Well into the twentieth century where most of Ireland was concerned, and into the twenty-first century for Northern Ireland.

[40] Pitt's first attempt to tie Britain and Ireland more closely together had been in 1785. He had sought to link the country to Britain by improving their access to trade and ensuring that the financial wealth of both countries would increase. Ireland would contribute to the costs of the navy, but only on a basis that was affordable and as their prosperity increased. However, the handling of the measure was badly bungled, with not enough time allowed to persuade the Irish parliament of the benefits, and it was eventually dropped. Inadequate consultation was a feature of Pitt's early days in power. It partly resulted from his character, but was inevitably more significant before he had developed a track record of credibility and competence.

Those who came after Fitzwilliam, such as Camden and Castlereagh, saw this as "an awful warning"[41].

Although Pitt was sympathetic to the catholic cause, it was not clear what he had discussed with Fitzwilliam about his appointment the previous November. Pitt's reaction suggests that their discussion would not justify, and he did not condone nor expect, Fitzwilliam to behave as he did. Fitzwilliam would have known anyway that Portland had never adopted this position, publicly or otherwise, and that George III was against it. Fitzwilliam appears to have ignored their views and acted in accordance with his own regardless.

Meanwhile, Ireland's own radicals were coming to the fore, determined to dismantle the status quo. The roll-call was lengthy, but included James Napper Tandy (1737-1803), Lord Edward Fitzgerald (1763-1798) and, the most celebrated, Wolfe Tone. All were associated with the United Irishmen and France in the aftermath of the French Revolution. The views of radicals such as Fox and Paine were often influential. Napper Tandy had a chequered career as a revolutionary, while Edward Fitzgerald is best known as one of the aristocratic leaders of the uprising. He was captured and mortally wounded in Dublin just before the 1798 rebellion itself. Wolfe Tone is frequently referred to as the father of Irish republicanism. His early career was conventional (although at the age of 22 in July 1785 he did elope with and marry a 16 year old, subsequently changing her first name as well as her last!). It included Trinity College and studying to become a barrister. When he then chose to become a political writer and pamphleteer, he still aimed to take a reasoned line that set out both sides of an argument. He helped form the Society of United Irishmen in 1791, first in Belfast and then in Dublin[42], sought to redress catholic grievances, arguing for their political rights and with those protestants prejudiced against them, and blamed Ireland for getting the (English) government it deserved.

---

[41] R.F. Foster, 'Modern Ireland: 1600-1972', London, Allen Lane, 1988, p264

[42] Tone had set out three key objectives for the Belfast and Dublin Societies. These were: "a union among all the people of Ireland to counter the huge weight of English influence in the country; a radical reform of parliamentary representation as 'the sole constitutional mode' by which such influence can be countered; and the inclusion of Irishmen of 'every *religious* persuasion'." See Marianne Elliott's summary of her 'Wolfe Tone: prophet of Irish independence', 1989 and 'Partners in revolution: the United Irishmen and France',1982 in the Dictionary of National Biography (DNB).

Although Tone's views became more revolutionary in April 1794, when he foresaw a militant backlash and a welcome for the French if they sought to assist Ireland rather than conquer the country, the initial reaction of the government was to see him as a nuisance rather than a threat. However, when Fitzwilliam was replaced by Camden as Lord Lieutenant in February 1795, it became clear that Tone would not be rehabilitated. Instead, he was given a few weeks to leave the country or be charged with treason. He fled to America.

Tone was to some extent the victim of the war with France (as well as of Camden's reaction to the crisis Fitzwilliam had caused), with views then being seen as treasonable that would hardly have been noticed previously. R.F. Foster says in his influential 'Modern Ireland' that "The nature of Ireland's peculiar crisis [at the turn of the nineteenth century] ... was precipitated by an international dislocation: the French wars from 1793, too often divorced by historians from the Irish scene."[43] From America, Tone went to France in early 1796, continuing to stress that the United Irishmen brought together Catholics and other radicals with the overall objective of Irish independence. By July that year he had persuaded the French Directory that their support for Ireland, provided the invasion was seen in this light and the force was large enough to prevent civil war, would suit both countries in their continuing campaigns against Britain. The Irish revolution was to take place when the French landed.

It took some time to assemble an invasion fleet of the necessary scale (nearly 15,000 troops, almost three times as many arms), and it did not sail until mid-December 1796. Things went well until the fleet arrived off Ireland, but at this point the weather intervened, the fleet was dispersed and only fifteen of the original forty-three ships made it back to France. Tone compared the British escape to that from the Spanish armada. But the element of surprise had now disappeared, and Britain would be better prepared the next time. What also changed from September 1797, when Bonaparte and the second Directory seized power, was that Tone now had to negotiate with different officials and the French expected that the Irish uprising would have to take place before, rather than at the same

---

[43] Foster, op cit, p259

33

time as, the French invasion. In other words, the French were now only prepared to help those who took the initiative first.

Eventually, the Irish did rebel in mid-1798, though weakened by the capture and death of Lord Edward Fitzgerald in Dublin, and with James Napper Tandy hindering rather than helping as an agent in France. A smaller French fleet sailed in September, with the British aware of the objective. Tone knew there was little hope of success. The British attacked the fleet off Ireland, with the weather again intervening, and Wolfe Tone was captured and brought to Lough Swilly in County Donegal on 31st October before being taken to Dublin. He was found guilty of treason and requested, as a soldier in the French army, that he be executed by a firing squad. The British decision was that he should be hung. He committed suicide instead. The 1798 rebellion was already over.[44]

Pitt brought in the Act of Union with Ireland in 1800 (based on that with Scotland in 1707) to take effect from 1st January 1801. Pitt's aims were both to give the Irish political and social stability and to ensure they became an ally against France.[45] A further objective would have been to enhance Westminster's control. Although Pitt had hoped to couple this with Catholic emancipation and relief, it soon became clear that this was unacceptable both to George III and the Protestant aristocracy. These developments would have to wait. Even then, it took the use of "secret service" money, patronage and other inducements to get the Act passed and for the Irish parliament to vote itself out of existence.[46] Pitt and Portland

[44] See Foster, op cit or Thomas Pakenham, 'Year of Liberty', London, Abacus, 2000 for a description of the military events of the Irish uprising of 1798 and the British response.
Tone had not achieved the objectives he had set out in 1796. He said they explained his motivation ever since the Society of United Irishmen had been founded in 1791. They were:
"To subvert the tyranny of our execrable Government, to break the connection with England, the never-failing source of all our political evils, and to assert the independence of my country—these were my objects. To unite the whole people of Ireland, to abolish the memory of all past dissensions, and to substitute the common name of Irishman in the place of the denominations of Protestant, Catholic and Dissenter—these were my means."
Wolfe Tone, 'Memorandums', 1796. His wife and surviving son published all his writing in 1826.
[45] Hinde, op cit, p68
[46] Winn, op cit, p96 says, for example, that "Sir William Newcomen was suspected of being bribed [for his support] … against the wishes of his constituents. Certainly

maintained that the rules of propriety had been bent rather than traduced, an illustration of influence rather than bribery.[47]

Pitt sought to introduce the Emancipation of Catholics Bill subsequently, but resigned when George III vetoed the measure. Pitt was later to suggest that he had not done enough to prepare the King for this step (though it is doubtful that he could have been successful since George III felt bound both by duty and his conscience, and the Cabinet and parliament were divided on the matter).

There was again an Irish uprising in 1803. This was led by Robert Emmet and had been discussed with the French. However, it was much more limited than the 1798 rebellion, largely being restricted to Dublin and its surroundings. It fizzled out in confusion when the arms store blew up and Emmet's supporters then dragged the Lord Chief Justice from his carriage and killed him. Emmet was captured shortly afterwards. He was hanged and beheaded in Dublin in September 1803.[48]

## Legacy

At the turn of the century France was about to become a "monarchy" again with Napoleon as "king" (and did in fact become an Empire from 1804), but the rules had changed in any case. Protestant Britain was still pitted against catholic France and her continental allies, but the stakes had been raised. The effects of the French revolution had been seen across the Channel, and its horrific impact for individual people and for institutions beyond the aristocracy understood – even its own leaders were unceremoniously removed and executed. Britain's monarchy and elites – whether aristocratic or not – remained in power, and its institutions, such as parliament, were subject to challenge. The example in France did not necessarily dull or dilute the demands for change, but was to contribute to the ways in which they were

---

a substantial debt that he owed to the government was written off and his wife was raised to the Irish peerage ..."

[47] The Ireland parliament had come into independent existence only eighteen years earlier in 1782. The Library Ireland website quotes Grattan as saying of the parliament after the Act of Union, "I sat by its cradle and followed its hearse." See http://www.libraryireland.com/

[48] Winn, op cit, p63

expressed and the objectives sought. In the future, they would come to be characterised as reform rather than revolution.

Although Britain and British people were appalled as the extreme and cynical bloodshed grew in France, the government became increasingly nervous that the rebellion might spread to Britain. (Even if this was not a real anxiety, a "conservative" government and a protestant monarchy had a duty to ensure it did not take place. Hence, the short shrift that Fox and other Whigs received for their continuing support for the revolution after 1792.[49]) Ireland was a catholic country and recognised as a potential ally of France. Pitt had sought to neutralise this through the Act of Union and would have gone further through Catholic emancipation had he been permitted. Potentially, and in reality after 1798, Ireland was seen to provide France with the opportunity to open a "second front" and as a base for invasion of Britain.

Britain must have felt itself beset on both sides. Not only was it assailed by much of the continent, but American attitudes were still hostile and it was seeking to expand commercially and profit by trade in its own right. America was keen to show that its future development did not depend on Britain as an intermediary. For example, it was keen to trade directly with Europe so that its exports to Britain did not become Britain's re-exports to the continent – as had happened in the past.

In this sense Britain was besieged from left and right – politically as well as geographically. France and America were both republics, but they had shrugged off their monarchies through different routes. One had rebelled against its internal aristocratic rulers; the other had fought a war to get rid of colonial rule. The message for Britain was clear: its days as a monarchy might be limited too. In addition, Britain politically and geographically was caught between the revolutionary aims of America and its French counterpart on the one hand, and what had become the ambitious, and more grandiose, less republican, intentions of Napoleon on the other.

It is little wonder then that Colley says that: "... the half-century after ... 1776 [was] ... one of the most formative periods in the making of the modern world and – not accidentally – in the forging of British

---

[49] See Appendix

identity. These were the years in which the monarchy and the governing class became authentically and very effectively British, and both ordinary working men and unprecedented numbers of women were drawn into national affairs and especially national defence as never before."[50]

## Britain's Military Defences

The military defences designed to protect the country from Napoleonic invasion included the volunteer militia, Martello Towers, Weedon and the Royal Military Canal between Rye (Winchelsea) and Hythe that effectively cut off Romney Marsh from the rest of the country.

Cookson[51] says that the home garrison consisted of about 95,000 people in 1810, having been as large as 110,000. He explains that it was not unusual for the inland areas "to be training 20 per cent or more of their men. But when enrolments under the Defence Act are counted as well, the figures suggest something like a total mobilisation in the most threatened areas." Cookson quotes areas such as Debden (an Essex parish) to illustrate this, with the whole county of Essex expecting to mobilise 50 per cent of its male population. He refers to the Horse Guards' map of home defence, whereby volunteers from as far away as Scotland and North Wales could be drawn into a protective cordon around the south east if necessary.

Martello Towers were designed in 1804 and started to be built the following year. They were chosen in preference to the initial plan (never approved) to flood the Dungeness flats if necessary. There were 103 towers originally, 74 along the Kent and Sussex coast and the remaining twenty-nine in Essex and Suffolk. "They were built of brick, 13 foot thick on the seaward side, stood about 30 foot high

---

[50] Colley, op cit, p7   Colley makes a similar point on p149: "The half-century that followed the outbreak of the American war would be one of the most formative and violent periods in the making of modern Britain and in the making of the modern world – a time of accelerating industrialisation and urbanisation, of growing class consciousness and demands for reform, of revolution in France, and of war in Europe so massive that it swept into every other continent. Virtually every European state in this period would undergo political change, military reorganisation, and social and ideological upheaval."
[51] JE Cookson, 'The British Armed Nation 1793-1815', Oxford, Clarendon Press, 1997, pp41-59

and were equipped with a cannon on the roof."[52]  Only nine are still in their original condition.

Robert Banks Jenkinson the MP for Rye from 1790[53] (even though he did not become 21 until 1791) was made Warden of the Cinque Ports in 1806.  He had previously been colonel of the Cinque Ports Fencible Cavalry from 1794 to 1799.[54]  He followed William Pitt as Warden and was to be succeeded by Wellington after his death in December 1828.  Thorne says that he was made Warden to compensate him for sensibly turning down the premiership on Pitt's death.[55]  He chose instead to join other followers of Pitt, such as Canning, Castlereagh and Perceval, in excluding themselves from Grenville's government.  Although the role of Warden was already a sinecure by this stage, Jenkinson was symbolically important given his previous background and profile in home defence.

The Royal Ordnance Depot at Weedon (near Daventry, Northamptonshire) was built between 1804 and 1816.  It was partly constructed to provide a refuge for the government if they were forced to flee London and in case it proved inadequate as an arsenal.  It comprised "eight storehouses ... to receive, store and dispatch ... muskets brought to and from the Depot by canal boats on the Ordnance Canal ... and Field Ordnance transported on the Turnpike roads ...   [There were] three workshops ... to allow maintenance of the muskets and Field Ordnance."[56]  The canal connection was created as part of the building work.[57]

---

[52] See http://www.ecastles.co.uk/martello2.html

[53] Thorne, RG (ed.), 'The House of Commons, 1790-1820', History of Parliament Trust, Secker & Warburg, 1986, volume 2, p471.  Jenkinson later became Lord Hawkesbury, and then as Earl of Liverpool was Prime Minister from 1812 to1827.

[54] His DNB entry says, "In the patriotic defence movement which followed the outbreak of hostilities Jenkinson was one of the first of the junior ministers to enlist in the militia."  According to http://www.regiments.org/regiments/uk/lists/fen1793.htm, "Fencibles were hostilities-only full-time regulars who were limited to home service (i.e. "de-fencible"), unless all members voted to go overseas. Thirty-four Fencible Cavalry regiments were raised in 1794-95, and most, if not all, were soon renamed "Light Dragoons".  These should not be confused with county yeomanry regiments (part-time volunteers for local defence) which formed at about the same time. Most regiments disbanded in early 1800 and the rest at the Peace of Amiens in 1802."

[55] Thorne, op cit, volume 4, pp300-305.

[56] See http://www.daventrydc.gov.uk/

[57] Anthony Burton says that "As late as the First World War there was a regular munitions traffic carried on ... But Weedon's days as a military depot came to an

The 28 mile long Royal Military Canal across Romney Marsh "was started in October 1804 and finished within two years. The construction of the defence works and gun emplacements (spaced every 500 yards) took longer. The complete defensive structure was finished in 1812, by which time it was redundant as the French navy had been defeated at Trafalgar ... and the threat of invasion had gone."[58] In 1823 William Cobbett was to refer to "the canal as a great military folly and a waste of public money".[59]

## Britain's Economic Defences

Alongside these physical defences, Britain evolved three main types of economic defence. They were designed to ensure that the country remained stable and could continue to trade. The categories were not mutually exclusive and they were rarely as passive as "defence" makes them sound. Often they involved being the first to act and being on the offensive. They were:

- sustaining the country's existing imports and exports as far as possible
- disrupting and reducing enemy trade, and
- developing new markets that would come in time to substitute for, if not fully replace, trade reductions in continental Europe and an independent America.

For an island such as Britain these economic measures were vital to its continued independent existence. They had been formulated on the basis of naval strength and their achievement would continue to depend on maintaining the country's naval dominance.[60]

## <u>Maintaining existing trade</u>

Although the demands of the war ensured that there was sufficient work for those people engaged in supplying it, the war did not affect most people on a daily basis. Nevertheless, they all had to be kept

---

end in 1965, and in 1984 it was sold." See Anthony Burton, 'Canal Mania',
London, Aurum Press, 1993, pp57-58
[58] See the 19th century Romney Marsh website at
http://www.liv.ac.uk/geography/RomneyMarsh/RM%20Hum%20and%20Nat/19th.htm
[59] See http://www.royalmilitarycanal.com/pages/facts.asp
[60] This was one of the reasons for the Copenhagen expedition in 1808 that seized the Danish fleet and made sure it was not available to Napoleon. The action also heightened the impact of the orders in council (see below).

in productive work if the riots that had been prevalent in the eighteenth century were to be avoided. And, regardless of this, all the population had to be fed. Poor harvests in 1794 and 1795, and again in 1799 and 1800, had resulted in the inevitable disorder. In 1795 the protests had included Pitt's windows being broken and the mob stoning George III's coach when he opened Parliament. These were sufficiently recent events for the government still to recall them vividly. Hinde says that, for the authorities, "... a mob planting a Tree of Liberty in a park in Dundee was a much more alarming phenomenon than a mob rioting for bread".[61] This was because they believed they would always be faced with the poor and hungry and could do little for them.[62] Nevertheless, they would no doubt prefer that food riots should not be necessary at all.

Briggs[63] makes the point that "In the countryside a 'moral economy' was acknowledged which in practice allowed for the expression of discontent through ritualised behaviour (including tolerated but circumscribed violence) when food prices were high ... In the cities, however, there was already more uncertainty about motivation and behaviour." He cites the examples of the Wilkes riots in 1763 and the Gordon Riots of 1780 to illustrate his claim of unritualised urban protest.

Briggs underlines the impact of reductions in trade, and therefore the availability of work, by pointing out that there were strikes by the Spinners' Union in 1808 and 1810, and by Preston weavers in 1808, for higher wages. Not everybody was benefiting from the additional demands generated by the Napoleonic Wars. "New laws against ... combination had been passed in 1799 and 1800, but they did not stop such action."[64]

---

[61] Hinde, op cit, p32

[62] This was not dissimilar to the view promulgated by (Thomas) Robert Malthus. Having previously criticised William Pitt, he published in 1798 his influential tract on population change and the means to prevent population growth outstripping food supply. In other words, his view was that the poor had only themselves to blame.

[63] Asa Briggs, 'A Social History of England', London, Weidenfeld & Nicholson, 1983, p203

[64] Ibid, p225. The Combination Act 1800 was repealed in 1824. The Trades Unions then gained in strength.

## Disrupting and reducing enemy trade

After Trafalgar it became clear that Napoleon could no longer invade Britain. The halving of Lloyd's insurance rates from 1806 to 1810 demonstrated British control of the seas. As a result, Napoleon concentrated on economic warfare instead. It had become routine over the years for all countries, but particularly Britain with its dominant navy, to disrupt and reduce enemy trade as an integral part of war. Britain usually specified and regularised this practice through emergency legislation, or 'Orders in Council'[65]. This had already happened on several occasions in the 1790s to restrict, for example, French trade in the Caribbean or supplies of grain to France. The revived war with France after 1803 was accompanied by renewed trade embargoes.

On the 16th May 1806 the Foreign Secretary Fox[66] informed neutral countries that the King had decided "to direct that the necessary measures should be taken for the blockade of the coast, rivers and ports, from the river Elbe to the port of Brest, both inclusive" – a distance of about 800 miles. This blockade would not affect neutral powers so long as "... the said ships and vessels so approaching and entering (except as aforesaid), shall not have been laden at any port belonging to or in the possession of any of His Majesty's enemies; and that the said ships and vessels so sailing from said rivers and ports (except as aforesaid) shall not be destined to any port belonging to or in possession of any of His Majesty's enemies, nor have previously broken the blockade." In other words, neutral ships were permitted to cross the blockade so long as they had been loaded, or were to be unloaded, at a British or allied port.

Napoleon responded with the Berlin Decree of 21st November 1806. In this he laid out how Britain was breaching both international and natural law by its operation of the blockade. He declared that "this monstrous abuse of the right of blockade has no other aim than to prevent communication among the nations and to raise the commerce and the industry of England upon the ruins of that of the continent". He decreed among other things that, as a result, "the

---

[65] An 'Order in Council' is secondary legislation that has been issued by the Privy Council because an Act of Parliament or a Statutory Instrument would be inappropriate (e.g., for reasons of urgency at a time of emergency).
[66] See http://www.napoleon-series.org/research/government/diplomatic/c_continental.html

British Isles are declared to be in a state of blockade and all commerce and all correspondence with the British Isles are forbidden".[67]

Britain retaliated by introducing more stringent Orders in Council during 1807[68]. In January Grenville's government extended the existing coverage and they were strengthened further by the Portland government in November that year. The latter included the stipulation that "only by going through a British port, and paying duties and obtaining a licence, could a neutral [ship] trade with an open European port". According to Spencer Perceval, "The object … was not to destroy the trade of the Continent, but to force the Continent to trade with us". British merchants grew increasingly alarmed as they became aware of the impact (as Briggs explains in 'The Age of Improvement'). Even the licences to get round the blockade proved unpopular, as in their view excessive bureaucracy and unwarranted interference were impeding their prospects. This complaint had to be taken seriously for, as Stone and Stone say in a different context, "It was argued first that it was commerce which had 'caused England to rise so high in the political scale of Europe', and second that English merchants were different from, and superior to, those of foreign countries, since they had adopted the gentlemanly values of elite society."[69]

Thomas Jefferson had drafted the Declaration of Independence and then followed Benjamin Franklin as America's minister to France from 1783.[70] In this capacity he witnessed the early stages of the French revolution and was said to sympathise with the reasons behind it, if not always the results. He had therefore gained revolutionary credibility both at home and abroad by the time he became the third American president after Washington and Adams from 1801. He was more sympathetic to the French position than Washington and bought the Louisiana Territory (not the current state) from Napoleon in 1803. Relations between Britain and America got worse after 1805, partly because of the Louisiana sale

[67] Ibid
[68] There were twenty-four of these in total. See Asa Briggs in 'The Age of Improvement: 1783-1867', 2nd edition, Harlow, Longman, 2000, p143.
[69] Lawrence Stone & Jeanne C Fawtier Stone, 'An Open Elite? England 1540-1880', Oxford, Clarendon Press, 1984, p24
[70] See Conor Cruise O'Brien, 'The Long Affair: Thomas Jefferson and the French Revolution', Chicago, University of Chicago Press, 1996

and the resulting failure to ratify frontiers. As might be expected, the loss of Britain's first empire in America still rankled with some people more than twenty years later. For example, Lord de Blaquiere said in the House of Lords in July 1806, "I would ask ... if this is a time to prostrate ourselves to America when that country has done everything but spit in your face."[71]

Jefferson spent much of his second term from 1805 trying to keep America out of the Napoleonic Wars. Both France and England interfered with the neutrality of American shipping (e.g., stop and search of their captains), and the trade embargo Jefferson attempted to impose on both countries proved unpopular with Americans as well. This prevented American ships from trading with Europe and banned the export to America of goods manufactured in Britain.[72] British merchants became even more concerned as the effects on trade and, ultimately on their prosperity, became clear.

Britain's economic situation deteriorated during 1808, with both exports and imports reducing. Consequently, the price of corn increased and demand slackened. The Manchester weavers went on strike in 1808, for example, because reduced imports meant less work and lower pay. But there was also an impact on France and her Empire of this economic approach. Napoleon was soon forced to relax the system.

**Developing new markets**

The imperative generated by the Napoleonic Wars provided some of the impetus towards the development of Britain's next empire. For Colley this followed shortly after, and resulted from, the loss of a first empire in America.[73] For Briggs in 'The Age of Improvement' much of it took place after 1815.[74] The two are not mutually exclusive and Britain certainly was able to take a dominant role after

---

[71] As recorded in a speech in the Lords on the American Intercourse Bill on 8th July 1806. Quoted on p24 of S King-Hall & A Dewar, 'History in Hansard 1803-1900', London, Constable, 1952
[72] The Embargo Act 1807 was repealed in March 1809 and replaced by the Non-Intercourse Act. This permitted trade with all countries except France, Britain and their colonies.
[73] For example, Colley, op cit, p145
[74] For example, Briggs, op cit, p141

Waterloo.  It had reinforced its command of the seas with victory on land, this was recognised by other European countries and it had freed up military and other capacity with the end of the Napoleonic Wars.  Also, of course, the the Industrial Revolution (i.e., the shift towards industrial processes of manufacture with its economic and social consequences) was underway as another motor for growth.

Britain sought to develop new markets in South America, where Bolivar's views would be likely to help.  The Peninsular War was to change the Portuguese and Spanish positions too, with the Portuguese empire ruled from Brazil from 1808.  In Turkey and Persia Britain capitalised on their increasingly friendly attitude in response to Russia's ambitions.  The other main options were expansion of the East India Company (now that the government had more influence over the Company's activities following the Board of Control Pitt had put in place through an Act in 1784) and in the Cape Colony obtained from the Netherlands in 1795.  Canada was an established territory and New South Wales was beginning to be opened up, but there was not yet any market to speak of.[75]

Simon Bolivar (born in Caracas in 1783) aimed to unite all South America, following Napoleon's example in Europe.  However, he soon became disillusioned with Napoleon whom he thought had "betrayed republican ideals" by becoming Emperor and King of Italy.  The Caracas junta declared itself independent of Spain after Napoleon made his brother Joseph King of Spain in 1808 at the start of the Peninsular War.  In 1810 Bolivar went to Britain in search of aid for Venezuela, but only came away with "a promise of neutrality".  This was the start of his push for South American independence.

Castlereagh as Secretary for War and Colonies in Portland's government from March 1807 was at the centre of many of these developments.  For example, he had become head of the East India Board of Control in Pitt's second administration (and was later accused of corruption and excessive influence in this role by the House of Commons in 1809[76]).  Gray says that "On 13 September 1806 … news reached England that 1,600 British troops … had captured Buenos Aires, one of the largest commercial centres in

---

[75] See Appendix
[76] See Chapter 5 below

44

Spanish South America. Dazzled by the prospect of new and unlimited markets for British goods, the prime minister immediately sent reinforcements to the river Plate. Whitehall was full of grandiose plans for seizing the entire continent of South America. Grenville decided to send Sir Arthur Wellesley to take Mexico: Windham (1750-1810) [Castlereagh's predecessor in the Grenville government], outbidding even this, sent Colonel Craufurd with 4,000 men to sail round Cape Horn, occupy Valparaiso and Chile, and then march across the Andes to join forces with the British army in Buenos Aires, a thousand miles to the east."[77]

Gray goes on to say that "the news of ... ignominious surrender at Buenos Aires [in late 1807 or early 1808] put paid to all hope of a new British American Empire"[78], but not of the opportunity for trade.

Australia's Dictionary of National Biography identifies a key role in this expedition for Richard Bourke, a future governor of both Cape Colony and New South Wales (and the future father in law of Dudley Perceval, one of Spencer Perceval's six sons). It says that "...as quartermaster-general with the unsuccessful expedition to South America [in 1807 he] ... took part in the siege and storming of Montevideo and in the expedition against Buenos Aires."[79] The possible expedition to Mexico was not pursued.

---

[77] Denis Gray 'Spencer Perceval – The Evangelical Prime Minister. 1762-1812', Manchester, Manchester University Press, 1963, p160
[78] Ibid, p161.
Harvey, op cit, pp211-212 says that "The opposition was further discouraged by the conclusion of the Buenos Aires expedition, their major military venture while in office. Lieutenant-General Whitelocke, the commander appointed by Windham ... had met heavy resistance from the rebel colonials and on 7 July 1807 agreed to evacuate his troops. Both his own troops, and the people at home, who had had such extravagant expectations from the opening up of South America to British trade, were enraged by this capitulation. Whitelocke was court-martialled and, on 18 March 1808, sentenced to be cashiered."
C.R. Fay, 'Huskisson and His Age', London, Longman Green & Co, 1951, p73 says Canning and Huskisson were to make South America "the spearhead of their democracy" - this was the subject of Huskisson's last contact with Pitt before his death in 1806.
[79] The DNB entry goes on to say that "In 1809 he was appointed permanent assistant in the Quartermaster-General's Department. He served in the Peninsula, where his knowledge of Spanish proved useful, and in 1812-14 he was stationed at Corunna as military resident in Galicia; he was favourably noticed for his services and was promoted colonel on 4 June 1814." He was later Governor of Cape Colony in 1825 and of New South Wales 1831. His daughter Mary Jane Bourke married Dudley Perceval in 1827.

Gray also says that "By the time the [Ministry of All the] Talents fell there was a British expeditionary force nearly everywhere, except where there ought to have been one."[80]  It fell to Canning and Castlereagh in the Portland administration from 1807 to tackle this situation.  Hinde says  that "The Cabinet ... became seriously worried [in late 1808 that] ... Napoleon's next step should be to extend his control indirectly over the Spanish colonies in South America, and Castlereagh busied himself with plans, and even actual preparations, for military expeditions to various parts of South America. "[81]  These were not pursued and Castlereagh may have been more circumspect in 1808 as a result of the earlier failures and the potential for conflagration closer to home.

To summarise, Britain was holding its own internationally in the run up to 1809 – but only just, and this required constant vigilance.  The threat of invasion had disappeared, but the blockades were taking their toll on Britain as well as on other countries.  The alliance Napoleon struck with Russia in 1807 at Tilsit threatened to make the position worse.[82]  The treaty was said to contain secret clauses that allowed for a grand alliance against Britain if it persisted in the war.  The start of the Peninsular War the following year made the international situation even more perilous.

---

[80] Gray, op cit, p160

[81] Hinde, op cit, pp191-2.  She goes on to say that "Fortunately, none of these rather doubtful expeditions actually got under way. Only one military expedition [by Moore] was launched at this time.  It went to Sweden and it was a disastrous failure."

[82] The treaty of Tilsit followed the defeat of the Russian forces at Friedland.  Britain had aimed to assist the Russians, but had sailed too late to be of any help.

## 2.    THE CHANGING NATIONAL CONTEXT

Thomas Creevey, the Whig MP and social observer whose letters provide an insight into this period, said that "The years 1807 to 1810 were momentous ... in the destiny of England ..."[83] There is much to support his view as several Chapters, including this one, show. It provides the domestic backdrop in Britain and Ireland to complement the international run-up to 1809 in Chapter 1.

After Pitt's death in January 1806 (see Appendix), the 'Ministry of All the Talents' became the government from February that year. According to Thorne, George III's initial choice as Prime Minister had been Liverpool (Hawkesbury at this stage), but he chose to remain outside the government, joining other ex-Pittites such as Canning, Castlereagh, Perceval and Portland who refused to serve with Fox. They were against the Talents ministry in public ("splendid pretence and pitiful performance" according to Perceval), but Gray[84] says that they were more defeatist in private. Pitt's friends were split into three "intolerant sects" (in Castlereagh's words) that were unlikely to stand against Grenville. In Wendy Hinde's words:

"... like most contemporary politicians, [Pitt's friends] still felt an instinctive reluctance to oppose the King's government, especially when it was new to office. The result was that they found it almost as difficult to agree on tactics as on a leader."[85]

### Grenville's 'Ministry of All the Talents'

Grenville's "Ministry of All the Talents" lasted little more than a year from February 1806 to March 1807. (Gillray called them the "Broad Bottoms" - meaning both a coalition and ready targets - as in his cartoon of 20th February 1806 in Figure 2 as they entered government.) It excluded a number of former Pitt supporters, but included Fox. It failed to provide the stability being sought after Pitt and, indeed, it would be difficult to better Hinde's description of the effects that ensued:

---

[83] Quoted on page 67 of John Gore (ed.), 'The Creevey Papers', London, The Folio Society, 1970 (from Batsford 1963)
[84] Gray, op cit, p63
[85] Hinde, op cit, p144

"... the Talents themselves were hardly a happy crew. Both Grenville and Fox wished they could dispense with Sidmouth and his importunate friends. But not many people thought they could make their own alliance stick, and while the Pittites were trying to detach Grenville, the Foxites were busily seeking recruits from among Pitt's friends. Everybody praised the virtues of moderation but few managed to practise it; and those who loftily proclaimed their intention of not getting mixed up in all the political caballing could not refrain from adding to the general uncertainty by assiduously passing on every scrap of political gossip that came their way." [86]

*Making-Decent; — i.e. — Broad-Bottomites getting into the Grand Costume.*

**Figure 2: 'Making-decent; - i.e. - Broad-Bottomites getting into the grand costume',** © National Portrait Gallery, London

After the death of Fox that September, Grenville strengthened his position by winning a general election. One hundred Irish MPs from

---

[86] Ibid

66 constituencies had been added as a result of the Act of Union in 1801, giving a total of 658 MPs in the House of Commons. 87 of these seats were contested, with the result that Grenville could usually expect to rely on 349 supporters in the new Parliament. There were 92 opposition MPs, while 208 were neutral and 9 independent.

Grenville's government had two pressing issues to deal with. The first concerned the erratic behaviour of Princess Caroline, the estranged wife of the Prince of Wales. The examination of her alleged adultery and treason became known as the 'delicate investigation'. Among other things she had claimed that an illegitimate child was adopted. George III prevented her exclusion from court, much to his son's irritation, and the King and the Prince of Wales continued to clash over several issues, including the latter's mistresses and his treatment of Princess Caroline. She was keen that 'The Book' recording the conclusions of the investigation should be published as it supported her position. Grenville insisted as Prime Minister that its publication would be inappropriate and that it be withdrawn. Perceval, a key adviser to Princess Caroline, is said to have burned 500 copies and the government bought back others. Not all copies were found, however, and it was published some years later. Despite the warning that had led to the inquiry in the first place, Princess Caroline continued to behave in an extreme fashion.

The second was an issue with much wider implications that had substantial ramifications for Britain's place in the world and for her sense of moral superiority. This was the abolition of the slave trade[87]. Although Grenville had failed to persuade Canning to join the government, he adopted the advice Canning had previously offered Pitt that abolition of the slave trade be made a government issue. Grenville saw the Act passed at the beginning of March 1807, thereby bringing to an end what had previously been an annual vote left to the consciences of individual MPs.

Perhaps emboldened by this significant success, the government sought to take the next step in promoting civil rights by commissioning Catholics into the army. Catholic emancipation had

---

[87] Slavery itself was not abolished in Britain until the Slavery Abolition Act of 1833 and later in the colonies.

been a critical and long-standing issue for the Whigs. The lesson from Pitt's resignation in 1801 was that the King was not prepared to countenance it, but this did not deter the Whigs from continuing to press the matter. Nor could it; it had become their distinctive rallying call. Sidmouth (previously Prime Minister as Addington) was the one member of the Cabinet who continued to be against the measure. George III sought written assurances from Grenville that he would not pursue it. This remained an issue of conscience for the King, but it also provided the opportunity he had been waiting for to get rid of Grenville's government. Grenville refused to provide the assurance asked for and consequently his ministry was dismissed by the King. When he learned of this outcome, Sheridan observed "that 'he had known many men knock their heads against a wall, but he had never before heard of a man collecting bricks and building a wall for the express purpose of knocking out his own brains against it.'"[88]

George III knew he could count on the leading ex-Pitt supporters who had excluded themselves from Grenville's government (i.e., Canning, Castlereagh, Liverpool and Perceval) and who had been discussing their return with the King since June 1806. They were to feature as prominent members of the Cabinet in the administration ostensibly led by Portland. However, as Portland provided little leadership or co-ordination, there was every chance of the confusion in Europe being mirrored by chaos at home.

**The "Portland Government"**

The Portland government that replaced Grenville's in 1807 was already the fifth administration of the century. At a time when we are used to governments lasting four or five years, the effect of these frequent changes of ministry should not be underestimated. The impact was lessened of course by the continuity of people and policies from one government to the next. On this basis, some historians have concluded that one thread runs through Pitt's two administrations and the government of Addington that separated them up to 1806, and another from 1807 through the governments of Portland, Perceval and Liverpool to 1827. For example, Gray[89] sees the Perceval government as an extension of Portland's, and

---

[88] Quoted by Gore, op cit, p66
[89] Gray, op cit, pp471-473

50

therefore considers the two governments as one (given Perceval's key roles in both), while Thomas Creevey[90] took the same view of the Perceval and Liverpool governments. In any case it may be that the surface similarities were more marked than underlying differences for good reason. Other Prime Ministers, especially Pitt's contemporaries, sought to emulate the standards he had set as Prime Minister[91] and the speed of transition from one government to the next left little time for changed policies to emerge other than where they were fundamental.

While Pitt's second administration had been ended by his death, the others had concluded because of resignations. In two of these cases (Pitt in 1801 and Grenville in 1807) the resignations had been precipitated by differences between the Cabinet and the King over the civil rights of Catholics. This reinforces two perspectives: firstly, that Catholic emancipation (in its widest sense) was a major issue of conscience and principle that could assume over-riding importance at a time of major war with (largely catholic) France and her empire; and, secondly, that despite this huge national risk, militarily and economically, the war with France could not have been total war to the exclusion of all else. An alternative explanation might be that resolving the Catholic issue would leave Britain free to concentrate its efforts on Napoleon's ambitions on the continent by closing the back door in Ireland. In other words, it was difficult at this time to separate the Catholic issue from questions of defence and national interest. Indeed, Addington's resignation as Prime Minister came about partly over issues of defence.[92] Grenville had brought the two together in his government's concern to enable Catholics to take up army commissions.

---

[90] Gore, op cit, p103 and Creevey's note of 10th June 1812 in which he refers sarcastically to the continuation of the Perceval government: "... such is the worthy *new* Administration" of Liverpool. It reflects his disappointed and jaundiced view of the Prince Regent's appointment of Liverpool rather than a Whig as Prime Minister on 8th June 1812.

[91] Colley, op cit, p190 says that, "Pitt was the prototype on which subsequent British politicians such as Liverpool, Canning, Peel, William Gladstone and hundreds of lesser men would consciously base their careers."
Boyd Hilton, "Sardonic grins and paranoid politics: Religion, economics and public policy in the *Quarterly Review*" in Cutmore, J. (ed.), 'Conservatism and the *Quarterly Review*', London, Pickering & Chatto, 2007, p41 says "Pitt ... had begun to be invested with the mythical qualities of a national saviour, a type of conservative nostalgia that was actually rather frightening, since the more Pitt was lauded the more his loss seemed catastrophic".

[92] See Appendix

William Cobbett's view when the Duke of Portland's administration took over in March 1807 was that "... it is the King's prerogative; a prerogative which he possesses, and which he ought to possess, to change his ministers whensoever he pleases, and without being liable to be questioned or taunted respecting it by any power on earth."[93] It was on the advice of Lord Hawkesbury that the Duke of Portland was made Prime Minister, even though he was already nearly seventy and unwell. These apparent deficiencies ensured that he would not be competing with the other leading contenders in Canning, Castlereagh and Perceval. As such he was a compromise candidate who could be expected to stand above their disputes. The key question was whether he would seek to adjudicate and mediate between them, or whether "stand above" might come to mean "stand aside".

He faced some difficulty in bringing a government together. As J Steven Watson says, "There was no man anywhere, since the deaths of Pitt and Fox, of sufficient stature to subdue the petty quarrels of ambitious and able men. Sidmouth and Canning would never serve together. Canning would serve with Castlereagh or with Perceval or with Hawkesbury, but not under them."[94] The upshot was that they were all in the Portland Cabinet apart from Sidmouth. As Table 1 shows, there were eleven members of the Cabinet initially (including Portland himself) and thirteen from mid-1809 when a further two posts were brought in. Only three of them were in the House of Commons (Perceval, Canning and Castlereagh)[95].

Portland had briefly been Prime Minister over twenty years before[96] as the last of three Whigs prior to Pitt's first administration. He had then joined Pitt's coalition government from 1794 as Home

---

[93] Cobbett's *Political Register*, volume XI, 4th April 1807, p532. Surprisingly, this does not seem to have been said sarcastically or tongue-in-cheek. Cobbett was not yet fully embarked on the unconventional transformation that would see him become a radical in later life. Robert Southey and the Duke of Portland would be just two of those who made the more usual journey in the opposite direction from reformer to reactionary as they aged.

[94] J Steven Watson, 'The Reign of George III 1760-1815', Oxford, Oxford University Press, 1960, p443

[95] Robert Banks Jenkinson had been made Lord Hawkesbury and joined the House of Lords at Pitt's request at the end of 1803 and was briefly Leader from May to June 1804.

[96] See Appendix

Secretary. From his original position as a radical Whig, he had become disillusioned with them by now, and had been moving in this direction for some time (at least since 1792 and his breach with Fox). This would have been confirmed to the extent that he felt betrayed by the unilateral action Lord Fitzwilliam sought to take on Catholic emancipation in Ireland in 1795. Although the Tory party had yet to come into existence[97], other than during elections, he stood against reform and had adopted views that, if not reactionary, were at least consonant with protection of the status quo. He viewed himself as a staunch supporter of George III and a "servant of the crown". Not surprisingly, he had an excellent relationship with the King. Inevitably, his lack of action, let alone leadership, quickly led others to see him as a figurehead.

**Table 1: The Portland Cabinet March 1807 to October 1809[98]**

| First Lord of the Treasury | Duke of Portland |
|---|---|
| Chancellor of the Exchequer | Spencer Perceval |
| Lord Privy Seal | Earl of Westmorland |
| Lord President of Council | Earl Camden |
| Lord Chancellor | Lord Eldon |
| Home Secretary | Lord Hawkesbury (second Earl of Liverpool from December 1808) |
| Foreign Secretary | George Canning |
| Secretary for War and Colonies | Viscount Castlereagh |
| First Lord of Admiralty | Lord Mulgrave |
| Master-General of Ordnance | Earl of Chatham |
| President of Board of Trade | Earl Bathurst |
| Secretary-at-War (from June 1809) | Lord Granville Leveson-Gower |
| President of Board of Control (from July 1809) | Earl of Harrowby |

The first pressure on the Portland government came on the 9th April 1807 as a result of Thomas Brand's somewhat opaque motion on Catholic emancipation. This was that 'it is contrary to the first duties

[97] Gray, op cit, p111 says "To attempt to divide the 1807-12 parliament neatly into whigs and tories would … be about as helpful as trying to group members according to the colour of their hair." Similarly, Hilton prefers the term 'conservative' at this stage rather than 'Tory'. See, for example, his 2007 Chapter on the *Quarterly Review* already referred to.
[98] After Gray, op cit, p471

of the confidential servants of the Crown to restrain themselves by any pledge, expressed or implied, from offering to the King any advice which the course of circumstances may render necessary for the welfare and security of any part of His Majesty's extensive dominions.' Harvey[99] says that "The opposition were confident of winning, but when the Commons divided at six the following morning the result was 258 for the government and 226 against." Cobbett's reaction[100] was "What in all the world could have produced this sudden change!" The Portland government had a majority of 32 in a Parliament that had previously produced a majority for the Ministry of All the Talents government.

## 'No popery' election

Portland then sought the dissolution of Parliament in late April. Hinde[101] says that, despite the recent general election the previous autumn, "The King at once agreed, hoping that the dissolution would 'be productive of every advantage expected of it'."

On the face of it 'No popery' was an obvious slogan for Portland's government to choose for their election campaign. In modern parlance, it put "clear water" between themselves and the recent Whig campaign for Catholic emancipation and army commissions. It also had the merit of distancing them from Pitt's position in 1801. It seemed to be saying to the electorate that, while several of Pitt's friends had been in the out-going Cabinet, they should be reassured this did not automatically imply a return to the previous policy. In addition, it could be important that the Portland government found a slogan that people would recognise and would bring internal factions together; internal unity would be especially valuable in the face of the external threat from Napoleon. Catholics readily provided an "out-group" that the people might be expected to rally against (especially in a protestant country at war with a catholic

---

[99] Harvey, op cit, p201. Hinde, op cit, p157 refers to this as Catholic emancipation. The Portland government had a majority in early April over a Whig motion referring to "condemnation of the change of government and of the King's attempt to tie the hands of his ministers permanently on the Catholic issue". Following the government's subsequent victory on 15th April by 244 to 196 against the House of Commons regretting the change of Ministers, the King granted a dissolution on 25th April.

[100] Quoted in the *Times Literary Supplement* in its 9th January 1964 review of Gray's book on Spencer Perceval

[101] Hinde, op cit, p158

empire). The Portland government was not above taking advantage of prejudices. On the other hand, this strategy also had its risks. Not all the out-going ministers were against Catholic emancipation, so adopting this slogan could have split the Cabinet. It also encouraged the Whigs to come up with an alternative competing platform.

Perceval was known to be a staunch opponent of Catholic emancipation.[102] For example, he had spoken against the petition for Catholic relief in May 1805, claiming that the measures were inappropriate and would encourage other demands. He sustained this view throughout his career and his stance on the issue was to raise severe difficulties for the government in 1808 (see below). George III was another long-standing opponent. It was likely that Portland opposed it too, but he had been closely involved with Pitt in the Act of Union and closing down the Irish parliament, bringing Irish MPs into the House of Commons. More significantly, however, Canning and Castlereagh were moderates. Not only did they not oppose Catholic emancipation, they could see the political benefits of pursuing this. As Harvey says, the issue for them was "… whether the government should serve the King actually or only nominally. It was because men like Canning and Castlereagh were willing to be the King's servants in more than name that they gave up their personal commitment to Catholic relief and co-operated with the anti-Catholics in order to oblige the King …"[103]

Faced by this single slogan, the Whig opposition were encouraged to come up with another. This was 'No corruption'. It had the advantage of reflecting their long-standing stance against patronage. As Hinde says, "…they did their best to blacken the reputation of their opponents, both individually and collectively."[104] But it was not enough to secure their return to office. Of the 658 MPs, the seats of 102 were contested. This was more than in the 1806 election and perhaps reflected public distaste for Whig opposition to George III. The Portland government might expect to have 388 supporters in the new Parliament (depending on the issue raised), an increase over its position in 1806 (of 79 over the 309 non-Grenville MPs, but of 296 compared to the previous opposition

---

[102] Arguably, his views reflected religious rather than political considerations.
[103] Harvey, op cit, p200. For others, such as Grenville and Howick (the younger Grey), their principles were more important than pleasing the monarch.
[104] Hinde, op cit, p158

to Grenville on all issues). An analysis for the Treasury in March 1808 indicated that the Parliament comprised 378 Portland supporters, 256 opposition, 10 "hopeful" (i.e., potential supporters of Portland) and 14 doubtful. The Treasury then re-allocated the last two categories to reach a final analysis of 389 pro Portland and 269 con.[105]

## The new Parliament

The House divided on the King's Address to the new Parliament on 26th June 1807. The minority against the speech was 255 (larger than the Whig opposition had expected), with 350 supporting it. The King felt vindicated in having called the election and Portland justified in having adopted a national platform for the first time. The government was essentially a collection of departments rather than an overall government. There was no overarching policy and it "staggered along". The 1964 *Times Literary Supplement* review referred to above describes it as "the Cabinet of all the Fribbles" to contrast it with the Ministry of All the Talents that preceded it. This would mean that it comprised trivial people, or was concerned only with frivolous issues. This is extreme and unjust. It involved several politicians who were to prove their dedication, expertise and stamina, including three future Prime Ministers in Perceval, Liverpool and Canning.

The conventional wisdom is that the lack of co-ordination was largely due to Portland's poor leadership. However, Perceval was to turn this on its head when he explained in a letter to Huskisson on 21st August 1809 that "It is not because the Duke of Portland is at our head that the Government is a Government of departments; it is because the Government is and must essentially be a Government of Departments that the Duke of Portland is at our head." He saw the government as comprising separate departments because it "... is constituted with so many of equal or nearly equal pretensions ..."[106]

'No popery' associated all those in Portland's government with the status quo and a reactionary stance. But corruption was a charge levelled at both sides. A number of observers including Cobbett

[105] Thorne, op cit, vol 1, pp188-226
[106] Harvey, op cit, p198

and the *Edinburgh Review* "saw 'the seeds of revolution in the present aspect and temper of the nation.'"[107] (It should be remembered though that both Cobbett and the *Edinburgh Review* might be expected to take the Whig position and neither could be considered impartial.) Gray continues, "One observer noted that the ten leading ministers in the Commons had been returned by a total of 1,214 electors, [about] 120 apiece. Even this did not present a true picture, for Perceval's constituents alone accounted for over half the total [720]: no other minister on the list represented as many as 100 voters."[108] Revolutionary change continued to be out of the question, and even modest domestic reform might have to be put on the back-burner for the moment. But it had been postponed rather than abandoned. Parliamentary division lists for the remainder of 1807 and 1808 indicate that Ireland and the war with France predominated.

Perceval remained as Leader in the House of Commons, though Hinde says that Canning was the chief spokesperson for the Portland government in the House. Although the two are not necessarily mutually exclusive, this discrepancy does indicate how a biographer may tend to favour their subject. Perceval may have been chosen originally to balance Canning and Castlereagh, but his successful performances as attorney-general and in opposition to Grenville had been recognised. In March 1807 Lord Mulgrave had referred to him as 'the ablest man in the House of Commons'. Canning was recognised as the most effective orator after the deaths of Pitt and Fox, but Perceval used his legal skills to the full in debate.

As Foreign Secretary, Canning exercised considerable influence. An early demonstration of this was the action in Copenhagen designed to keep the Danish navy out of Napoleon's control. This took place during the summer recess[109] at the beginning of

---

[107] Gray, op cit, p139

[108] Ibid, p139, though Perceval's constituency was not contested in the general election of 1807. Indeed, there was no electoral contest in Northampton from 30th May 1796, three weeks after Perceval was induced to become the MP, and June 1818. The figure of 720 voters represents the number of votes cast for Perceval at the May 1796 election.

[109] Even though the country was at war, Parliament was in recess for half of most years. Gray, ibid, says on p110 that "The majority of members of the House of Commons were self-avowed amateurs, who thought six months in twelve ample time to be devoted to politics."

September 1807. It was followed by strengthened Orders in Council on 11 November. The government was to win all three divisions over the Copenhagen bombardment, even though it turned out to be more excessive than Canning had intended, in January and February 1808.[110]

Perceval's industriousness and capacity for work were similar to Pitt's. The government's finances, especially at a time of war, consumed much of his attention. But he still made time to tackle two issues in 1808 that offended his religious and evangelic fervour. This did not extend to Catholicism, let alone the Catholic church; rather this fervour led in his case to a bigoted approach to Catholics.

The first of these concerned his stance against additional grant for the catholic seminary at Maynooth. The issue was to cause particular difficulties for the government, with his refusal to countenance any increase in funding threatening a split. The government had reduced majorities in divisions on 29th April and 5th May 1808. Hinde says that "Perceval, who usually showed such moderation and good sense, could only see the intractable and explosive affairs of Ireland through an opaque haze of religious bigotry."[111] The second was his attempt to revive the issue of resident curates on which he had already been defeated twice (in April 1805[112] and a year later). Absentee ministers and impoverished curates was a real issue, and Perceval wanted to see a minister living in every parish who was sufficiently well-paid to provide "an example to his parishioners and a source of charity" rather than someone from outside who only came in to officiate at services. However, Francis Burdett's counter-argument was that poverty had previously been a badge of honour for religion and Perceval would alienate curates from the masses. The Bill was defeated in the Lords again. "All a discouraged Perceval could do was submit the facts of clerical poverty to the King and recommend

---

[110] Harvey, op cit, p211 says there were six divisions.
[111] Hinde, op cit, p189
[112] See Gray pp23-25. The original Bill in April 1805 gave "bishops power to enforce residence in all livings under £400 a year and, when the living exceeded that sum, compelling the rector to pay his resident curate a minimum of £200 a year."

a grant of £100,000 a year for four years to raise all livings to a minimum of £50 a year."[113]

Although Daniel O'Connell was to become much better known later, he had protested against the Union in 1800 in his first public speech. He was particularly opposed to the abolition of the separate Irish parliament that accompanied the Union's implementation. O'Connell abhorred violence[114] (and, like Cobbett, preferred constitutional remedies), and consequently had not participated in the 1798 or 1803 Irish rebellions, but he also deplored both the principle of unequal treatment for Catholics and the impact in practice for individuals such as himself. Although some Catholics had been permitted to become lawyers since 1793, the scope for promotion was limited. O'Connell had joined the bar in 1799, but despite proving very successful (it is said that he was known as "Counsellor O'Connell" long before he was described as "the Liberator"), he had not been able to advance further in the profession twenty-five years later. He became prominent in the Catholic Committee in November 1804 and by 1808 was its effective leader. His policy was to oppose such civil disabilities and petition Parliament continually for equal rights for Catholics. Predictably, the most recent petition was defeated in May 1808, but it did at least result in a division in Parliament. Further efforts were to be made in 1810 under the Regency, and in 1811 when the Committee was re-named the Catholic Board to ensure that it was not outlawed. He was to found the Catholic Association in 1823.

**The Convention of Cintra**

Wellesley (the future Wellington) was still an MP and Chief Secretary in Ireland when in May 1808 there was a popular uprising in Spain against the French occupation. This provided an opportunity to strike directly at Napoleon in Europe, rather than relying solely on distant and possibly obscure revolutions in South America. Wellington had just been promoted lieutenant-general and lost no time in promoting this point of view to a sympathetic government.

---

[113] Perceval to George III 25 May 1809 and *Annual Register* 1809 p344.
[114] Maurice R O'Connell, 'Daniel O'Connell: The Man and His Politics', Dublin, Irish Academic Press, 1990

Sir John Moore's army was already engaged in the Peninsula with what amounted to a small expeditionary force of 7,000 men. An army of 9,000 had been assembled in Ireland with a view to supporting uprisings in South America, but Wellington was now ordered to lead these troops to the Peninsula and join up with the Spanish and Portuguese forces. He expected to be reinforced by a further 5,000 men already off southern Spain. More optimistic about the prospects in the Peninsula than for the future of the Union in Ireland, he temporarily gave up his duties as Chief Secretary in June 1808. Before he arrived in Portugal, however, Wellington had acquired two superiors, Dalrymple (1750-1830) and Burrard (1755-1813). They were certainly senior to him, but had little recent experience of active service. It is unclear why Moore was not given the overall command[115] or whether the Duke of York's role as army commander was significant in preferring seniority to ability.

By late August Wellington and his army had disembarked in Portugal and were heading towards Lisbon when they were attacked by Junot at Vimeiro. The battle on the 21st proved a decisive defeat for the French but Burrard prevented Wellington from pursuing their remaining troops. On the following day Dalrymple instructed Wellington not to advance further and soon agreed to the French request for an armistice. The French were required to relinquish control of Lisbon and other fortresses they held in Portugal, and their troops were to leave the Peninsula. However, they would be transported back to France in British ships, could re-enter the war immediately and were permitted to take with them their arms and equipment and anything they considered private property. The latter could, and no doubt would, include whatever had been looted in Portugal. These concessions, under what has become known as the Convention of Cintra, were extreme. Wellington was required to sign the armistice even though he did not agree with the terms. He sought leave to return to his post in Ireland in order to make his views apparent.

News of Wellington's victory at Vimeiro reached London on September 1st, and they were still celebrating when the terms agreed under the Convention of Cintra became known to the government and the King three days later. Nobody could believe it.

---

[115] Perhaps because he was a Whig according to Peter Spence, 'The Birth of Romantic Radicalism: War, popular politics and English radical reformism 1800-1815', Aldershot, Scolar Press, 1996, p74

The terms then became public knowledge on the 15th September. Although Cintra had its advantages in the removal of the French army from Portugal and their loss of two fortresses, the British public inevitably concentrated on what they saw as the humiliating terms that allowed the defeated French forces to be repatriated. An inquiry became inevitable.

On 22nd December 1808 the Board of Inquiry reported a second time (at the King's insistence) on the armistice and the terms that had been agreed. While the armistice was supported, the Board's views of the terms were mixed, with three out of the seven members indicating that they were against them. No further military proceedings followed, but the two senior generals Burrard and Dalrymple were never deployed on active service again. Castlereagh was keen to protect Wellington over Cintra: "My first object is your reputation; my second is that the country should not be deprived of your services at the present critical conjuncture."[116] Castlereagh was successful "in preventing Wellesley being sacrificed to the public outrage, but at considerable cost to his own public standing."[117]

The inquiry report was to have a significant impact on the futures of both Canning and Castlereagh, with the former blaming the latter for the humiliating terms agreed at Cintra - though not necessarily overtly. This was the start of their enmity. 1809 saw it deepen considerably. It was also to have an impact on Wellington and Napoleon. At about this time Wellington persuaded Castlereagh that 30,000 men would be sufficient to hold Portugal. The die was cast.

---

[116] Castlereagh's Correspondence, vol 6, p454, 26 September 1808
[117] Harvey, op cit, p216

## 3.   PEOPLE AND THE PATTERN OF POPULAR EXPERIENCE

Much of the attention in the two preceding Chapters was on political leadership and inter-country tensions and developments.  These were significant factors in setting the conditions, and in some cases generating the pressures, for reform and transition.  However, this is only part of the story.  The balance now needs to be redressed by considering the impact of changing social structures and the effects for, and by, the majority population in Britain.  What part did people in general play as a result of the years before 1809 and their experience subsequently?

Asa Briggs[118] has identified five factors as significant in moving from a society characterised by the status quo to one where change and fluidity were more readily apparent.  They were:
- individual mobility
- increasing wealth
- but also continuing poverty, so that there was growing and more readily apparent inequality,
- population growth, and
- inadequate, but developing, education.

These began to be influential in the course of the eighteenth century, with this trend continuing, and in some cases becoming more marked, thereafter.

In this instance, the first of these factors refers to social status, but it could equally well relate to better transport and communications. Briggs himself has drawn attention to contemporary improvements in this area.[119]  They are addressed in the following Chapter. Developments in trade contributed both to increasing wealth and to more malleable social status as some merchants used their money to acquire property and estates, buying their way into the company of the landed and the titled.  However, the money could only be used once.  If it was invested in fixed assets at home, it could not be used for trade abroad - except in those circumstances where the former provided security for loans that were to be repaid through

---

[118] Asa Briggs, 'The Age of Improvement: 1783-1867', 2000, pp12-14
[119] Asa Briggs, 'A Social History of England', London, Weidenfeld & Nicholson, 1983

trade, a considerable risk given the uncertainties.[120] No doubt some merchants wanted to signal their success to the outside world, and ensure that there was something tangible to leave to future generations. But it is not clear how widespread or sustained this practice was. Certainly, Stone and Stone argue that the elite were less open to outsiders coming in than it often appears. For some merchants, investing in land and property seems to have provided an alternative, but usually temporary, haven while trade was under stress. Briggs quotes from a 1760 letter indicating that trade and the consequent new wealth percolated through all tiers of society, changing all the population, not just the aristocracy and the gentry.[121] He argues that automatic deference decreased as a result and the status quo was less readily accepted. The horizons for most people had been raised. They now expected and anticipated something better. This was to become even more apparent in the nineteenth century.

Overarching all these factors, however, was the division of people into 'optimists' and 'pessimists', "those who welcomed change and dreamed of its limitless possibilities and those who tried to resist or to challenge it"[122]. At one extreme were not only the engineers, merchants and entrepreneurs who sought to develop new ideas and markets, moving on from what had gone before, but also those individuals who grasped the opportunity to better their circumstances and those of their families. They were prepared to step into the unknown.[123] At the other pole were those who harked back to what had gone before. It might prove less inviting than the future, but at least it was known. By contrast the future was uncertain, and something of a threat - a threat that was more real to those who had most to lose in the way of status and privilege, as well as wealth. The examples of the French revolution and American independence were recent and provided poignant lessons: "... the aristocracy will rather go to hell with Satan rather

---

[120] See Stone and Stone, op cit for further detail on this argument.
[121] Briggs, 2000, op cit, p12
[122] Ibid, p12
[123] Briggs also makes the point (ibid, p22) that this was often a necessity for religious Dissenters if they were to overcome the civil disabilities that they were otherwise subject to.

than with any democratic devil", as Richard Lovell Edgeworth (1744-1817) wrote in 1793[124].

This is one of the differences between **hope** and **history**; one group looks forward, the other finds security in the past. For some people there would have been ambiguity, but for both individuals and society as a whole this dissonance and tension can only be ignored for so long. Eventually, it has to be resolved - or it will resolve itself in conflict, as had happened in France, America and Ireland.

## Population Growth

EP Thompson[125] sees three major influences at work in the first half of the nineteenth century  Those were the huge population increase between 1801 and 1841 (a rise of over 70% from 10.5m to 18.1m), the industrial revolution and the political counter-revolution from 1792 to 1832.[126]

Wrigley and his colleagues have provided detailed population analyses for various periods. For example, Wrigley and Schofield set out the compound annual percentage growth rates every five years from 1541 to 1871 for England[127]. Examination of the Tables in their publication shows that, prior to 1786, the compound annual rate was only 1% or more on three occasions and these were all in the sixteenth century. From 1786 the compound annual rate only fell below 1% in the five years up to 1851. And even on this occasion it was 0.99% per annum. The contrast between the nineteenth century in England and the preceding 250 years could hardly be more marked. Furthermore, in the thirty years to 1831,

---

[124] Quoted in Butler, op cit, 1972, p110. An alternative lesson might be that the future can best be moulded by engaging with it and helping to shape it. Involvement was preferable to confrontation and sedition. It generally took people in Britain with power and influence some time to see that this might be a more useful lesson. Others (for example, Pitt) had been advocating parliamentary reform in the 1780s, but this may in part have been a way of deflecting more far-reaching "real" reform. Inevitably, war with France had become a more pressing priority since.

[125] EP Thompson, 'The Making of the English Working Class', London, Penguin, 1980, p216

[126] Charles Abbot promoted the Population Bill that led to the first census in 1801 and, as Speaker of the House of Commons from 1802, continued to press for a number of administrative reforms.

[127] Wrigley, E and Schofield, R., 'The Population History of England 1541-1871: A Reconstruction', Cambridge, Cambridge University Press, 1981, pp178-181

the compound annual rate never fell below 1.3%. After 1831 it never quite reached it, though coming close in the fifteen years from 1856 to 1871. Population growth in England was therefore particularly marked up to 1831, as it was up to 1841 for Great Britain as a whole.

The question, following Malthus' 'Essay on the principle of population' in 1798, was whether the food supply could keep up with this rate of increasing population or whether prices would have to rise to maintain the balance of supply and demand. Wrigley and Schofield demonstrate that, up to the time when Malthus' essay appeared at the end of the eighteenth century, the previous 250 years provided substantial supporting evidence for his contention that food prices increased as population grew. After 1800, however, the link was quickly broken. Population grew throughout the nineteenth century, but the price index turned down from 1811 and began to increase again only very slowly after 1841.[128] Malthus' arguments came to be abandoned in the second half of the nineteenth century.[129] By 1871 the population had reached 22m, but overseas trade and food imports had expanded, and at home agricultural yield had improved, industry had grown, and transport and distribution networks had been transformed. Malthus' views were no longer relevant in what had become a very different country, trading and operating throughout much of the world.[130]

William Hazlitt had long disagreed with Malthus' conclusions, writing several articles accusing him of having stolen the ideas in the 'Essay' from an earlier writer called Wallace. Malthus' views were also anathema to William Cobbett. Richard Ingrams says that,

---

[128] Ibid, pp402ff. Donald Winch, 'Riches and Poverty: An Intellectual History of Political Economy in Britain 1750-1834', Cambridge, Cambridge University Press, 1996, p8 describes Wrigley as "revisionist" and says that, to Malthus, land was the one fixed element on the supply side in land, labour and capital. This might be correct where an individual country is concerned (though it ignores the impact of agricultural improvements), but it fails to take account of the colonial expansion that had already taken place. Subsequently, the pressure on land and space at home was one of the causes of further expansion abroad and another empire. See below.

[129] Briggs, 2000, op cit, p29

[130] Dependence on other countries, even colonial ones, has its disadvantages as well as its benefits - particularly if this is trade in order to feed and clothe your population. This is why Diamond 2005 makes failure of a trading partner one of the key factors that could contribute to risk in other civilisations. It is of course one of the perils of inter-dependence in a globalised world.

"Cobbett's fierce denunciation of Malthus, which he kept up till his dying day, sprang from his natural aversion to parsons and his objection to all forms of birth control (particularly when urged on the lower orders by an economist). His political instinct, as so often, was right, because it was Malthus' theory about overpopulation which underpinned the disastrous economic policies, or lack of them, of successive governments."[131] Southey and Coleridge were others who found Malthus' views repugnant and argued most vehemently against them.[132]

In each of the four decades to 1841 the population of Britain increased by at least one-seventh or 14% to over 18.5m. Recent expertise attributes this primarily to increasing births rather than reductions in deaths (for example, Britain became a younger country, where "more than 60 per cent of people were less than 24 years old during the first half of the nineteenth century"[133]), whereas earlier writers saw the latter as partly responsible, drawing attention to the declining death rate after 1790[134]. GM Trevelyan says "... after 1780 the death-rate went down by leaps and bounds ... In 1750 [it] had been 1 in 20 [in London]; by 1821 it had fallen to 1 in 40."[135]

Comparing the 1801 and 1811 censuses[136], the population of Britain (excluding Ireland) appears to have been just over 12m in 1809, with 9.5m people living in England, over 0.5m in Wales and the remaining 1.8m in Scotland. All three parts of the country had increased their population at similar rates since 1801. Between 1801 and 1811 the overall population increase was 14.7% or 1.6m from 10.9m to 12.6m. As a result of the Napoleonic war, there had been an increase of more than a third to 641,000 people in the army

---

[131] Richard Ingrams, 'The Life and Adventures of William Cobbett', London, HarperCollins, 2005, p126
[132] See below for more detail on Robert Southey and his views on Malthus. Southey wrote 'On the State of the Poor' in the *Quarterly Review* at the height of the Luddite riots in 1812 and was one of the first to "attribute increasing misery of the poor to the manufacturing system" (Winch, op cit, pp323-325).
[133] In Hilton, op cit, 2006, p5
[134] For example, Watson, op cit, p524
[135] G.M. Trevelyan, 'English Social History: A Survey of Six Centuries Chaucer to Queen Victoria', London, Longmans Green and Co., 1944, pp341-343
[136] It is worth noting that the census only provided numbers until names were included from 1841. Age structure is available from 1851, the first census at which the population was predominantly urban rather than rural.

or navy at the latter date. Several English "counties" exceeded the general one-seventh rate of increase (Chester, Kent, Lancaster, Middlesex, Nottingham, Staffordshire, Surrey, Sussex and the East and West Ridings of Yorkshire). This was also the case for Brecon, Cardigan, Carnafon and Flint in Wales, and for Argyll, Ayr, Edinburgh, Lanark and Renfrew in Scotland. Lanark's increase was 45,053 or 30.7% from 146,699 to 191,752. This was by far the largest increase in percentage terms. Only Lancaster (Lancashire) came close with an increase of 155,578 or 23.1% from 672,731 to 828,309.

The Lanark figures require some explanation. Robert Owen's development at New Lanark might have been symptomatic of other factory initiatives in the area, but this would not explain a 31% increase on its own. It is largely due to the inclusion of Glasgow in the Lanarkshire figures. The city had begun to thrive as a port in the late eighteenth century and was becoming an important manufacturing centre in its own right at the start of the nineteenth. Its population would increase exponentially as a result of additions from the Highlands in the 1820s.

As in 1801, Middlesex, Lancashire and the West Riding of Yorkshire had the largest populations with over half a million people each in 1811. The factory system was only just beginning to make its mark, and these population figures would comprise small groups of workers, mainly out-workers.[137] The impact of spinners and weavers, and of cotton and wool, could be seen on either side of the Pennines. Bohstedt cites one estimate in which 75,000 weavers in 1795 had increased to 225,000 by 1811.[138] This continuing growth in population (roughly doubling every fifty years), and the increasing move towards urban areas as the Industrial Revolution took hold, led to severe social problems in time. Although these mostly came after the turmoil of the Napoleonic wars, observers such as Cobbett noted that agricultural labourers had to contend sooner than this with worsening conditions. He blamed the Poor Laws and increasing enclosures for their reduced state (though it is clear from elsewhere that some communities

---

[137] Chapter 4 refers below to the employment legislation that was repealed in the first decade of the nineteenth century as the weavers lost their ancient, but paternalistic, protection.
[138] Bohstedt, J., 'Riots and Community Politics in England and Wales 1790-1810', London, Harvard University Press, 1983

sought to mitigate the worst effects of social change by the use of local taxes through the Poor Laws).

Increasing growth in population, and the accompanying perception (whether accurate or not) that this could mean reduced opportunities and heightened risks at home, were among the factors that were to impel some people overseas in time. This was particularly the case for those who had no readily marketable skills other than their muscle and, then as now, for those whose skills were in greater demand elsewhere. Labourers would particularly fall into this category, whether urban or rural. Some people were to take advantage of the new worlds opening up (e.g., in America). Others saw their future options being best served in the colonial expansion taking place  A burgeoning empire required a growing band of recruits who could conquer new territories, continue to keep them subjugated and police both the new additions and the old. A larger population readily supplied the staff required, while their engagement overseas took some of the pressure off their consumption and potential disaffection at home. Both parties benefited from the arrangement - particularly if there was no other war at the time (as was the case up to 1815 and Waterloo). In many circumstances colonisation became a substitute for war. It distracted attention from domestic difficulties and provided a safety valve and outlet for ensuring energy was put to productive use.

This is not to say that there weren't "pull" factors at work as well as these "push" ones.[139] Empire, like Everest, was something that had to be conquered because it was there. Curiosity will have played its part, but once explored the next step was to ensure an area's natural resources were opened up, and used or protected, for Britain's benefit. Security came with additional land mass, the forces to control it and growing numbers of settlers. Serving the country will have had intrinsic virtues that attracted some. Others will have seen themselves as "missionaries", taking the social as well as religious values of Britain and, in their view, "civilisation" beyond its shores.

---

[139] The conclusions of this section concur with those of Diamond 2005 who uses the "push/pull" analogy to explain Viking expansion (op cit, pp185-187). He says that population pressure and lack of opportunities at home are the main "push" factors in all historical expansions, and good opportunities and empty areas to colonise overseas the main "pull" ones.

## Life expectancy

Life expectancy was about 36 or 37 for those born in 1801. It was higher for those living in rural areas compared to urban ones, for women compared to men, and varied considerably by social class. It should be remembered, however, that life expectancy is an average that, at this stage, was significantly affected by the high infant mortality rate, with about one-sixth of babies not making it to their first birthday. This had changed little by 1901.[140]

Of the people referred to as active in 1809 (see the chart on pages 18-19 above), only Byron and Shelley had died by the age of 36 and they were hardly representative. The next youngest deaths were Jane Austen at 42 and Simon Bolivar at 47. Most people in the chart lived well beyond this age. Henry Addington (Viscount Sidmouth) and Robert Owen were the longest lived at 87, but several others lived into their 80s. Robert Owen was also the person who died last – in 1858, seven years after the Great Exhibition and well into Queen Victoria's reign.

## Urban growth

Boyd Hilton[141] draws attention to nine towns that grew fast in the first half of the nineteenth century. Four of these, Bradford, Liverpool, Huddersfield and Manchester, all increased at more than 6% per year between 1801 and 1851. FML Thompson[142] says that there was a particular "urbanising ... spurt" in the first half of the nineteenth century. This was not primarily to develop new towns, but to ensure that the size of existing ones increased. Briggs looks at the growth of towns after the 1801 census, a "landmark in social history", concluding that in 1801 there were only 15 towns with 20,000+ populations, whereas by 1851 there were 28, and by 1891 there were 63.[143]

---

[140] It should be noted in connection with longevity that Patrick Colquhoun in his 1806 'Treatise on Indigence' (see below) refers to 471 people aged 80+ in 55 workhouses he surveyed in 1805. These included 5 people aged 100+.

[141] Hilton, 2006, op cit, p6

[142] FML Thompson (ed.), 'Cambridge Social History of Britain 1750-1950: Volume 1 Regions and Communities', Cambridge, Cambridge University Press, 1990

[143] Briggs, 1983, op cit, p216. The Census was the "landmark" to which he refers, but it took place because people were aware of, and interested in, the population and social changes taking place around them. There was also some dispute about

Charles Tilly[144] has illustrated how much more marked was the urbanisation of Britain in the nineteenth century compared to the remainder of Europe. In 1800 10.5% of the population in England and Wales lived in cities of 100,000 or more. This was a lower proportion than in European Turkey (13.3%) and similar to that in Denmark (10.7%) and Holland (9.3%). No other country exceeded 6% at this stage; Ireland was at 3% and Scotland at 0%. Tilly says that by 1900 39.0% of the England and Wales population lived in cities of 100,000+ people. The proportion had increased fourfold, but the number of people involved had increased 13 times from under 1m to nearly 13m. At this period 16.1% of the Ireland population, and 30.8% of the Scotland one, now lived in cities of 100,000 or more. Meanwhile, Holland, Denmark and European Turkey had each increased their proportions to about 20%. No other country came close and the proportion across Europe as a whole was 10.1% of inhabitants living in large cities.

FML Thompson says that 24% of the population lived in towns over 10,000 people in 1801. He includes the following Table to vividly demonstrate the marked growth of large cities in Britain over this period.

**Table 2: Percentage of the population of England and Wales living in towns 1700-1951**[145]

| Date | Towns 2,500 – 10,000 | Towns 10,000 – 100,000 | Towns over 100,000 | All towns |
|---|---|---|---|---|
| 1700 | 5 | 2 | 11 | 18 |
| 1750 | 6 | 6 | 11 | 23 |
| 1801 | 10 | 13 | 11 | 34 |
| 1851 | 10 | 19 | 25 | 54 |
| 1901 | 9 | 25 | 44 | 78 |
| 1951 Census | 1 | 16 | 55 | 72 |

Sources: 1700 & 1750 – Corfield, 'Impact of Towns', Table II; 1801, 1851 &1901 – Law, 'Growth of Urban Population', Table XI

---

whether the population was increasing or decreasing - see John Clarke, 'The Price of Progress: Cobbett's England 1780-1835', London, Granada Publishing, 1977, p19
[144] Charles Tilly, "Misreading, then rereading nineteenth century social change", p341. In Wellman, B and Berkowitz, SD, (eds), 'Social Structures: A Network Approach', Cambridge, Cambridge University Press, 1988
[145] After FML Thompson, op cit, p8

## Population density

The Vision of Britain website makes the point that the overall population of Britain in 2001 was more than six times what it was in 1801. Population density overall has therefore increased by the same factor. However, "in 1801, the City of London contained over 400 people per hectare, while in 2001 only two local authorities contained over 100 per hectare."[146] This was inevitable since, before the advent of affordable transport, you had to live close enough to your workplace to be able to reach it on foot each day. However, the implications of this population density should not be under-estimated. The ravages of smallpox were to be checked over time following the discovery of vaccination after 1796, and the impact of cheap gin had been reduced by the controls introduced by the 1751 Act (high taxation and proscribed retailing by distillers and shopkeepers). Nevertheless, living in cramped conditions in slum housing was still the norm in urban areas such as London - as was grinding poverty.

## The Pattern of "Popular" Experience[147]

Patrick Colquhoun collated considerable statistical information on late eighteenth and early nineteenth century conditions in order to draw conclusions about the improvements to society he wished to see. He is partly remembered now for his proposals on the police, but he inquired into a wide range of areas relevant to social reform. For example, in 1814 he audited the resources of the empire.[148] In his 'Treatise on Indigence' in 1806 Colquhoun calculated the social structure of England and Wales at the start of the nineteenth century.[149] This treatise has informed the conclusions of many historians, including EP Thompson and Boyd Hilton.[150] It included proposals for the criminal system, friendly societies, education and apprenticeships. He identified 128 possible occupations that might be suitable for the men, and 46 for the women, who made up the

---

[146] See http://www.visionofbritain.org.uk
[147] "Popular" is used in the sense, and only in the sense, of the people's majority or general experience.
[148] Briggs, 2000, op cit, p146
[149] Patrick Colquhoun, 'A Treatise on Indigence', London, Hatchard, 1806. See Table 3 below.
[150] EP Thompson, op cit, pp59-61. Boyd Hilton, 2006, op cit, includes Colquhoun's table on social structure on pp127-8.

seven million people he described as being of "inferior stations". (By this he means the poor who had received no education.)

Appropriate diet also played its part. According to Colquhoun, his observations were that about 25 out of every 30 males of the 1000 balloted for the militia he considered too small to be "fit for the army or navy".[151]

Leaving aside his views of appropriate (i.e., different) male and female occupations, it should be clear that he generally sought to resist the paternalistic attitudes of his time. For example, he said, "In the superior and middle stations in society, the task of educating an offspring and placing them usefully in the world may safely be consigned to parents and guardians; but the poor have no efficient parent or guardian but the legislature. They may have the will, but they have not the ability ... [or opportunity or funds]"[152] Colquhoun drew a series of enlightened conclusions from this, including the view that national systems were required, backed by legislation that balanced encouragement and restraint. He proposed this mechanism as both a route out of poverty for the individual and the means by which society as a whole could make the most effective use of the human capital it had available. Crime and indigence would be reduced by giving people the education and skills to help themselves. He saw education as the defining characteristic of a civilised society. But he also recognised it as a feature that was in the interests of society as a whole. Richard Lovell Edgeworth took a similar line and had entered politics in Ireland in order to campaign for improved education of the poor.[153] These views were very close to those put forward by Robert Owen and discussed below.

## Poverty and Employment

Colquhoun distinguishes what he sees as "virtuous" poverty from indigence. He says that poverty is necessary in any society in order to encourage the supply of labour as a route to improvement. Indigence, on the other hand, can be unavoidable but is otherwise reprehensible. He specifies the reasons for indigence that he sees

---

[151] Colquhoun, op cit, p159
[152] Ibid, p161
[153] Edgeworth and his daughter Maria published 'Practical Education' in 1798 and subsequently 'Essays on Professional Education' in 1809.

as avoidable. Table 3 sets out his conclusions about social structure at the start of the nineteenth century. As might be expected, this social structure shows a marked pyramid effect, with the tiers of society based on the income levels achieved. 100,000 people are members of families with an annual income over £1,000. Almost 900,000 people live in families with income between £200 and £800 per annum. The families of two million people have annual incomes between £100 and £200, and the remaining 6.3m people live in families with incomes under £100 per year. Figure 3 illustrates these ranks within society as a hierarchical pyramid.

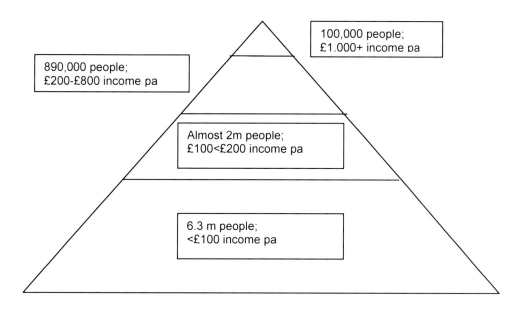

**Figure 3: Social hierarchy in England and Wales, 1801-1803 on the basis of Colquhoun's analysis of social structure[154]**

On the basis of Colquhoun's analysis of social structure, the median annual income was £55. Of the England and Wales population of

---

[154] This is similar to the "ascending series of cubes representing the relative numerical strengths of the social order" with which Robert Owen took aback the Dukes of York and Sussex when they visited New Lanark. Their visit is cited on p209 of Owen's 'Life' and on pp42-43 of the introduction to Robert Owen, 'A New View of Society and Report to the County of Lanark', edited and with an introduction by Vic Gatrell, London, Pelican, 1970.
See Colquhoun's discussion of indigence, op cit, pp9-15

about 9.3 million people in 1801, over three million people lived in families that had a higher income than this figure and more than three million in families with a lower income. Two million people lived in families with incomes at this level. Colquhoun states that in 1803 more than 1,040,000 people were receiving relief (of whom only 83,000 were in workhouses).[155] This is the number of people referred to as "Paupers ..." in Table 3 below. Colquhoun complains on their behalf that they have rarely been given the useful work required under the Poor Law. Family income of £10 was well below subsistence levels.

In 1803 the poor rate had increased to £5.3m[156] (or one-seventh of the rental value of all property of £38m). The total expended on relieving the poor had risen to £7m, including private benevolence. Colquhoun makes the point that the poor rate had increased much more rapidly than had the population in recent years.

Understandably, perhaps, Colquhoun provides no figures for a living wage. This would have been affected by a range of factors - as it is today. They would include personal expectations, comparable wages elsewhere and the extent to which payment was in kind as "truck" rather than as money. For example, an artisan might find £55 an appropriate level, matching his expectations, whereas £100 might be unacceptable to a farmer. Further factors would be the price of corn, the size of family to support, age, the ability to supplement diet with home-grown produce and parish location (hence cost of living and local wages).

---

[155] Ibid, p54. The Poor Law of 1722 had put the responsibility on parishes to build workhouses. They were able to refuse relief to those who would not enter one. The 1782 Act permitted the provision of outdoor relief and parishes joining together as unions.
[156] Ibid, p36

## Table 3: Colquhoun's analysis of the social structure of England and Wales, 1803[157]

| Occupational category | Number of families | Number of persons | Average annual income per family (£) | Cumulative population total |
|---|---|---|---|---|
| King | 1 | 50 | 200,000 | 50 |
| Temporal peers and peeresses | 287 | 7,175 | 8,000 | 7225 |
| Spiritual lords or bishops | 26 | 390 | 4,000 | 7615 |
| Baronets | 540 | 8,100 | 3,000 | 15,715 |
| Eminent merchants, bankers, etc | 2,000 | 20,000 | 2,600 | 35,715 |
| Knights | 350 | 3,500 | 1,500 | 39,215 |
| Esquires | 6,000 | 60,000 | 1,500 | 99,215 |
| Persons in higher civil offices | 2,000 | 14,000 | 800 | 113,215 |
| Lesser merchants, trading by sea | 13,000 | 91,000 | 800 | 204,215 |
| Principal warehouseman, selling by wholesale | 500 | 3,000 | 800 | 207,215 |
| Manufacturers employing capital in all branches (wool, cotton, iron, etc) | 25,000 | 150,000 | 800 | 357,215 |
| Gentlemen and ladies living on income | 20,000 | 160,000 | 700 | 517,215 |
| Persons employing capital in building and repairing ships, etc | 300 | 1,800 | 700 | 519,015 |
| Persons educating youth in universities and chief schools | 500 | 2,000 | 600 | 521,015 |
| Eminent clergymen | 1,000 | 6,000 | 500 | 527,015 |
| Shipowners letting ships for freight only | 5,000 | 25,000 | 500 | 552,015 |
| Persons keeping houses for lunatics | 40 | 400 | 500 | 552,415 |
| Persons of the law, judges down to clerks | 11,000 | 55,000 | 350 | 607,415 |
| Liberal arts and sciences | 16,300 | 81,500 | 260 | 688,915 |
| Persons in lesser civil offices | 10,500 | 52,500 | 200 | 741,415 |

[157] Ibid, pp23-24

| Occupational category | Number of families | Number of persons | Average annual income per family (£) | Cumulative population total |
|---|---|---|---|---|
| Persons employed in theatrical pursuits, musicians, etc | 500 | 2,000 | 200 | 743,415 |
| Persons employing professional skill and capital as engineers, surveyors, master builders, etc | 5,000 | 25,000 | 200 | 769,415 |
| Freeholders of the better sort (i.e., mainly or only freeholders, though some would also have been farmers) | 40,000 | 220,000 | 200 | 989,415 |
| Persons in the education of youth of both sexes | 20,000 | 120,000 | 150 | 1,109,415 |
| Shopkeepers and tradesmen dealing in goods | 74,500 | 372,500 | 150 | 1,481,915 |
| Persons employing capital as tailors, mantua makers, milliners, etc | 25,000 | 125,000 | 150 | 1,606,915 |
| Naval officers, marine officers, surgeons, etc | 3,000 | 15,000 | 149 | 1,621,915 |
| Military officers, including surgeons, etc | 5,000 | 25,000 | 139 | 1,646,915 |
| Lesser clergymen | 10,000 | 50,000 | 120 | 1,696,915 |
| Dissenting clergymen and itinerant preachers | 2,500 | 12,500 | 120 | 1,709,415 |
| Farmers | 160,000 | 960,000 | 120 | 2,669,415 |
| Innkeepers and publicans, licensed | 50,000 | 250,000 | 100 | 2,919,415 |
| Lesser freeholders | 120,000 | 160,000 | 90 | 3,079,415 |
| Clerks and shopmen to merchants, manufacturers, shopkeepers, etc | 30,000 | 150,000 | 75 | 3,229,415 |
| Artisans, handicrafts, mechanics, and labourers, employed in manufactures, buildings and works of every kind | 445,726 | 2,005,767 | 55 | 5,235,182 |
| Military and naval half-pay officers, pensioned | 4,015 | 10,000 | 45 | 5,245,182 |
| Labouring people in mines, | 40,000 | 130,000 | 40 | 5,375,182 |

| Occupational category | Number of families | Number of persons | Average annual income per family (£) | Cumulative population total |
|---|---|---|---|---|
| canals, etc | | | | |
| Hawkers, pedlars, duffers, etc | 800 | 4,000 | 40 | 5,379,182 |
| Seamen in the merchant service, fisheries, rivers, canals, etc | 67,099 | 299,663 | 40 | 5,678,845 |
| Marines and seamen, in the Navy and revenue | 38,175 | 150,000 | 38 | 5,828,845 |
| Labouring people in husbandry, including earnings of the females | 340,000 | 1,530,000 | 31 | 7,358,845 |
| Confined lunatics | 2,500 | 2,500 | 30 | 7,361,345 |
| Common soldiers, including non-commissioned officers and militia | 50,000 | 200,000 | 29 | 7,561,345 |
| Persons imprisoned for debts | 2,000 | 10,000 | 25 | 7,571,345 |
| Paupers producing from their own labours in miscellaneous employments | 260,179 | 1,040,716 | 10 | 8,612,061 |
| Vagrants, Gypsies, rogues and vagabonds, thieves, swindlers, coiners of base money, in and out of prisons, and common prostitutes (incl. wives and children) | ? | 222,000 | 10 | 8,834,061 |
| Chelsea, Greenwich, Chatham pensioners | 30,500 | 70,500 | 10 | 8,904,561 |

The first two of these factors led to the Speenhamland system of supplementing low wages from the poor rate. This was first introduced in the Speenhamland area of Berkshire from 1795, and has become known by that name as it spread. For example, when a loaf of bread cost 1 shilling (1/-, or 5p in the decimal system) a married man with two children was guaranteed 7/6 (37.5p) per week to support his family of four. This comprised 3/- (15p) for himself and 1/6 (7.5p) for each of the other three. When bread rose by 3d to 1/3 (6.25p), the poor relief guarantee for this family increased to

9/- (45p). This was made up of 3/9 (18.75p) for the man and 1/9 (8.75p) for each of the other three people.[158] This was effectively a minimum wage, but it had a number of unforeseen consequences as the price of corn increased and the poor rate grew accordingly. For Malthus it encouraged large families, which would not have happened in his view if wage levels had been adjusted instead. It no doubt encouraged some paupers to regard this as their permanent state.

Leaving aside different rates for married men and the rest of their families, a poor rate of £5.3m in 1803 equates to support of almost 2/- (10p) per week per person for 1.04m paupers. Others had to be supported through the poor rate as well, but their numbers are probably offset by paupers who received only periodic or temporary relief. Assuming that an average family was indeed four people, £5.3m poor rate would therefore amount to support of perhaps 8/- (40p) per family per week on average. This equates to a family income of £21 per year. Combined with the £10 income Table 3 suggests they might earn through their own efforts, this would result in a family income of £31. This level of income was the same as might be earned by an entire family working as labourers in husbandry (see Table 3). As with the benefits trap today, it is easy to understand why some families might have found permanent pauperisation preferable to the alternatives.

One measure of the subsistence level was Perceval's attempt to ensure that resident curates received a minimum living of £50 a year.[159] Hilton says that the wage required for subsistence was more difficult to calculate than fifty years earlier (£20 in 1759), not least because of "the sharp fluctuations in prices caused by bad harvests".[160] However, he implies that it could be upwards of £100. On the basis of Colquhoun's analysis of social structure and its representation in Figure 3, this would suggest that 6.3m people, or two-thirds of the population of England and Wales, were living below subsistence levels.

EP Thompson makes the point that "It was a matter of policy to increase the dependence of cheap reserves of labour ... [This] was endorsed as heartily by landowners as by manufacturers. But

---

[158] See http://www.workhouses.org.uk/index.html for the basis of these calculations
[159] See above
[160] Hilton, 2006, op cit, p126

whereas it fitted the conditions of the Industrial Revolution like a glove, in agriculture it contested (at best) with older paternalist traditions (the squire's duty to his labourers) and with the tradition of earnings based on need ...; while (at worst) it was reinforced by the feudal arrogance of the aristocracy towards the inferior labouring race. **The doctrine that labour discovers its own 'natural' price, according to the laws of supply and demand, had long been ousting the notion of the 'just' wage.** [my emphasis]"[161]

EP Thompson considers particular types of employment (such as farm labourers, artisans and weavers) throughout the eighteenth and nineteenth centuries, concentrating on the impact of the Industrial Revolution and the rise of working class radicalism. He indicates that averages are unlikely to be found in either the field or factory, and may not prove helpful even if they are. Of more value to any consideration of a living wage, and the interaction of this with expectations, are the examples he cites of consumption, and how these relate to "standards and experiences". In 1801 over a third of the population were employed in agriculture (35% according to Boyd Hilton[162]) and this still involved 28% of families in the 1831 census.[163] GM Trevelyan says that a number of writers "who shared the life of the common people ... leave an impression of ... health and happiness as well as much hardship".[164] He cites William Howitt's 'Rural Life in England' for the period from 1802 and George Borrow's 'Lavengro' from 1810 onwards as examples of this.

William Cobbett's 'Rural Rides' was first published in 1830 and refers to journeys in the 1820s. However, Cobbett had come up against rural poverty among southern agricultural workers in Hampshire as early as 1804.[165] Trevelyan argues that this experience was not characteristic of rural England beyond the south. Agricultural wages in the north could be expected to benefit from competition with industrial growth and increased employment in factories. Trevelyan's view is supported by Bohstedt's inclusion of figures that show agricultural wages broadly keeping pace with

---

[161] EP Thompson, op cit, pp 243-244
[162] Hilton, 2006, op cit, p8
[163] EP Thompson, op cit, p233
[164] GM Trevelyan, op cit, p473
[165] Ian Dyck introduction to William Cobbett, 'Rural Rides', London, Penguin, 2001, footnote 11 on p xxv

the cost of living[166]; as it is by Fay[167] who points out that northern agriculture focussed on the staples of meat and milk (rather than crops as in the south).

## Education

A general education system began to appear from 1810, with the Church of England playing its part from 1811.  In advance of that, however, apprenticeships, access to education and the nature and availability of education itself were significant issues.  Colquhoun made a number of proposals in his 1806 'Treatise on Indigence' reflecting his belief that education was a critical indicator of civilisation (see above).  Robert Owen (see Chapter 7) was another passionate advocate of education, both for its own sake and as a means by which individuals might shape and master their surroundings.

A distinction needs to be drawn between formal and informal, everyday (what would now be called "street-wise") education. Children and young people had always learnt from adults and from their peers.  In most instances this was to prove sufficient for day to day living and ensured that skills passed from one generation to the next.  But it also encouraged a degree of inflexibility, not to say rigidity, that ensured each successive generation was largely restricted to the experience and position of the preceding one.  It would be rare for someone, such as James Watt, to transcend those limitations.  Where they did they were driven by curiosity and a personal thirst for knowledge, or they were encouraged by parents with the time and enthusiasm to foster their learning (such as James Mill with his son John Stuart).

This was accepted, if not acceptable, in a society in which change was itself limited.  It became much less accepted in a society that wanted, and needed, to develop in order to realise its potential at an aggregate level.  This required skilled and educated individuals who could contribute as merchants and entrepreneurs, or at least knew enough to act as foremen and overseers of other people (the NCOs of industry).  But there was a balancing act to be struck.  There was no point in educating people generally ("the masses") if they were to

---

[166] Bohstedt, op cit, p185
[167] Fay, op cit, pp43-44

remain in unskilled employment that offered no prospects of advancement. In this scenario education was only likely to increase expectations and lead to disaffection when these were not fulfilled.

On the other hand, enlightenment (and enlightened individuals[168]) was one of the drivers that saw education as a right for all rather than a privilege of the few. Others saw that society as a whole would benefit if individuals were helped to realise their potential through education. As the average age decreased, with more children and young people, this became a necessity - as it would as the pace of change increased through the century. If individuals were to become contributing members of the industrial workforce, there were certain basic skills (for example, in counting and the rudiments of reading) that could prove beneficial. Formal education would ensure they were imparted.[169]

From Table 3 it can be seen that, at the start of the nineteenth century, 2000 people were members of families engaged in education at the main universities and schools. Another 120,000 were part of families that were educating youth more generally. Colquhoun calculated that there were 20,500 families in total in education. These small numbers are one indicator of the limited access to education at this stage.

Gillian Sutherland has drawn attention to the importance of Sunday schools in developing basic skills at the start of the nineteenth century, particularly with regard to reading (a permissible act on the Sabbath).[170] Sunday schools were already in existence, whereas the development of day schools might require new buildings and

---

[168] It is always a mistake to under-estimate the impact that individuals with vision and determination can make more widely. Diamond, op cit, p306 is surely correct when he says, "Leaders who don't just react passively, who have the courage to anticipate crises or to act early, and who make strong insightful decisions of top-down management really can make a huge difference to their societies. So can similarly courageous, active citizens practising bottom-up management." At the extremes it is worth contrasting the allied anticipation of the necessity of regenerating Germany after World War II by introducing a staffed office for this purpose from **1940**, with the absence of any agreed planning for the next steps after the Iraq invasion in 2003.
[169] Lancaster's monitorial system was one way of ensuring (very) basic skills were passed on to large numbers.
[170] Gillian Sutherland, 'Education', pp 119-169 in FML Thompson (ed.), 'Cambridge Social History of Britain 1750-1950: Volume 3 Social Agencies and Institutions', Cambridge, Cambridge University Press, 1990

would require paid staff. Individual benevolence, as well as the church and charities, inevitably had the most impact. But, even where formal education existed, the addition of another wage, no matter how small, was a competing attraction that was more important to most family finances. And, even where this was less of a consideration, education brought with it implications of control as well as opportunity. There was also the issue of families having to pay. This made formal education a luxury that few could afford.

There were therefore several grounds for resisting education. The authorities first sought to ensure that conditions at work were improved for children and young people (from the Health and Morals of Apprentices in the 1802 Act on). They subsequently restricted employment as an alternative to education, either by age and/or hours of work. For example, the Factory Act of 1833 did not permit children under eight years of age to work in textile factories at all, and restricted those aged between eight and thirteen years to eight hours of work a day. It also created an inspectorate to enforce these regulations. These, and other developments like them, were much needed improvements, but their coverage was far from comprehensive. Agriculture, for instance, was omitted.

Compulsory education was yet to come. Even after the 1870 Act parishes were permitted to compel attendance, but did not have to. The Education Act of 1880 made elementary schools routine in every parish, with all children between five and ten years of age being required to attend on a full-time basis (though attendance had only reached 82% by 1895). Elementary education did not become free until the Fees Act of 1891 abolished the requirement on parents to pay to keep their children out of work.[171]

## Conclusion

In summary, therefore, the start of the nineteenth century saw a rapidly growing population, but with poverty a prominent factor for the majority. Regardless of whether access to the elite was open to all, it contained relatively few people by definition. Over six million, or more than two-thirds of the population, lived in families with incomes less than £100, over three million people in families with

---

[171] Ibid, p145

incomes less than the median of £55 and over a million (one-ninth of the total) were classed as paupers and depended on poor relief.

The population was concentrated in a few counties, with density already most marked in London.  Lancashire and the West Riding of Yorkshire on either side of the Pennines had the largest numbers of people, but other areas of the country were also growing fast. People were moving from rural areas into the towns, a movement that was rapidly gathering pace.[172]

Formal education was one route by which individuals could improve their circumstances, but this was only available to most people through Sunday schooling.  This would remain the situation for the majority of the population for most of the nineteenth century, despite more enlightened people viewing access to education as in the interests of society as a whole.

While many may have accepted the circumstances in which they found themselves, or not been aware that alternatives existed, and others sought refuge in the familiarity of the past, a few sought change (in the sense of progress and not just for its own sake). There were radical models around, but these did not necessarily relate to the realities of working-class experience.  Even if they did, there was an example across the Channel of the unforeseen and unfortunate consequences of revolution and precipitate transformation.  There was a risk of over-turning the foundations of civil and civilised society as well as tackling the excesses that needed to be curbed.  There was also the issue of patriotism when the country was at war with the French empire.  Even if the revolution had proved an acceptable model for other reasons, this alone might have precluded its adoption.

The over-riding aspiration remained reform, but with a preference that this should be predictable, managed and therefore manageable.  This would help ensure that change was synonymous with continued development and improvement, and at a human pace.  More rapid change might be superficially attractive, but there was little point if it could not be sustained.

---

[172] In 1809 Potts published his New Gazetteer.  His inclusion of canals in a new map of England and Wales was another illustration of how the country was changing.

## 4. WHAT WERE PEOPLE DOING AND HOW WAS THIS CHANGING?

Weight was an issue in 1809, but usually in the sense that poor diet and poverty often went together. However, when Daniel Lambert died on 21st July 1809 in a Lincolnshire inn he was said to have weighed 52 stone 11lb.[173] In order to bury him, a wall and window of the inn had to be moved in order to get him out. Daniel Lambert clearly made his mark on his surroundings and is remembered 200 years later by newspapers such as the Liverpool Echo and Birmingham Evening Mail that refer to him as "famous fattie".

His fellow countrymen left their mark as well: physically in the case of roads and canals, or books and paintings; equally indelibly, if less obviously, in the case of social and economic change. This Chapter focusses on the impact of such people, both the general population and some particular individuals, while Chapters 5 and 6 concentrate on the political impact and significance of 1809.

### Communications and Trade

Britain's traditional patterns of trade abroad were being restricted by the effects of war with France and by the trade embargo against both France and Britain that America had introduced to replace their ineffectual attempt to remain neutral. Even so, several London docks were completed in the first years of the nineteenth century as the country planned ahead for an island's future of maritime trade. They included the London docks (completed in 1803), the West and East India docks (1806), Surrey and East County docks (1807) and Commercial docks (1815). The inevitable gap between planning and realisation was fortunate. The new docks proved a further spur to both opening new markets and making this a realistic option. Another reason for these developments, according to Brown, was that "the Committee of West Indian merchants threatened [in 1793] to transfer their trade elsewhere"[174] if this was not done. Internal trade within Britain continued to be one of the main drivers for improved communications and communication routes.

---

[173] This is four times the average for adult men now, and was five or six times the average weight then when people's diets were limited and they were smaller.
[174] R. Brown, 'Society and Economy in Modern Britain 1700-1850', London, Routledge, 1991, p149

Both the movement of people and the movement of freight had increased during the eighteenth century. But trade was to prove a more prominent impetus to development than passenger traffic.[175] Producers who wanted to get their goods to market more efficiently, to reduce their costs and delays, or to open up new markets, had two main options. Either they could press the powers that be for change or they could fund the developments themselves.[176] In some instances their initial funding might lead other people, or perhaps the government, to support them. In other words, private speculation had proved its worth and drew in other investors. This was a pattern that started with canals but was repeated even more obviously with railways from the 1840s and 1850s. 1807 was the start of a four-year boom for joint stock arrangements in order to develop canals.[177]

Transporting produce by road was not an option unless the market was very close. Private turnpike trusts had been in existence since 1706, but there was no national scheme for roads and it was generally up to individual parishes to maintain them.[178] Unless you had far to go, or much to carry, it was as quick by foot. For most people, this was the only affordable means of moving around. If you lived close to a river or the coast, a boat might provide an alternative for the better off. Transport on horseback and by stagecoach increased as the quality of roads improved. Brown[179] says that journey times reduced by 80% between 1750 and 1830. But he also says the elliptical spring was not patented until 1805. The significance of this was twofold: it reduced the cost of

---

[175] At least prior to the advent of railways towards the middle of the 19th century. Up to this point most people did not venture further than they could walk - with the inevitable consequence for limiting their expectations and horizons. Even labour mobility was said to be restricted to short distances (e.g., A Redford, 'Labour Migration in England', Manchester, Manchester University Press, 1926 cited by Hilton, 2006, p675).

[176] Stone and Stone, op cit, p16 say "They [country landowners] also improved communications by sponsoring canal and turnpike Acts in order to get their produce to market."

[177] Hilton, 2006, op cit, pp 131 and 647

[178] The exception to this prior to 1809 was the Commission for Highland Roads in 1803 to open up this area of the country. From 1810 to 1835 the government spent £0.75m to improve the road from London to Holyhead so that people and exports could reach Ireland more rapidly (according to Brown, op cit, p135). The converse might also apply, but the possibility of two-way traffic with Ireland seems not to have been at the forefront of deliberations.

[179] Brown, op cit, pp143-145

constructing coaches, and, as importantly, it improved comfort for passengers.

The internal movement of freight meant transportation by water. Since the rivers had been made as navigable as possible by 1720, further development depended on canals.[180] There was a period of canal building up to the 1770s that ended with the Chester Canal. A dormant period then followed as a result of the war with America, but economic activity increased again from 1783. The 1790s are described as "canal mania"[181], with 51 Acts of Parliament between 1791 and 1796 allowing the building of new canals.[182] Asa Briggs says that 42 new canals costing £6.5m capital were planned in the 1790s.[183] The benefits extended beyond Britain with Thomas Telford being knighted in Sweden in 1809 for his help with their canals.

By 1830 the period of canal building was largely over, though they continued to be built during the following decade[184]. At this stage there were more than "4000 miles of navigable waterways".[185] The canal network had overcome major engineering challenges that were to prove beneficial for later aspects of the Industrial Revolution. An extreme example, perhaps, is the perpendicular lift invented by John Woodhouse and installed at Tardebigge on the Worcester-Birmingham canal in 1809.[186] Early mistakes with different canal sizes were rectified (though this was hardly a unique error and seems to beset all developments from railway gauges to inventions up to our time where there are competing producers). Canals fostered economic development by improving transport and opening up new markets for produce. They provided employment, particularly during the labour-intensive building phase. They

---

[180] Adam Smith in the 'Wealth of Nations', 1776 says that "Good roads, canals, and navigable rivers, by diminishing the expense of carriage, put the remote parts of the country more nearly upon a level with … the town. They are upon that account the greatest of all improvements."

[181] The title of Anthony Burton's 1993 book already referred to in Chapter 1.

[182] Brown, op cit, p152

[183] Briggs, 1983, p230

[184] Christian Wolmar, 'Fire and Steam: A New History of the Railways in Britain', London, Atlantic Books, 2007, p54

[185] Brown, op cit, p152

[186] J Gregory and J Stevenson, 'Britain in the Eighteenth Century, 1688-1820', London, Longman, 2000, pp281-286. This section also lists all canal and turnpike Acts in this period.

therefore increased spending power. They reduced prices of food and materials, and made coal more widely available - both for factories and for people to keep themselves warm.

In the final analysis, however, canals also had significant limitations. Britain's hilly topography was one issue, as was the country's climate. Water levels fell in summer, while canals could be ice-bound in winter. They provided fixed routes that were dependent on the producers and their markets not moving. Although it was said that nowhere was more than fifteen miles from a navigable waterway, this could be a significant distance for alternative forms of transporting freight (especially given the condition of roads). Transferring freight to and from the barges was often prohibitive as costs were increased by the requirement for local transportation. Traffic was often one-way, leading to significant down-time as empty barges returned to their starting-points to be refilled. Although the ideal might be to transport freight both ways, this occurred less frequently than might be wished. For example, a barge that had been carrying coal to a factory could not then be used to take away the finished textiles without significant, perhaps costly, protection for the latter load. The distribution networks onwards from their drop-off points were limited.

Most significant, though, was the absence of competition. This ensured that canals had a heyday in the first decades of the nineteenth century. But once alternative forms of transportation developed, this was bound to be brief. The roads were in a lamentable state when canals flourished, with both ultimately dependent on horses (and their towing power) for speed. It would be the 1840s before railways developed apace after the Rocket trials at Rainhill in 1829 prior to the opening of the Liverpool and Manchester railway in 1830.[187] Wolmar calls this the "first railway", with the railway operator carrying passengers as well as freight, although Richard Trevithick had been working with high-pressure steam engines since obtaining his first patent in 1802[188] and the Stockton-Darlington line had opened in 1825. James Watt had perfected the steam engine for industrial purposes as early as 1775, and he and his partner Matthew Boulton (who was to die in 1809)

---

[187] Wolmar, op cit, pp36-42. Fay, op cit, p20 says that Liverpool and Manchester merchants saw the development of railways as an opportunity to remove the canal monopoly.
[188] Briggs, 1983, p234

installed a number of the low pressure machines in factories. However, these were different to the engines that George Stephenson first developed for railway locomotion.

Pickfords was one of the companies that relied by 1809 on the canal network for the movement of goods. At this stage it was a general haulier, and as such dependent on canals for much of its trade. The company history describes 1809 as a "slump". This loss of trade was a foretaste of the crisis that was to emerge more obviously in 1811 as a result of the Napoleonic wars.

Canals were valued for their military purposes, where they were often the only realistic option for transporting large amounts of munitions. For example, the Bedfordshire militia oversaw the transport of 22,000 muskets from the arsenal at Weedon to London in 1809.

## Employment and Professions

Both Gregory and Stevenson[189] and Joyce[190] include tables on the distribution of the labour force in the early years of the nineteenth century. The former provide this as percentages of the occupied population, while the latter includes the actual numbers. Each is based on Cole and Deane's analysis of British economic growth.[191] Table 4 combines the two, but restricts the coverage to the first years of the nineteenth century.

It can be seen from Table 4 that the number of people employed overall increased significantly (by 29%) over this twenty-year period. This is in line with the population increase of one-seventh (14%) each decade, or a doubling every fifty years (as discussed in the preceding Chapter). With the exception of the category of public service and professionals, the number of people engaged in each area of occupation also increased. It needs to be remembered, however, that the balance within these occupational categories could, and indeed did, change. For example, Joyce concludes that

---

[189] Gregory and Stevenson, op cit, p293
[190] P Joyce in FML Thompson (ed), 'Cambridge Social History of Britain 1750-1950: Volume 2 People and their Environment', Cambridge, Cambridge University Press, 1990, p133
[191] P Deane and WA Cole, 'British Economic Growth, 1688-1959', Cambridge, Cambridge University Press, 1969

there was "a decisive shift to manufacture ... [and] the decline of agriculture was inexorable".[192]  This picture is reinforced by the changing pattern of percentages in the lower half of the Table.

**Table 4: Estimated distribution of the labour force 1801-1821**

| Number of people (m) | | | | | | |
|---|---|---|---|---|---|---|
| **Year** | Agriculture Forestry Fishing | Manufacture Mining Building | Trade Transport | Domestic Personal | Public service Professional | **Total occupied population (m)** |
| 1801 | 1.7 | 1.4 | 0.5 | 0.6 | 0.3 | 4.8 |
| 1811 | 1.8 | 1.7 | 0.6 | 0.7 | 0.4 | 5.5 |
| 1821 | 1.8 | 2.4 | 0.8 | 0.8 | 0.3 | 6.2 |
| | | | | | | |
| Percentage of total occupied population | | | | | | |
| **Year** | Agriculture Forestry Fishing | Manufacture Mining Building | Trade Transport | Domestic Personal | Public service Professional* | **Total occupied population (m)** |
| 1801 | 35.9 | 29.7 | 11.2 | 11.5 | 11.8 | 4.8 |
| 1811 | 33.0 | 30.2 | 11.6 | 11.8 | 13.3 | 5.5 |
| 1821 | 28.4 | 38.4 | 12.1 | 12.7 | 8.5 | 6.2 |

* Gregory and Stevenson include 'other' in this category.  Hence the percentages exceed what might be expected from Joyce's figures of people.

One illustration of this switch towards increased factory production can be seen in changes that took place at this time in the woollen trade.  Paternalistic approaches to employment were removed in the ten years from 1803, with the regulations covering the woollen trade repealed in 1809.[193]  This is amplified by the website on Calderdale's weavers, which says "Woollen workers believed their jobs were safeguarded by statutes dating from Tudor times and demanded that their livelihoods were entitled to protection by enforcement of the law. Factory masters argued that the old laws were archaic and an obstacle to the development of the industry. Parliament appointed a Select Committee in 1803 and again in 1806 to investigate the issues.  In 1809 the government repealed all existing legislation, the woollen trade was thrown open to the forces of the free market; the new order, the factory age had arrived".[194]

---

[192] Joyce, op cit, p132
[193] EP Thompson, op cit, p578
[194] See http://www.calderdale.gov.uk/wtw/timeline/1800_1810/1800_1810_1.html

The weavers were at the cutting edge of the Industrial Revolution as the nature of their employment changed. Their disaffection with these changes in employment practices, and reductions in wages in particular, made them a case study both for EP Thompson and for Bohstedt's analysis of riots[195]. EP Thompson says that, "... at the same time as wages were screwed lower and lower, the number of weavers continued to increase over the first three decades of the nineteenth century; for weaving, next to general labouring, was the grand resource of the northern unemployed".[196] This concurs with the figures already quoted from Bohstedt (see above).

EP Thompson goes on to say that "Fustian weaving was heavy, monotonous, but easily learned. Agricultural workers, demobilized soldiers, Irish immigrants - all continued to swell the labour force".[197] Similarly, Bohstedt states that "Irish peasants, many of them experienced cottage-weavers, poured into Manchester in the 1790s." He sees cotton hand-loom weavers as classic exemplars of "proto-industrialisation".[198] By this he means the exploitation of abundant cheap labour using hand techniques of production, rather than power-driven machinery. This exploitation was made all the easier because weaving was a full-time occupation before the widespread adoption of powered machinery in the 1820s.[199] Despite the ease with which the weaving task could be learned, apprenticeships had been introduced in 1782. The only purpose in this was to provide employers with additional cheap labour through pauper children and maintain the downward pressure on wages.

The weavers had been seeking a minimum wage since the 1790s in order to protect themselves against pressures to reduce wages - regardless of whether these were brought about by reduced demand as a result of the wars, an increase in the labour force supply or the machinations of unscrupulous employers. The minimum wage had been supported by the more competitive employers who saw an opportunity to put their less scrupulous rivals out of business. When the demand was finally rejected by the House of Commons in 1808, after expectations had first been raised that it would be approved, the weavers had no other

---

[195] Bohstedt, op cit
[196] EP Thompson, op cit, p307
[197] Ibid, p307
[198] Bohstedt, op cit, pp131-132
[199] Ibid, p134

recourse but to strike (of which more below).  Although prosperity was to return to the weaving trade in the two years immediately after the strike (1809 and 1810), the reprieve was only temporary.[200] The Lancashire spinners also formed themselves into a general union from 1810.[201]

Bohstedt's overall conclusion is framed in terms of the changing circumstances of Manchester.  He says that "... conventional explanations of working-class solidarity in this period - hardship, proletarianisation, ideological radicalisation - are not sufficient to explain the workers' *capacities* for collective action nor in what way that action was new.  To understand that history one must recast it in the light of Manchester's community politics.  The crucial fact is that the textile workers ... were new groups of workers in 1790, 'created' and assembled by the appearance of new technology and by Manchester's rapid industrial growth.  Both geographically and culturally they were recent immigrants into a new urban industrial world."[202]

It would be a mistake to over-generalise from the weaving trade to employment generally.  Weaving is of particular interest to EP Thompson and Bohstedt because of the special nature of the changes and the political consequences.  The same is the case for agricultural workers and led Cobbett (amongst others) to various conclusions about their mistreatment.  It was happening to most traditional forms of employment faced with the changed, and changing, arrangements of supply and demand in order to avoid being overtaken by alternatives, improvements, imports and new markets.[203]

Despite what Table 4 might appear to indicate, professions such as medicine, law and banking were beginning to coalesce and were to form themselves into colleges and societies at this time or shortly afterwards.  For example, the Royal College of Surgeons was

---

[200] Ibid, p157

[201] Ibid, p130

[202] Ibid, p126

[203] Not all forms of employment were traditional.  For example, Wolmar, op cit, pp31-32 distinguishes ordinary labourers from the "navigators" who built the canals and their successors, known as navvies, who made the railways possible.

formed in 1800.[204]   The Law Society was founded in 1825, though its predecessor had been called for in 1823 to tackle the "'pettifoggers and vipers' disgracing the profession".[205]   The Stock Exchange became regulated on 3rd March 1801, moved into a new building in 1802 and produced its first rule book in 1812.[206] Rothschild moved from being a warehouseman in Manchester to become a merchant banker in London between 1808 and 1811.[207] There were almost 700 country banks by 1815, all of which could issue their own notes alongside the Bank of England, many of which had been founded by Quakers (such as Barclays or Gurneys), and some of which overstretched themselves and went bankrupt when their debts proved more extensive than their reserves.[208]

Even the Bank of England could no longer guarantee to convert notes into gold after 1797 as a result of the Napoleonic Wars:   "... the Government was obliged to protect the gold reserves for the war effort by declaring the Bank's notes inconvertible. This 'Restriction Period', as it was known[209], continued for six years after the end of the war, until 1821.   Because of the consequent shortage of coin the Bank issued £1 and £2 notes to keep the wheels of trade turning; but, inevitably, prices rose generally and this provoked a fierce debate and the setting up of a Parliamentary Select Committee which attributed the country's difficulties mainly to the Bank's over-issue of paper. The Committee argued that a paper currency which had ceased to be convertible into gold or silver coin could only be kept up to its proper value by limiting its quantity, in that way it would become again a sound currency."[210]

---

[204] See Virginia Berridge in FML Thompson, Vol 3, op cit, pp171-242 on developments in health and medicine.

[205] See http://www.lawsociety.org.uk/aboutlawsociety/whoweare/abouthistory.law Interestingly, the Bar Council did not come into being until 1894.  There seems to have been less urgency to protect the public from barristers or to regulate the profession, perhaps because this area of the law was more visible to the public and it was assumed that the courts served this purpose.

[206] See http://www.londonstockexchange.com/en-gb/about/cooverview/history.htm

[207] Hilton, op cit, p155.  He also has a section on "Commerce and the Quasi-Professions" pp141-151 as well as the section on "Business Classes" pp152-156 from which this example is drawn.

[208] This might provide a "warning from history" given the global downturn or "credit crunch" from 2007 that has affected some banks.

[209] After Pitt's Restriction Act of 1797.

[210] See http://www.bankofengland.co.uk/about/history/major_developments4.htm Ricardo's criticisms in this respect, and the bullion report, are referred to below.

With regard to industrialists, FML Thompson says "... the manufacturer, as an entrepreneur and employer, was typically a merchant-manufacturer. The modern industrialist, as owner of the means of production and direct manager and employer of the production workers, was of course beginning to appear: this is what Richard Arkwright, Robert Peel ... Josiah Wedgwood, Matthew Boulton, and the others ... were all about. They were the harbingers of the future, but down to 1815, and indeed for many further decades, the great bulk of industrial production was organised and managed on more traditional lines, while the early industrialists themselves were successful precisely because they were good at trading and marketing."[211]

The means of production was evolving in the direction of factories rather than independent outwork, with more trades (such as weavers) being drawn in. Technological developments and new inventions made this feasible.[212] Working in groups rather than as individuals should in theory be more efficient; production processes were shared, increasingly mechanised and ultimately "engineered". The raw materials were now delivered to, and the finished products collected from, one location without any necessity for these to be re-distributed to, or gathered from, workers at home. This made options for bulk distribution and transportation more realistic. It was now the workers who had to travel to the factory, or more likely to re-locate. Given that transportation accounted for a significant proportion of the finished costs, the employers were shifting an aspect of these on to the workers.

Initially, the focus was on reducing costs and improving processes. However, the products themselves developed as technology and new processes expanded what was available and new markets generated additional and innovative demands.

---

[211] FML Thompson, Vol 1, op cit, p31. Gavin Weightman, 'Industrial Revolutionaries', London, Atlantic Books, 2007, p21 says "The key figure ... was perhaps not so much the skilled artisan as the talented entrepreneur or businessman. Men such as Matthew Boulton and Josiah Wedgwood combined both skills."
[212] See Weightman, op cit and Christine Macleod, 'Heroes of Invention', Cambridge, Cambridge University Press, 2007

## Dispute and Dissent

In advance of this, though, various workers were to express their disaffection. They were expected to work long hours - increasingly long hours in some trades. Cunningham says that "By the early nineteenth century the working day in [textile] factories lasted from 6am to 7pm or 8pm with only one hour for meals; that is to say twelve or thirteen hours of actual work as opposed to the ten-hour norm" or the accepted benchmark of sixty hours per week.[213] They had few, if any, rights, little protection in many industries and their wages were rarely adequate compensation. The new machinery appeared to threaten their livelihoods, and often did. From where many workers stood, the benefits looked to be all one way.

It would be an exceptionally brave, perhaps foolhardy, employer who was prepared to buck the trend of their industry. Even if they had the vision or imagination to adopt a different approach, there were always the risks of being less competitive, and perhaps going bankrupt at the extreme, or at least of being ostracised by other factory owners. On both these counts, as well as others, Robert Owen stands out (see Chapter 7 below). Religious principles might require a different stance, but these were as likely to determine which type of employment was pursued as the approach then taken within it. Even Joseph Rowntree (1836-1925) and Titus Salt (1803-1876) were viewed as philanthropists and their initiatives were in any case still some time off. Historians can discern an enlightenment period, but this was primarily intellectual, far from universal and often an attitude that did not necessarily translate into action. Employers in 1809 frequently had other priorities that meant their behaviour appeared far from enlightened.

Disorder and riot were long-standing traditions in Britain when immediate reaction was inevitable, or when alternative means for people to express their views were closed off or having little impact. Perversely, collecting people together in one place might be expected to make this group behaviour more likely. Alternative forms of negotiation would have to be found if such mob protest was to be avoided. On the other hand, the sources of discontent were usually at hand too. This made the search for alternative,

---

[213] H Cunningham in FML Thompson, Volume 2, op cit, p280. The Ten Hours Act was introduced in 1847.

more ritualised mechanisms inevitable and more pressing if the escalation of discontent was to be avoided.[214]

In the meantime, however, traditional forms of protest were to be pursued again in 1809 and subsequent years (the Luddite revolt, for example), but there were also other non-violent illustrations and exemplars, such as non-conformist traditions in religion.

## Religion

The Act of Toleration in 1689 required Protestant dissenters from the Church of England to register their meeting houses, but they were otherwise permitted to worship freely.[215]   Roman Catholics continued to be excluded for over a century until they were allowed from 1791 to worship "with unlocked doors" - provided the chapel was registered.[216]   By the turn of the nineteenth century, therefore, people were worshipping openly in accord with their religious beliefs.  It would be another twenty-nine years, however, before the Catholic Emancipation Act of 1829 gave Catholics the right to sit in Parliament.

James Obelkevich says that "Between 1790 and 1815 the main influences on British religious life were the great events of revolution, war and reaction.  In no church could there be business as usual while the fate of nations hung in the balance."[217]  But the Anglican and Dissenter perspectives were very different. Obelkevich says that the older Dissenting churches, but not necessarily Methodists, took a different political stance to Anglicans generally: they were more likely to support the French Revolution and reform in Britain, and to advocate peace in the war rather than outright victory over France.  Inevitably, "the Anglican majority ... [viewed such] Nonconformists [as] disloyal and unpatriotic.  [They

---

[214] Vic Gatrell on p43 of his introduction to Robert Owen, op cit, makes the point that New Lanark provided this example: "What the village portended was clear: that the relationships, close, deferential, and interdependent, which were thought peculiar to pastoral Britain, were capable of reconstitution within industrial society." In other words, Owen had extended ritualised behaviour in rural areas (see references to Briggs elsewhere) to the factory community, with both employer and employee seeing how their interests were better served by cooperation than conflict.

[215] See http://www.buildinghistory.org/Church/Nonconform.htm

[216] Ibid

[217] See his Chapter on religion in FML Thompson, Vol 3, op cit, pp311-356, p326.

were] determined to crush the Revolution and to close ranks against dissent and reform of any kind."[218] He goes on to add by way of emphasis that Parliament, dominated by the established Anglican church, sought in 1811 to restrict "itinerant preaching, one of the keys to their success. The lesson drawn by Dissenters was that they were at odds not just with the established church but with the entire system of aristocratic rule and privilege."

Alongside these Nonconformists, Methodism continued to increase in popularity while the Anglican church separated into its Evangelical and traditional adherents. According to Obelkevich, "Perhaps a tenth of the clergy (largely from Cambridge) were Evangelicals; the 'Clapham Sect', a circle of rich businessmen and their families living near Clapham Common in London, provided the lay leadership."[219] William Wilberforce (1759-1833) and Spencer Perceval were two of the most well-known Evangelicals and prominent proponents of this wing of the church in Parliament. The Evangelicals were criticised on several counts. In particular, they were said to be "eager to suppress the pleasures of the poor while turning a blind eye to those of the rich".[220] And, in even more emotive language, "Radicals attacked them for telling the poor to 'starve without making a noise'".[221] Although this view does not necessarily accord with Wilberforce's leading role in the anti-slavery movement, nor with Perceval's personal benevolence and support for charitable causes, it would hardly be surprising if the Evangelical movement were to be limited to a restricted and rarefied circle.

On the other hand, evangelism in its broadest - and usual - sense was both the defining characteristic of Methodism and was prevalent among other Nonconformist churches as well.

[218] Ibid, p327

[219] Ibid, p323

[220] However, Boyd Hilton has pointed out (in a personal communication) that "Wilberforce, Hannah More (1745-1833), Thomas Gisborne (1758-1846), Thomas Chalmers (1780-1847) et al all started with the need for 'the reformation of the manners of the great'". He says (2006, op cit, p178) that "... there is no denying the gradual permeation of the new Puritanism, even among the aristocracy", though this was an uphill task during the Regency, a time more "notable for rakes" than "godly nobles".

[221] Obelkevich also says, "[Their] opponents were numerous and highly critical. In their view Evangelicals were no more than puritanical humbugs, obsessed with their own souls, complacent about being 'saved', ... They were accused of being humourless, anti-intellectual ... and philistine ... There was **some truth** [emphasis added] in all these criticisms." Ibid, p323

Obelkevich concludes that "the combined forces of Non-conformity and Methodism were making deep inroads" among those who had previously been identified as Anglican.[222]

Watts analyses the 1851 religious census, which counted all those worshipping at the various services on 30th March 1851.[223] He shows that 17% of the England population by this stage, or nearly 3m people, worshipped as Protestant Nonconformists. In Wales it was over 45%. Although numbers and percentages were less in 1809, religious dissent already accounted for a sizeable proportion of the population. More significantly, perhaps, this minority was growing rather than shrinking. The importance of religious affiliation cannot be over-stated. It provided the Nonconformists with an acceptable and publicly sanctioned means of expressing views and beliefs that could vary in significant ways from the mainstream. Religious beliefs might be shaped by a particular political perspective or vice versa - it hardly mattered. Both reflected a certain world view and the political undercurrents that determined this. There might be some personal disadvantages and costs to demonstrating this dissent, but these were decreasing. At least the physical penalties were unlikely to be as severe as those to which participation in mass demonstrations and riots might lead.

As Obelkevich says in relation to Methodism:
"[It] grew fastest, significantly, in the period of heightened social strain in the first half of the nineteenth century. For those making the difficult transition from a traditional way of life to a more individualistic and competitive one, Methodism did much to ease the way. ... There was also an element of social protest. ...
"[Another] suggestion has been that during the years of social unrest around 1800 Methodism prevented a possible revolution."[224]

Religion was an alternative form of dissent. But it was also a safety-valve, reducing pressure in a controlled way. It could dilute the impact of other changes in society, or at least deflect attention from them, without endangering people or property. Riots by

---

[222] Ibid, p326
[223] Michael Watts, 'The Dissenters, Volume ii: The Expansion of Evangelical Nonconformity', Oxford, Clarendon Press,1995. Watts addresses the issue of those people who were counted several times if they attended more than one service.
[224] Obelkevich, op cit, pp324-5

contrast lacked this element of control and might result at any time in physical risk.

## Riot

Riots have been a characteristic means of protest in Britain[225] - not only up to the nineteenth century, but more recently as well (over, for example. race in the early 1980s, coal-mining in the mid-1980s, the poll tax later that decade and community tensions again in the first years of the twenty-first century). They have proved a fundamental way of demanding change and addressing inequity. In some instances, an intransigent political leadership may have meant people considered this the only way to register the strength of their opposition and the depth of their views. In their opinion the constitutional parliamentary process had proved, or was thought, to be ineffective and they were unable to rely on it. Thwarted expectations generally are a potent explanation of most instances of this form of dispute and dissent, and provide an alternative to the "rational response" theory that riots reflect real grievances or hardship.

Inevitably, therefore, there have been many writers on riots and the significance of this form of protest over the years. Two in-depth studies of this period have been conducted by John Bohstedt and Charles Tilly. Tilly[226] analysed more than 8000 contentious gatherings (as he described them) by sampling thirteen of the 62 years up to 1820. This work is referred to in Chapter 7 below given that his conclusions mainly relate to the years after 1809. Bohstedt sampled all riots in the 20 years up to 1810 that were reported in two newspapers (the Observer and Morning Chronicle, or substitutes when these were not available) and in the Home Office's general Domestic Correspondence file. There were a total of 617 riots in his sample, by which he means a crowd of at least 50

---

[225] It should be remembered that by definition these have always involved a minority of people. This is not to disagree with the strength or significance of the views expressed, let alone their appropriateness or the sincerity with which they were held in many instances. What it does mean though is that Britain has not pursued the revolutionary approach adopted by majorities elsewhere (even in 1848), let alone the covert tactics of coup or assassination.

[226] Charles Tilly, 'Popular Contention in Great Britain 1758-1834', London, Harvard University Press, 1995

people acting in a hostile fashion against people or property.[227]  He stopped short of the start of the Luddite riots in 1811.

Figure 4 sets out the incidence of riots over this 20 year period. This indicates that the period 1804 to 1809 was largely quiet, with the exception of the weavers' actions in 1808.  The spinners were to strike in 1810 on forming their union, and there was a lead-up period prior to the Luddite riots getting underway in earnest from 1811.   Bohstedt examines the incidence of riots against food prices, and concludes that people's expectations of prices were just as important as rising prices themselves.  There were few food riots after 1801.

Number of riots in England & Wales 1790-1810

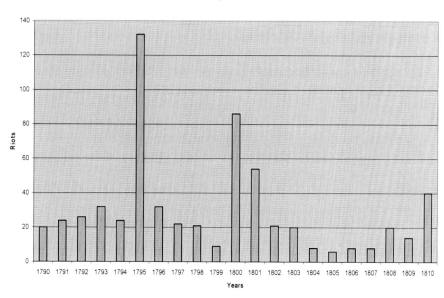

**Figure 4: Incidence of 617 riots in England and Wales 1790-1810** (after Bohstedt's Figure 1 setting these against wheat prices)[228]

---

[227] Bohstedt, op cit, pp4-12
[228] Bohstedt's conclusion on p17 is "... rioting reached peaks in 1795 and 1800, years of high food prices.  But in both crises, still higher prices in the following year coincided with sharp drops in the incidence of rioting.  Some historians have continued to insist upon simple economic causation by suggesting that it was the steepness or suddenness of the price rise, rather than its absolute level, that touched off rioting.  That may well be.  But sharp rises in 1798-1799, 1804-1805, and 1808-1809 coincided with *decreases* in the incidence of rioting, while the dearth of 1810 was not nearly so riotous as the earlier crises."  It would appear that people's expectations were therefore vitally important.

A further conclusion would be that there was a link to the lows of the Napoleonic War. Considerations of patriotism alone would be sufficient to make riot or violent protest less likely at this time.

Bohstedt's analysis of the causes of these riots is shown in Table 5. He goes into further detail on the issues (and the limitations of the "rational response" theory)[229], but even this Table is sufficient to show that the issues in London were different to (and less likely to be food-related than) those elsewhere in the country. The military frictions identified in Table 5 refer to recruitment, mobilisation, mutinies and civilian-military brawls. Generally speaking, these issues could not have arisen while much of the army and navy were out of the country[230], and must have taken place before the period after 1803 when patriotism would be expected to reduce the likelihood of riot (and Figure 4 indicates there were insufficient incidents anyway).

**Table 5: Issues provoking riots in England and Wales 1790-1810** (after Bohstedt's Table 1)

| | Riots in England and Wales 1790 - 1810 | | | | | |
|---|---|---|---|---|---|---|
| | London | | Elsewhere | | Total | |
| Issues | Number | % | Number | % | Number | % |
| Food | 5 | 4.1 | 237 | 48.0 | 242 | 39.2 |
| Labour | 6 | 4.9 | 38.5 | 7.8 | 44.5 | 7.2 |
| Military | 31 | 25.2 | 102.5 | 20.7 | 133.5 | 21.6 |
| Political/Ideological | 17 | 13.8 | 46 | 9.3 | 63 | 10.2 |
| Brawls | 20 | 16.3 | 14 | 2.8 | 34 | 5.5 |
| Miscellaneous | 43 | 35.0 | 46 | 9.3 | 89 | 14.4 |
| Other | 1 | 0.8 | 10 | 2.0 | 11 | 1.8 |
| Total | 123 | 100.1 | 494 | 99.9 | 617 | 99.9 |

This analysis is amplified in Table 6. As Bohstedt says[231], riots were more likely in urban than rural areas. This might be thought inevitable given the concentration of population, but it is worth noting that riots were as likely in smaller towns as in the large conurbations. For example, there were significant disturbances in

---

[229] Ibid, pp14-16
[230] Though incidents sparked off by people resisting press-gangs and other forms of forced service obviously could have done.
[231] Bohstedt, op cit, pp166-167

Nottingham in 1809 as well as riots in London when the actor-manager Kemble raised prices at the rebuilt Covent Garden theatre.[232]

**Table 6: Riots per 10,000 people of 617 riots in England and Wales 1790-1810** (after Bohstedt's Table 2)

| 1801 Population | Number of riots | Riots per 10,000 people |
|---|---|---|
| < 2,000[1] | 138 | 0.23 |
| 2,000<10,000 | 188 | 1.50 |
| 10,000<20,000 | 66 | 1.38 |
| 20,000<100,000 | 102 | 1.60 |
| > 100,000[2] | 123 | 1.36 |
| **Total** | 617 | 0.67 |

[1] Includes places for which the 1801 Census gives no population
[2] In other words London, including Southwark

Interestingly, this urban-rural split reflects Briggs' point about ritualised behaviour in the countryside providing an alternative outlet for disaffection. This form of protest had yet to develop or be adopted routinely in urban areas. Bohstedt makes a similar point about the ubiquity of rural disrespect for the gentry, linking riots to community politics.

The weavers strike in 1808 is of interest in this context because it covered much of the region around Manchester and therefore towns of various sizes. For example, it is said that support for the weavers could be found in Bolton and the other towns, but not in Manchester itself.[233] This industrial dispute had been brewing for some time, and it was to have a lasting influence. The first Combination Act in 1799 made labour gatherings illegal and may have been devised in large measure to counter the Weavers' Association, formed earlier that year to lobby for regulation of the cotton industry and avoid the necessity to appeal to magistrates. This Combination Act was rapidly followed by another in 1800 and by the Cotton Arbitration Act the same year. The latter provided for two independent arbitrators to resolve disputes or, in the event that they could not agree, for the matter to be referred to the justice of the peace.

---

[232] See page 3 above. It is not known whether either this or the Nottingham example were included in Bohstedt's sample.
[233] Bohstedt, op cit, p146

The weavers soon used this Act to refer a dispute with the employers over reductions in piece-rates. At first the indications were that they would be successful, but the position was rapidly reversed when legal opinion was sought by the employers. This concluded that the Act could not be used to regulate wages (in other words, determine a minimum wage). Consequently, "[b]y 1801 the weavers' grievances had taken their place beside the war, Parliamentary reform, and bread prices on the agenda of popular public meetings ..."[234] In deciding to strike in 1808, the weavers had first to set aside those obstacles that worked against collective action. Despite the introduction of apprenticeships, weaving required little skill, restricting the opportunities to bargain, and weavers had to counter the "putting-out" system which limited the likelihood that they would, or could, take joint action. According to Bohstedt, the proximate reasons for the strike were the "disastrous decline in wages", a broader view of the economic and political consequences of the war with France for the weaving industry and for prices, and a realisation that because "foreign conditions made markets unstable" weavers had to organise - and would have to act - regionally rather than locally. This would help ensure that they were not picked off separately by the owners.

The strike began in May 1808 as soon as the failure of the minimum wage bill became known. The first protest of two thousand weavers at St George's Fields in Manchester passed off peacefully on Tuesday May 24th. It was dispersed after the Riot Act had been read and the cavalry called out. The second protest took place the following day, again at St George's Fields, and now involving more than five thousand weavers (between 10,000 and 15,000 according to John Burnett[235]). In the meantime "Small parties of strikers collected shuttles (the key part of the loom ...) [forcing] weavers to leave work and close their shops".[236] Again the Riot Act was read. But this time the protesters did not leave. They said they might as well stay as go home and see their families starve. The situation was further inflamed by Joseph Hanson, a well-known local radical who had previously stood unsuccessfully as parliamentary candidate for Preston and was known as "the weavers' friend"[237].

---

[234] Ibid, p145
[235] John Burnett, 'Idle Hands: The Experience of Unemployment 1790-1990', London, Routledge, 1994, p53
[236] Bohstedt, op cit, p149
[237] Watts, op cit, p488

Although he may have encouraged the weavers to disperse, he also assured them that the minimum wage was a just cause and that they should continue to pursue it. He was arrested and, at his trial a year later in May 1809, was fined £100 and imprisoned for six months.

The jittery magistrates responded by forcibly breaking up the crowd, calling on the military to disperse the protesters. The military resorted to shooting and one man was killed as a result. This has led the protest to be compared to Peterloo - as has the magistrates' over-reaction. Perhaps as a result of this response, the strike spread to surrounding towns and remained solid for at least the next three weeks. But there were no more mass meetings in Manchester. Burnett says, "After a month's well-organised campaign the weavers won a wage advance of 20 per cent [compared to the 33.3% increase they had originally sought] ... and won a good deal of local sympathy".[238]

Bohstedt describes the strike of 1808 as "a transitional movement" and says that energies were subsequently re-directed towards "national political reform".[239] As one example of this, he refers to the seven United Englishmen who were deported after they sought parliamentary reform at this time and spoke out for "an equal representation of all the people of England".[240]

## Social Developments

RF Foster is one of those who have drawn attention to the fact that each country has its own accepted national narrative. Events are forced into this mould or, if they can't be made to fit, may be re-interpreted or ignored. For example, he says that "This [political correctness] often posits a highly questionable version of the order in which things happened, and requires a strangely limited notion of state, nation, allegiance and identity".[241]

---

[238] Burnett, op cit, p53
[239] Bohstedt, op cit, p219
[240] Ibid, p143
[241] RF Foster, 'The Irish Story: Telling Tales and Making It Up in Ireland', London, Allen Lane, 2001, p20. He goes on to say on the following page that "There is a need for a historical strategy that recaptures uncertainties and thereby unlocks contemporary mentalities; for instance, group biography, or local history, can re-create realities that are not forced into episodes in the preordained national narrative."

At first sight, therefore, it might appear that Bohstedt's view (that political energies were re-focussed on national reform after the 1808 weavers strike) is not sustainable. It does not conform to the accepted narrative for England and Wales. This is that dispute was primarily concerned with immediate local impacts for some time to come, and that national political reform only gained momentum in the 1820s. However, there was also much that belies this view and supports Bohstedt's analysis.

An urging towards reform took place at several levels in 1809 (as the following Chapters demonstrate). For example, Jeremy Bentham was writing on parliamentary reform - even if he had to circulate his 'Parliamentary Reform Catechism' privately in the first instance, with its publication being delayed to 1817.[242] At the same time Francis Burdett proposed a plan of reform, putting a motion in favour of democratic representation to the House of Commons. His proposal received negligible support at this stage and Burdett was incensed at receiving the endorsement of only fifteen MPs. According to Briggs, this "seemed to justify ... [his] earlier remark ... that the Commons was 'the only spot in the world where the people of England are spoken of with contempt'."[243] Even if they had not chosen to advocate reform publicly at this point, both Bentham and Burdett were thought of as radicals by now. This had not always been the case, but they had been radicalised by events. Bentham had been influenced by James Mill to see the benefits of democracy, becoming a fervent convert, and developed utilitarianism along these lines ("the greatest happiness of the greatest number"). Burdett had originally been a Tory (like Cobbett[244]), but had moved towards radicalism for a number of reasons. Unlike Fox, he was a patriot who had refused to be presented to Bonaparte in Paris some years earlier.[245] His position was further reinforced by the threat of invasion by France in the early 1800s and by a growing realisation in 1806-7 that the Ministry of All the Talents government was just as reliant on corruption as other administrations. Horne Tooke and Francis Place, as well as Cobbett, had a similar outlook, and the four of them proved mutually supportive. Burdett had failed to be elected for Middlesex in the 1806 election, but was returned for Westminster in 1807. This gave

---

[242] Briggs, 2000, op cit, p155

[243] Ibid, p157 and see below

[244] For example, Spence, op cit, p26; Ingrams, op cit

[245] Hilton, 2006, op cit, p91

him a metropolitan foundation in a constituency that was both influential and independent, and was prepared to be radical. His backing was similar to that enjoyed by John Wilkes thirty years before - as was his popularity (in the country if not in parliament).

The push for reform was underpinned by an increasing sense of inequity and inequality. This extended far beyond parliamentary representation to people's experience of daily life. For example, Hilton follows Rubinstein in drawing attention to a growing disparity in wealth. He says that about thirty people a year left personal unsettled property of £100,000 or more.[246] This is in sharp contrast to the significant role that charity and philanthropy played in the lives of most people. Frank Prochaska[247] says that "The need in poor neighbourhoods was often such that it could not be satisfied by spontaneous, informal acts of kindness; thus the poor organised. ... At their best, working-class charities were preventive."[248] The example Prochaska cites from this period is the West Street Chapel Benevolent Society in Seven Dials. This was a notorious area of deprivation in London (see Charles Dickens in 'Sketches by Boz', for example). Twelve men of the Benevolent Society met each week so that a campaign of relief and religious conversion could be planned for the days ahead.[249] Friendly Unions frequently performed a similar function. Bohstedt refers to the importance of friendly societies, and to the Union they formed in the north-west in 1800 to act as a "consumers' co-operative (selling food cheaply at a time of high prices)".[250]

Inequality flourished in the military as well as in civil society. William Cobbett highlighted in his *Political Register* the undeserved flogging of British soldiers at Ely in 1809. Their claims for back pay were categorised as mutiny, inappropriately in Cobbett's view, and he strenuously objected to the floggings that resulted - its use at all as much as its severity. He condemned the 500 lashes each soldier received as barbaric as well as undeserved. The government took the opportunity to prosecute him on the grounds of libel and encouraging insurrection. On conviction he was fined and

---

[246] Ibid, p129
[247] See his Chapter on Philanthropy in FML Thompson, Vol 3, op cit, pp357-393.
[248] Ibid, p364
[249] Prochaska refers to Anthony Highmore, 'Pietas Londinensis', 1810, pp920-1 as his source for this illustration.
[250] Bohstedt, op cit, p133

spent two years in Newgate prison from 1810.[251]

Poverty had been anatomised in recent years[252], but the impact of this was not widely appreciated or, if it was, had limited effect. This was as true of beliefs, values and attitudes, as it was of behaviours and actions, and cannot be explained by political concentration on the war with France or by individual pre-occupations or self-interest. Some people may have concluded that there was little that could be done (along with Canning and Malthus), or that there were other priorities. There may have been various explanations. None provided adequate or sufficient justification.

This is not to say that there was no progress in 1809. Advances in Britain and abroad included the British School opening in Birmingham to provide working class children with an education[253] and the Scottish Bible Society being founded to provide missionaries with bibles in countries such as Kenya, Korea and China.[254] Nevertheless, these were the exception rather than the rule. A general sensitivity and sensibility (to paraphrase Jane Austen) would first have to be created before social action and initiative became more widespread. The creative arts were to play a part in this.

Life went on as before for most people. At one extreme the Two Thousand Guineas was introduced to the racing calendar at Newmarket in 1809, providing the aristocracy with another outlet for indulgence and display. For those who had some money and time for hobbies and the pursuit of culture, museums still charged an entrance fee to ensure exclusivity.[255] Meanwhile the majority had little time and less opportunity for leisure. Work filled much of their waking hours from Monday to Saturday. It was not surprising then

---

[251] Cobbett was still there when Perceval's assassin John Bellingham was executed at the prison in May 1812.

[252] FM Eden, 'The State of the Poor', 3 volumes, 1797 (referred to by Bohstedt on p134 and by Briggs, 2000 in several places) as well as by Patrick Colquhoun in 1806.

[253] See Birmingham Post, 2003. Shortly to be followed by other British schools as the Lancaster monitorial system gathered adherents.

[254] See The Scotsman, 2002

[255] When the British Museum removed entry fees in 1810, attendances increased from 15,197 to 127,643 in 1824-5 and doubled to 230,000 by 1835. See Cunningham, op cit, p321.

that religion provided succour and support, as well as a refuge and release, from the drudgery and monotony of their existence.

## Inflation and Economics

Some changes resulted directly from the Napoleonic wars. As well as the more obvious military developments, these included Dartmoor Prison being opened on 24th May 1809 to house French prisoners of war initially (though it is unlikely that it could have been planned for this purpose several years before). The prison website says that "In 1809 the first French prisoners arrived [from their incarceration on prison ships or hulks], and were joined by American POWs taken in the war of 1812. At one time the prison population numbered almost 6,000. Many prisoners died and were buried on the moor. Both French and American wars were concluded [by] 1815, and repatriations began. The prison then lay empty until 1850, when it was largely rebuilt and commissioned as a convict gaol."[256]

On the economic front, David Ricardo criticised the inflationary policy of the government and the rising costs of the war. William Hazlitt was another critic. Ricardo was one of the most prominent economists of the time and, like Malthus, a follower of Adam Smith.[257] On 30th December 1809 Ricardo published 'The high price of bullion, a proof of the depreciation of bank notes'. In the following year Perceval as Prime Minister and Chancellor of the Exchequer was to disagree with Huskisson (previously at the Treasury, but out of office after Canning's duel with Castlereagh in 1809 until 1814) who had written the Bullion Report. Like Ricardo, the latter blamed the excessive circulation of paper money as the sole reason for depreciation, while Perceval thought the war with France was the primary cause. However, it is unlikely that either view was determined solely by monetary considerations; more likely these were influenced by their personal animosity as well. Ricardo's criticisms were supported by a House of Commons

---

[256] See http://www.dartmoor-prison.co.uk/history_of_dartmoor_prison.html Another camp for French and Dutch troops was built at Norman Cross, Cambridgeshire. According to Cambridgeshire archives, roughly 10,000 prisoners were held there between 1796 and 1816, of whom at least 1,700 died. Several thousand English troops were stationed there as guards. Items made by the prisoners can be seen at the Norris Museum in St Ives, Cambridgeshire.
[257] Winch, op cit, p9

committee report two years later. (This is referred to above in relation to the Bank of England.) He was subsequently to tangle with the government over the Corn Laws.

The Napoleonic wars were like most wars in being a mixture of boom and bust. There were increased production and consumption in the early years, as there needed to be, but these were followed by reduced demand as the continuing hostilities eroded confidence. 1809 proved to lie between the boom years before and the relative decline subsequently. But this decline was "relative". The overall wealth of Britain was increasing and this grew more rapidly once the full effects of the Industrial Revolution began to be felt and expenditure on the war reduced. The economic impact along the way included inflation, as well as wage reductions for those groups whose skills were no longer in demand. This had already begun to effect weavers and agricultural labourers, but it was to be more widespread in the period after 1809 (and in 1812 was to result in sustained machine-smashing at the height of the Luddite riots).

The loss of trade in 1809 was masked to some extent by new markets to replace those of the French empire, and increased trade with Spain and Portugal. Declining prosperity presaged the imminent trade crisis that was to follow in 1810 and 1811, and the disruption in Britain's economy as prices increased. Napoleon tried, but failed, to exploit this weakness. Matters improved for Britain inadvertently when the government took out more loans, thereby reducing food prices and improving confidence.

Despite their negative effects for Britain as well as France, the Orders in Council were not revoked until Liverpool became Prime Minister in 1812.[258]

Watson[259] says that William Smart's 'Economic Annals of the Nineteenth Century' is a key source for facts against which the conclusions of other books on the period should be measured. Smart concludes that, while imports increased in 1809, there was a much greater increase in exports as a result of "the opening up of the new markets in South America, and by the speculative fever

---

[258] Briggs, 2000, op cit, p145. He provides more detail on the effects of the Orders in Council over the five years from 1807 to 1812 on pp143-145.
[259] Watson, op cit, p597

which came to such an unhappy end in the following year".[260]   He goes on to refer to a report received in the House of Lords on 8th February 1810.   This said, "Instead of our exports to America amounting to £20m, including £12m to the United States, they now amounted to £25m, including £7m to the United States. The fears on the subject of cotton wool had proved groundless - a considerable supply was now obtained from other parts of America, and might also be procured from the East Indies."

Robert Peel underlined the point in a January 1810 parliamentary debate when he said that the French attempt to isolate Britain by reducing trade had not had the desired effect.   He reinforced the message by claiming that, "With regard to our internal commerce, while France has been stripped of the flower of her youth, England has continued flourishing, and the only alteration has been the substitution of machinery for manual labour."[261]   It is difficult to square this perspective with the experience of slump reported by Pickfords, but Peel may have been more concerned with making the patriotic point - or he may have been thinking of examples other than Pickfords.   One such is the growth of Liverpool at this time from the poor relation of Chester to a thriving port in its own right. This was as a result of trade across the Atlantic, particularly cotton one way and slaves the other - which might be said to amount to much the same thing (in the sense that cotton, like sugar, depended on slave labour for its production).   "Since Liverpool was near to the textile manufacturing areas of north-west Britain it became the country's main port of entry for cotton.  In 1802 half of Britain's cotton imports arrived through Liverpool. This increased to nearly 70% in 1812 and 90% in 1830."[262]

Despite Peel's positive analysis, the facts were more complex.  For example, Smart indicates that "there was a great decline in shipbuilding" throughout the empire.   This is one indication that merchants were anticipating a tighter period ahead.   Smart also

---

[260] William Smart, 'Economic Annals of the Nineteenth Century, Volume 1 (1801-1820)', London, Macmillan, 1910, p203

[261] Ibid, p204 quoting from the Hansard report of the January 1810 debate.

[262] See http://www.mersey-gateway.org This says "Cotton from America was first imported into Britain at Liverpool by William Rathbone IV (1757-1809) in 1784. Cotton was a product of slave labour so it is odd that an abolitionist like Rathbone should trade in it.  Earlier in his life William Rathbone IV had persuaded his own father, William Rathbone III (1726-1789), not to take a share in a slave trading voyage to Africa."

says that "Although economic legislation, with the exception of measures founded upon the agricultural deficiency, was very much elbowed out by the overwhelming interest in the war ...several projects bearing more or less on the industrial life of the country came before Parliament."[263]  This echoes the view expressed elsewhere that the war was not total, to the exclusion of all else (though it may have been more "total" than any previous foreign war).  Indeed, Smart refers to the political issues that were brought before parliament in 1809 (how could he not?) and states that "the fury of political parties never ran higher".

The 1809 Select Committee on Scottish labour adopted a position consistent with that already reached in relation to the demands of English weavers.  That is to say, they "... decided that the proposals to fix a minimum wage in the cotton industry, to limit the number of apprentices and to set prices for cotton goods were both impossible to implement and against the best interests of the industry."[264]

It is also worth noting the major impact that two engineers and inventors exerted on the economy of this period.[265]  Matthew Boulton has already been referred to in relation to his work with James Watt to refine the steam engine for factory production and as an early prototype of the new breed of employer.  He built many of the new machines himself as the foundations of the factory system were laid.  He was to die in 1809 and was buried on 28th August.  His work had proved to be a bridge from the pre-industrial society of the first half of the eighteenth century to the developing industrial world of the nineteenth.  The second also provided a link forward into future nineteenth century developments and, in addition, connected the world of invention with that of the arts.  He was Richard Lovell Edgeworth.  Winn says that "His finest achievement was the new road he laid across [his] estate [in Ireland], incorporating two ground-breaking design features that revolutionised road building for ever": camber and a top layer of broken stones or chips that were compressed into a smooth, hard surface as vehicles passed over them.  "These innovations were

---

[263] Smart, op cit, p204
[264] See http://gdl.cdlr.strath.ac.uk/haynin/haynin1005.htm a Strathclyde University website.
[265] These are of course but two examples out of many.  See Weightman, 2007, op cit and Macleod, 2007, op cit for many other examples.

adopted by road builders everywhere and foreshadowed John Macadam's techniques by three years."[266]

## Journalism and the Arts

Richard Lovell Edgeworth had 22 children[267] by four wives.  His eldest daughter was Maria Edgeworth[268] who wrote 'Castle Rackrent' (1800) and 'Ormond' (1817) among several other books. Her writing was admired by Walter Scott and is said to have influenced the novels of Jane Austen.  During the Irish famine in the 1840s she wrote 'Orlandino' to raise funds for the relief of poverty, distributed food and clothes, and encouraged her friends to provide further help.

'Castle Rackrent', her best known novel and a very brief one, went through five editions in the decade after its publication.  It is often identified as one of the earliest novels highlighting the importance of history in the Irish experience.  RF Foster says that "[it] was originally to be about a family called the 'Stopgaps'.  Given that they carry Irish history, so to speak, on their backs, it is an important conceit."[269]  Maria Edgeworth was much more prolific than Jane Austen, but like Austen felt most comfortable, and therefore best able to work, in the family environment she was used to.  Like

---

[266] See Winn, 2006, op cit, p92.  He says that Edgeworth was "an unsung hero of invention and innovation.  He inherited Edgeworthstown House in 1782 and ... put in a self-styled central heating system ... and filled the house with gadgets, such as sideboards on wheels ... Out in the yard, an ingenious pump fed water to cisterns in the house and automatically dispensed halfpennies to beggars for each half-hour they spent at turning the handle." He "... developed ... an early bicycle, an aerial telegraph system that could send a signal from Dublin to Galway in eight minutes, advanced carriage suspension springs, a horse-drawn railway for carrying peat across the estate, and a vehicle with caterpillar tracks that could traverse the local bogland." See also Desmond Clarke, 'The Ingenious Mr Edgeworth', London, Oldbourne, 1965.  Donald Davie, finding it difficult to judge Edgeworth's contribution, says that "A crank, one might argue, is only a genius who doesn't come off". See Butler, op cit, 1972, p34.  Edgeworth was a well-established member of the Lunar Society of Birmingham and in contact with several of its leading scientists.
[267] One of Edgeworth's daughters Lucy Jane (1805-1898), his "last surviving child" as she is described on the headstone, is buried at one end of Cambridge Mill Road cemetery while Charles and Sarah Gault who died at much the same time are buried at the other.
[268] There is some debate as to whether she was born in 1767 or 1768.
[269] Foster, 2001, op cit, p3  Sir Kit Stopgap is one of the characters in the story, but the main family are the Rackrents.

Austen she never married.  Marilyn Butler endorses the view expressed in the 1950s (by PH Newby and then by Walter Allen) that "Whereas Jane Austen was so much the better novelist, Maria Edgeworth may be the more important".[270]

Foster is not alone in saying that history does not progress in a predictable, linear fashion and that it would be a mistake to focus exclusively on the state rather than on individuals.[271] As long as the state is not autocratic or repressive, individual people will behave in a variety of different ways: diversity rather than uniformity is the defining characteristic of nations - even in colonial situations such as that of Ireland in the nineteenth century.[272] Wendy Hinde makes a similar point when she says that George Canning was aware that politics is about people as well as about power.[273] The importance of individuals should not be obscured by an over-concentration on the industrial revolution, despite its grave economic and social impact.[274]

This individualism shows up in many aspects of life.  It is still being wrestled with by economists, for example, in their attempts to explain people's financial decisions and choices.    Paul Muskett draws attention to the role of individuals in explaining whether a village took part in disturbances in East Anglia or stood apart: "... just as an unpopular employer, Poor Law overseer, or Magistrate could be the identifiable target for the relief of pent-up hostility and frustration, so an aggrieved villager might suddenly reveal

---

[270] Butler, op cit, 1972, p481

[271] Foster, 2001, op cit, pp37-57

[272] Foster goes on to say that "... history is not about manifest destinies, but about unexpected and unforeseen futures" (ibid, p54), or in the words of Lewis Namier "imagining the past and remembering the future" (ibid, p33).

[273] Hinde, op cit, p89

[274] Giorgio Riello and Patrick O'Brien draw attention in their 2004 LSE working paper to "society ... being radically transformed into something that broke decisively with tradition" as a result of the Industrial Revolution.  They identify Patrick Colquhoun and Robert Owen as two of the first people to recognise this and date their awareness to 1814.  But Patrick Colquhoun had already applied his statistical techniques to social structures (e.g., 'A Treatise on Indigence', 1806 - and of 7 social classes in 1815), and Robert Owen had made some changes at New Lanark by 1809 to improve conditions there.  He had others planned once his partners would let him proceed.  See 'Reconstructing the industrial revolution: analyses, perceptions and conceptions of Britain's precocious transition to Europe's first industrial society', *LSE Working Papers in Economic History*, 1 (2004)

unsuspected qualities of leadership when encouraged by the sense of being involved in a wider movement."[275] A prime illustration of this variety comes through in the ways individuals choose to characterise and describe their surroundings and the world as a whole. This is particularly obvious in relation to the examples of architecture, painting and writing (poetry, plays and novels) considered below, and this process of visualisation also comes through in other creative arts such as philosophy, music and pottery that are not considered here. By definition, these are new ways of seeing (hence "creative" arts). It is also apparent in developments in contemporary journalism, with exponents such as William Cobbett and William Hazlitt proving themselves to be classic exemplars of this art at any period. They commented on the world, but they also helped create it anew.[276]

It would not be possible here, nor would it be appropriate, to do more than mention in passing some of the key proponents (and inevitably, these are restricted to the few people identified as active on pages 18 and 19 above). They are included to provide both a sense of the surrounding cultural context of the time and to illustrate some of their individual contributions to a pervading pressure for change. Detailed surveys exist for those who want to explore particular aspects more thoroughly.[277] The artists referred to have transcended the "lurching" of generations as the preferences of one are discounted by the next. However, the stock of most of them has fluctuated over the years as fashions changed. This is particularly

---

[275] Paul Muskett, 'Riotous Assemblies: Popular Disturbances in East Anglia 1740-1822', East Anglia Records Offices, undated, p3

[276] EH Carr says this is also true of historians in 'What Is History?', London, Macmillan, 1961. The Palgrave edition of 2001 takes as its text the following view of history from 'Northanger Abbey' by Jane Austen: "I often think it odd that it should be so dull, for a great deal of it must be invention". This was certainly Jane Austen's view of history, as Claire Tomalin's biography makes clear (see below).

[277] An example would be Gillian Russell and Clara Tuite (eds), 'Romantic Sociability: Social Networks and Literary Culture in Britain, 1770-1840', Cambridge, Cambridge University Press, 2002. See also Iain McCalman, Jon Mee, Gillian Russell and Clara Tuite, 'An Oxford Companion to the Romantic Age: British Culture, 1776-1832', Oxford, Oxford University Press, 1999. On page 270 of the latter the key poets of the age are listed. The six main ones are said to be Wordsworth, Coleridge, Byron, Shelley, Blake and Keats, while George Crabbe and Robert Southey are among the longer list of those less well-known. John Keats (1795-1821) was 14 in 1809 and is omitted from the people listed as active on pages 18-19 above. The other seven are included, and many of them are referred to in the text on the following pages.

true of poets and painters[278], but has affected all of them to some degree.

Jane Austen, William Blake and Walter Scott (as a poet) are examples of some of those who were active at this stage. William Blake wrote 'Jerusalem' in 1804 for his book on Milton, and then worked on the 100 engravings between 1804 and 1818 that comprise his own edition. His poem reflects a roseate view of the countryside amid the grand aspirations.[279]

On the basis of six books, Jane Austen is one of the most highly regarded of novelists. This view was current in the early nineteenth century and her reputation has grown since. Asa Briggs says in 'A Social History of England' that, while her novels were admired by the Prince Regent (who read each book and kept copies in all his palaces), she was never as popular as her male contemporaries.[280] Elizabeth Jenkins says that "In his review of 'Emma' in ... 1816, Sir Walter Scott placed [her] in the foremost rank of innovators".[281] Scott said that she had re-written the rules of novel-writing by mimicking (in the sense of creating in a credible way, not repeating) "the current of ordinary life" more "immediately ... than was permitted" formerly. This accuracy reflects her talent and ear for dialogue, a realism that transcends the various forms that her individual books take (from the romance of 'Pride and Prejudice' to the satire of 'Northanger Abbey'). For Scott, she had "that exquisite touch which renders ordinary common-place things and characters interesting", while Jenkins says, "The occult power of creating

---

[278] See, for example, the changing fortunes of Constable and Turner, with the latter being much better known than Constable by contemporaries and then "re-discovered" through an exhibition celebrating the bi-centenary of his birth in the 1970s. The Tate Britain website http://www.tate.org.uk/britain/turner/biog_reputation.htm says that "Turner was always very aware of factors which affected his reputation and made full use of the wide circulation offered by print publishing to spread knowledge of his achievements. ... Turner's reputation has changed over time, partly because different generations have had access to different examples of his work."
[279] http://www.poetseers.org/the_poetseers/blake says that "Blake hated the effects of the Industrial Revolution in England and looked forward to the establishment of a New Jerusalem "in England's green and pleasant land." Colley, op cit, pp30-32 has a different interpretation of the significance of this poem.
[280] Briggs, 1983, op cit, p201
[281] Elizabeth Jenkins, 'Jane Austen: A Biography', London, Gollancz, 1948, p30

human personality - the rarest form of literary genius - ... invests Jane Austen's work with its extraordinary nature ..."[282]

Her private life was obviously a significant factor, giving her the time and space to translate her characters on to the page, deploying her talent to bring her stories and this inner world to life. This went beyond the usual traditions, but was recognisably part of it. For example, Stone says that "Novelists from Samuel Richardson to Jane Austen also made it ["infiltration of the elite by men of low birth but large fortune"] one of the two basic themes in the English novel, the second being the closely related issue of love versus money and status as the decisive factor in the business of marriage." [283] Claire Tomalin provides many illustrations of Jane Austen's view of the world and her interactions with family and friends.[284] Particularly pertinent here is "Her interest in history was, as she acknowledged, more to do with romance than with fact and date; and perhaps more still to do with making her family laugh."[285]

There were lengthy gaps between when Jane Austen wrote each novel and its publication.[286] There was also a significant ten-year gap between writing the first three books ('Sense and Sensibility', 'Pride and Prejudice' and 'Northanger Abbey') and the last three ('Emma', 'Persuasion' and 'Mansfield Park'). As Tomalin makes clear, "For ten years she produced almost nothing, and not until she was nearly thirty-five, in the summer of 1809, did she return to the working pattern of her early twenties."[287] This coincided with a

---

[282] Ibid, p251 where she also refers to this private judgement of Scott.

[283] Stone and Stone, op cit, p17. See also Jenkins, op cit, p30 who says that "... she was ... in direct descent from the masters of fiction who preceded her".

[284] Claire Tomalin, 'Jane Austen: A Life', London, Penguin, 1998

[285] Ibid, p68

[286] 'Northanger Abbey' and 'Persuasion' were published after her death in 1817.

[287] Tomalin, op cit, p169. Tomalin's biography contains one error that is pertinent to this book. She refers on pp94-96 to the link between the Austens, particularly Jane Austen, and William Chute, one of the Hampshire MPs. She says on p94 that "William Chute was educated at Harrow - where he was the statesman Spencer Perceval's fag, which may be what propelled him into Parliament ..." However, earlier on p94 and on p95 Tomalin indicates that Chute was born in 1757 or 1756, making him five years older than Perceval.
Thorne, op cit says in the History of Parliament 1790-1820 that the Hampshire MP WJ Chute (1757-1824) was only at Harrow for one year 1774-75 aged 17, while Spencer Perceval was at Harrow from 1774-79 aged 12-17. Their time at Harrow did overlap, therefore, but only for one year and Chute was indeed five years older.

move back to Hampshire (to a cottage in Chawton with her mother and sister) after ten years living in Bath when her parents decided to give up their Steventon parish and the rectory that had been Jane Austen's home since childhood. She had not been consulted on this, and like her sister and brothers was taken aback. It disrupted the familiar surroundings she had become used to and in which she felt sufficiently comfortable to work.

There could hardly be a greater contrast than between Jane Austen and Robert Southey in their productivity - at least as measured by the volume of their published output. Southey was best known initially as a poet, eventually becoming Poet Laureate in 1813 when Walter Scott declined the post and recommended Southey instead. But he also became well-known as an essayist, a biographer and a historian. The scale of his output was prodigious.[288] Regardless of talent, anybody would have been hard-pressed to produce so much and maintain its quality. He was not a hack, but inevitably some saw him in this light. He was frequently criticised for this and often in very scathing terms. For example, Byron was one of the first to satirise him in 1809. Lionel Madden says that "This is the first of Byron's satiric attacks in verse upon Southey [appearing in his first major work *English Bards and Scotch Reviewers*]. Unlike Byron's later writings these verses show no personal animosity towards Southey himself."[289] They include the lines:

"... Oh! Southey! Southey! cease thy varied song!
A bard may chant too often and too long:
...'God help thee', Southey, and thy readers too."

---

Christopher Tyerman, 'A History of Harrow School 1324-1991', OUP, 2000 gives no indication that it would have been possible for Perceval or anyone else to have been the fag master of someone five years older than himself.
[288] Mark Storey, 'Robert Southey: A Life', Oxford, Oxford University Press, 1997 lists Southey's publications on pp403-4. This excludes individual poems, essays, volumes of history and other contributions, but includes seven biographies (ranging from John Bunyan to Nelson) and a number of discrete histories (such as those for Brazil, Paraguay, Portugal and the Peninsular War). He never visited South America, but he didn't let this stop him. There was a connection anyway through his interests in and support for the people of Portugal and Spain in their struggle against Napoleon.
[289] Lionel Madden (ed), 'Robert Southey: The Critical Heritage', London, Routledge, 1972, pp130-1

Ten years later, though, Byron was to dedicate 'Don Juan' to "Bob Southey".

William Hazlitt produced a review in 1816 that was "violently hostile" to Southey.[290]  Posterity did not necessarily judge him any more kindly in the years after his death.  For example, both Bagehot in 1853 and Hawthorne in 1855 were very condemnatory.  In their view, Southey wrote too much and lived too little.[291]  It is fair to say that Southey would have been unconcerned.  He liked his isolation and knew what he wanted to achieve.  Southey said that, "Nothing provokes me like a waste of words ... I am a good poet - but a better historian."[292]  In Storey's view, "this sums up many of his virtues as a writer".[293]  Besides he had a large family to feed and his friend Coleridge offered an example of the risks if energies were channelled away from work.  In any case there may have been some re-dressing of the critical balance required.  Madden says that Hazlitt's negative review in 1816 should be compared with his temperate assessment some years later in 'Spirit of the Age' (dated 1825, though really 1824).[294]

Robert Southey and Coleridge devised the society they called Pantisocracy[295] (equal power for all) during the mid-1790s. Although they were unable to realise the vision in practice for lack of funds, Southey maintained this interest in co-operation rather than competition, with Robert Owen visiting him in 1816 and Southey going to New Lanark in 1819.[296]  Further connections between Southey and other aspects of this book include his views of Emmet and Malthus in 1803, his journey from being a Foxite in 1806 to a

---

[290] Ibid, pp219-222
[291] Ibid, pp448-9
[292] In a letter to his friend and political confidant John Rickman, secretary to Charles Abbot the speaker of the House of Commons from 1802 to 1817. Rickman was responsible for administering the first four censuses from 1801 to 1831.
[293] Storey, op cit, p172
[294] Madden, op cit, pp314-322
[295] The 'Dictionary of English Literature', London, Bloomsbury, 1997 defines this as an "ideal anarchistic society which preoccupied [Southey, Coleridge and others] in 1794-5 during [an early] phase of the French Revolution (from the Greek: pan = `all', isos = `the same', cratos = `power'). They hoped to establish a community on the banks of the River Susquehanna in the United States in which motives of gain would be replaced by brotherly love. They were unable to raise money, however, their ideas changed, and they abandoned their plan."
[296] Storey, op cit, pp249-250 and pp275-276. Also, see Chapter 7 below.

reactionary Tory ten years later (no doubt passing Cobbett on the way as they travelled in opposite directions), his changing opinions on reform, and as the first historian, including that for 1809, in the *Edinburgh Annual Register.*

Robert Emmet's limited attempt at rebellion in Ireland in 1803 has already been referred to in Chapter 1. It proved to be ill-prepared and was rapidly aborted. Emmet was hanged by the British authorities in Dublin that September. His fate obviously affected Southey deeply, who was both to write a poem on Emmet and, perhaps more memorably, commented that "If they mean to extirpate disaffection in Ireland by the gallows, they must sow the whole island with hemp".[297] It is not clear whether the revolutionary principles Southey held at this stage extended to the emancipation of Catholics. His association with the Whigs, and particularly with the Foxite wing, would suggest that they did. Later, they most certainly would not.

The second edition of Malthus' treatise came out in 1803. As might be expected, Southey was to rail against this deterministic view of poverty and the poor. Like Hazlitt and Shelley were to argue later, Southey said that "... poverty, vice and misery were the result not of immutable laws of Nature, but of a social system that was far from perfect". The bottom line for Southey was that "Malthus ... was **destroying any possibility of hope** [my emphasis] ..."[298] Given that Southey identified closely with the oppressed, and the principles he espoused resulted from the necessity to champion their cause, it is not surprising that he saw this charge as unforgivable.[299]

---

[297] Storey, op cit, p162. This view was expressed in a letter on 28th September 1803 to John King. Southey's poem on Emmet appeared in 'Iris', the Norfolk and Norwich weekly newspaper edited by Southey's friend William Taylor.

[298] Ibid, pp163-4

[299] See Chapter 3 above for Cobbett's condemnation of Malthus. It is interesting to note that The Economist in May 2008 describes Malthus as "a false prophet" in commenting on the 2008 riots that were triggered across the world by rising food prices.
(See
http://www.economist.com/research/articlesBySubject/displayStory.cfm?story_id=1 1374623&subjectID=348918&fsrc=nwl which refers to Malthus' "abiding fallacy" and describes him as "the pessimistic parson and early political economist [who] remains as wrong as ever".) Malthus' views may seem appealing on the surface, but they leave little opportunity for human agency to bring about change.

Fox's death in 1806 may have been the immediate catalyst for Southey's changing views to become apparent. He had welcomed Grenville's "Ministry of All the Talents" government initially and saw their resignation in 1807 as unnecessary - especially over army commissions for Catholics, and even more so when they were replaced by a government with "an old woman at their Head"[300] (i.e., Portland). But he had already moved some distance from his position in the early 1790s. According to Harry Jones, he wrote then of the early years of the French Revolution that "Few persons but those that have lived in it can conceive or comprehend what the memory of the French Revolution was, nor what a visionary world seemed to open on those who were just entering it. Old things seemed to be passing away, and nothing was dreamt of but the regeneration of the human race."[301] This was clearly the Southey of Pantisocracy days. By 1808 he took the view that "... I am swimming with the stream, but it is the stream that has turned, not I." Storey adds that "Southey the pragmatist, with his eye for the main chance, begins to take over from Southey the man of principle."[302] He was still holding out for reform at this point, but had firmly rejected revolution: "...I cannot but see that all things are tending towards revolution, and nothing but reform can by any possibility prevent it".[303]

This is similar to the irritation William Cobbett had felt at the confusion between reform and revolution in Britain. The first was required; the second was to be avoided if the example of the French Revolution was anything to go by. Prochaska says that even somebody as radical as Coleridge viewed the revolutionary mentality as a form of hysteria.[304]

---

This was what most sparked Southey's contempt. It is to his credit that his reaction was immediate.

David Craig says in his PhD thesis ('Republicanism becoming conservative: Robert Southey and political argument in Britain, 1789-1817', University of Cambridge, 2000) that Southey did not fully understand Malthus. It might be argued, however, that this did not matter. It was more important that he understood, and anticipated, the common reaction.

[300] Storey, op cit, p184

[301] Harry Jones, 'Free-thinkers and Trouble-makers: Fenland Dissenters', Wisbech, Wisbech Society and Preservation Trust, 2004, p13 in the section on William Godwin.

[302] Storey, op cit, p180.

[303] Ibid, p194 where this quotation is taken from one of Southey's reviews.

[304] Frank Prochaska, 'The Republic of Britain 1760-2000', Allen Lane, 2000, p34

But Southey still had some distance to travel. His preference for reform began to dilute in 1809, when his support for parliamentary reform was confronted by the more far-reaching changes that Burdett foresaw as necessary and Curwen's Bribery Act (see below) implied. He also distanced himself from making peace with Napoleon, whereas this was often the position of those who supported reform. By the time he came to write the history of 1809 in the *Edinburgh Annual Register* he had rejected reform in favour of the existing system. Like Spencer Perceval and other Tory politicians (see below), Southey concluded that this "has made us the prosperous, the powerful, the free, the happy people that we are". Reform was now "the direct road to anarchy"[305] whereas the consequences of the current arrangements were known. Why sacrifice certainty in favour of the potential hazards of the unknown?

By this point Southey's views exemplified the forces of reaction. By 1816 he aligned himself with those who thought the Government should have absolute power - as had his friend John Rickman ten years earlier. Not surprisingly, he was accused of political apostasy. But he shrugged it off: "It is the world that has changed, not I."

Kenneth Curry[306] has traced the founding of the *Edinburgh Annual Register* from its beginnings in 1808. It had been started as an alternative reference source to the *Annual Register* begun in 1758, but it never sold well and folded in 1826. Sir Walter Scott had ceased to be editor from the 1816 edition published in 1820 (though he had never done more than dabble in what was a passing interest), and was involved in the eventual bankruptcy proceedings along with the publishing business he had set up to produce it. Scott and Southey had distanced themselves from the *Edinburgh Review* when it cast aspersions on the fighting ability of Spain and her people, Britain's allies against Napoleon. John Murray was also involved in the *Edinburgh Annual Register* initially, but his efforts

---

[305] Storey, op cit, p195

[306] Kenneth Curry, 'Sir Walter Scott's *Edinburgh Annual Register*', Knoxville, University of Tennessee Press, 1977. There were four publications that are easily confused: *Annual Register, Edinburgh Review, Edinburgh Annual Register* and *Quarterly Review*. The latter two were started in 1808 and 1809 respectively and John Murray was involved in both. They are covered here. The *Quarterly Review* for the first time gave the Tory government a mouthpiece to counter the Whig influence of the *Edinburgh Review*.

were always primarily directed towards the *Quarterly Review* "to counter the opposition influence of the *Edinburgh Review*"[307]. Murray gave up his share in the *Edinburgh Annual Register* in 1812 when he could already see its limited potential and that it was not going to develop as planned. The number of copies printed had reduced from 3000 at the start to 1750 by the 1817 volume.[308]

Southey "wrote the historical section for the first four years, amounting to four substantial volumes of several hundred pages each".[309] His "...part in it grew until he was practically writing the whole of the political commentary in [each] volume."[310] Southey was helped by his friend Rickman who provided him with many of the background documents he required, and may have written some segments on his behalf. Southey was to be paid £400 per volume. However, he withdrew when he ceased to be paid properly as the *Register*'s financial difficulties became more pronounced. Scott became the historian himself for the years 1814 and 1815, but even this failed to boost sales sufficiently.

Southey's close friendship with Samuel Taylor Coleridge allowed him first to rent Greta Hall, Keswick from Coleridge, and then to purchase the whole of it as his family grew. Coleridge was allowed to remain there on his return to Keswick. Like Scott and Southey, Coleridge also had an interest in publishing. His involvement proved to be more short-lived, however, with his paper called 'The Friend' lasting from August 1809 to March 1810.

Southey was a neighbour of Wordsworth, but their relationship developed more positively after Southey supported William and Dorothy following the early death of their brother. As one of the most popular art forms at this time, the impact of poetry and poets could be considerable among certain sections of society. If "history is the new gardening" as a TV executive is recently quoted as saying, poetry was similarly popular, and indeed influential, at this point. Poets were expected to, and did, comment on issues of the moment - in prose as well as in their poems. For example, following the Convention of Cintra in 1808[311], Wordsworth published a critical

---

[307] Ibid, p7
[308] Ibid, pp12-13
[309] Ibid, p3
[310] Storey, op cit, p201
[311] See Chapter 2 above

pamphlet under this title in 1809. Eric C Walker describes this as Wordsworth's "first skirmish" with Wellington.[312] It then grew into a full-blown quarrel after Waterloo and Wordsworth's response in the 'Thanksgiving Ode'. In Walker's view, Wordsworth's enmity reflected in part his hostility to Wellington's serial philandering and the effects of his adultery on his wife.

Crabbe and Blake were outside the Lake District group, as were Byron and Shelley. George Crabbe and William Blake were in their forties at the start of the nineteenth century, while Wordsworth, Coleridge and Southey were in their twenties. Byron and Shelley were still children.

George Crabbe is best known for his poems 'The Village' and 'The Borough'. The latter was published in 1810 and was re-printed in a second edition four months later. It introduced Peter Grimes and his abuse of apprentices, as well as what his DNB entry describes as other "depraved characters". Contemporary reviewers criticised his view of life as overly harsh[313], but to Crabbe it was realistic. As a Church of England clergyman, first in his birthplace of Aldeburgh in Suffolk and then with livings in Lincolnshire and a parish in Leicestershire, he was in a position to know the realities of life for most people. 'The Village' was published in 1783 while he was still in Suffolk. Although some reviewers thought he had exaggerated the oppression of rural life, others held him in high regard at the time for his vivid descriptions of both people and places. He would have hardly come to the attention of a patron such as the Duke of Rutland (to whom 'The Borough' is dedicated) without a public reputation, nor would Crabbe have been given parishes around Belvoir Castle without this approval. Crabbe's son, also called George and a clergyman, but not a poet, was to produce a biography of his father that was published by John Murray together with a new edition of Crabbe's poems. Despite this, Crabbe's reputation was soon to decline[314] and has only been revived in

---

[312] Eric C Walker Chapter on 'Marriage and the End of War', p212 in Philip Shaw (ed), 'Romantic Wars: Studies in Culture and Conflict, 1793-1822', Aldershot, Ashgate, 2000

[313] For example in the November 1810 issue of *Quarterly Review*, published by John Murray (see below). See Humphrey Carpenter, 'The Seven Lives of John Murray: The Story of a Publishing Dynasty, 1768-2002', London, John Murray, 2008

[314] According to his DNB entry, the "… decline of his reputation was the result of two factors: the Victorian reaction against the neo-classical poets of the previous

recent years, particularly by the popularity of Benjamin Britten's first opera 'Peter Grimes'. (Britten himself provides another connection with Aldeburgh of course.)

William Blake has already been mentioned in relation to his poem 'Jerusalem'. This was prepared for his book on Milton, on which he had begun to work while living from 1800 to 1803 at the Sussex house of his patron William Hayley. By this stage Blake was known both as a poet and as an engraver, illustrating his own and others' works. In May 1809 he decided to counter what he perceived to be rejections by the Royal Academy by exhibiting his watercolour and other paintings at the family home, in the hope that his talents as a painter would be recognised alongside his existing reputations as a poet and as an engraver. His DNB entry says that "The display may have lasted until June 1810, when Charles and Mary Lamb saw [the] paintings."[315] Elsewhere this exhibition is described as "commercially unsuccessful".[316] The single review of the exhibition was derisory and commissions fell away afterwards.

JMW Turner was already a famous artist with a number of exhibitions to his name and a professorship at the Royal Academy by 1809. He had begun to sketch Petworth that year. By contrast his contemporary John Constable was still unknown and would only begin to be recognised as a leading landscape artist in the mid-1820s. Even then his style was initially appreciated and commended by the French rather than by his fellow countrymen. The Society of Painters in Watercolours (SPW) was founded on 30th November 1804 with membership limited to twenty-four artists. The

---

century with whom Crabbe was linked because of his pervasive use of the closed heroic couplet; and the decline of the verse tale as a popular genre, evidenced by Sir Walter Scott's abandoning verse tales for the novel".

[315] The 'Spiritual Form of Nelson Guiding Leviathan' circa 1805-9 was one of the sixteen paintings in the exhibition. The companion picture of Pitt guiding Behemoth was also included. Both pictures are in the Tate Britain collection.

[316] See http://www.poetseers.org/thepoetseers/blake Blake's reputation has proved to be enduring more recently, for his poetry as well as for his painting. It is rare for a poem to be set to such memorable music as Parry provided in 1916, over a hundred years after 'Jerusalem' was written. Known today as the hymn rather than as a poem, it is difficult to envisage the words not being sung. Similarly, his poem 'Tyger' is said to be the most frequently included in anthologies. His paintings and engravings are not only represented in most major collections, but are often among the focal points of those collections. Against this, however, it has to be said that his paintings can evoke equally strong reactions against; they are often seen as pretentious rather than visionary.

rural and landscape artist Robert Hills (1769-1844) was the founding secretary and "was so highly thought of by his fellow Society members that they presented him with a plate to the value of 100 guineas in 1809 to celebrate his unremitting service to the Society since its establishment."[317] Turner and Constable were not members, and nor were the younger generation David Cox (1783-1859) and Peter De Wint (1784-1849) who formed an alternative New Society. This so closely overlapped with the SPW that the latter was dissolved in 1812, and the Society of Painters in Oil and Watercolour was formed instead. This lasted until 1820 when "those in favour of watercolour's independence re-grouped as the Old Water-Colour Society".[318]

John Soane and John Nash were well-established architects. Soane was a close neighbour of Spencer Perceval, both in Lincoln's Inn Fields and briefly in Ealing[319] (still a village outside London) in the early nineteenth century. Soane had re-modelled Pitzhanger Manor House in Ealing as a country retreat for his own family and it was later to become the residence of Perceval's unmarried daughters. Nash had been the architect for the crown estates since 1806. His previous private practice had already worked in Brighton - though not yet on the re-building of the Pavilion, a commission for the Prince Regent in 1815. Brighton provided a bolthole for the Prince of Wales (as he then was) and an opulent alternative to the King's preference for the simpler pleasures of Worthing. This gave the future Prince Regent a base within striking distance of London, but sufficiently separate from it. He could continue to irritate his father, and sustain his indulgent approach to life, with a degree of impunity. Nash was soon to be commissioned by the Prince Regent to develop the Marylebone area of London.

James Gillray had been closely associated with George Canning over a number of years. Despite feeding each other with ideas, they had maintained their independence. Pitt and Fox had died in 1806, but Gillray still had many domestic and foreign targets for his satirical cartoons - not least the French and Napoleon. He attacked

---

[317] Fitzwilliam Museum catalogue for 'The field calls me to labour' exhibition May to September 2008
[318] Ibid
[319] Soane sold Pitzhanger Manor House in 1810, having put it up for sale a year earlier. The sale to Perceval of the Elm Grove estate in Ealing had been agreed through Act of Parliament in 1808.

**Figure 5: 'An old English-gentleman pester'd by servants wanting places',** James Gillray, 1809 © National Portrait Gallery, London

the Ministry of All the Talents with relish, but had to be more circumspect once Canning became Foreign Secretary in Portland's administration from 1807. By this stage his skills and enthusiasm, as well as his sight, were beginning to dim. Although his caricatures were still being published to May 1809, if not later, he was now over fifty.[320] By the time Canning left office later that year, it would probably have been too late for Gillray to come to the fore again, even had his health held up.

---

[320] The National Portrait Gallery's collection of Gillray's work includes 'An old English-gentleman pester'd by servants wanting places'. This is the last Gillray cartoon held by this collection and is dated 16th May 1809. It shows George III being jostled by many leading contemporary politicians seeking preferment. Ironically, Gillray was to lose his sanity in 1810 like George III.

Isaac Cruikshank ("Crookshanks") (1764-1811) had worked closely with Gillray in the past, helping to invent the John Bull character. In 'French Generals Receiving an English Charge'[321], 28 April 1809, he lampooned not only Napoleon, but also the Duke of York and his affair with Mary Clarke. His sons Robert Cruikshank (1789-1856) and George Cruikshank (1792-1878) also became well known as caricaturists and illustrators.

While Jeremy Bentham viewed the world primarily through the prism of philosophy, William Cobbett and William Hazlitt had chosen the routes of journalism and essays as ways of having an impact on current values and re-shaping accepted norms. They were no less major commentators and advocates of reform for that.

Cobbett had started his *Political Register* in 1802, publishing parliamentary debates from 1803. In the early 1770s external reporting of these debates had been illegal, and parliament's attempts to arrest the printers had been resisted by John Wilkes. Wilkes swung into action on the basis that it was only the City of London that could conduct arrests within its boundaries. As the newly-elected sheriff of the City, Wilkes had the parliamentary officer who had come to seize the printers arrested. This pitted him directly against parliament (again) and on this occasion he outmanoeuvred the government. Cobbett's partner Hansard took over the role of printing parliamentary debates from 1812, while Wilkes is remembered as the father of the free press.[322]

Cobbett and Hazlitt both found Malthus' stance on population and poverty repugnant. For Cobbett this was part of his journey towards radical reform, while William Hazlitt's views had been influenced originally by Fox and the early years of the French Revolution. Hazlitt is said to have revered Napoleon, and wrote for *The Times* in the early nineteenth century, having become the son-in-law of the editor in 1808. At this point *The Times* was not yet part of the establishment, having been founded in 1785, but equally it was less extreme than the press that Cobbett represented. Hazlitt's views

---

[321] See page 153 in Chapter 5 below.

[322] Information in this paragraph comes from my earlier article on John Wilkes 'A man of principle at a time of change', unpublished, 2005, and from http://www.south-central-media.co.uk/tuppenny_press.htm More detail can be found in Arthur H Cash's biography, 'John Wilkes: The Scandalous Father of Civil Liberty', London, Yale University Press, 2006.

were less radical than those of Cobbett by this stage - or at any rate he found more conventional and acceptable means of expressing them.

Taaffe published his 'Impartial History of Ireland' in 1809, with its radical sub-text arguing that Pitt's Act of Union was not in Ireland's interests. The most significant publishing event of the year, however, was the introduction of the *Quarterly Review*[323]. This was launched by the publisher John Murray[324] (who was later to publish Jane Austen). It provided a platform for the views of the Tory government for the first time and was to become very influential. Walter Scott was an adviser and George Canning was to be involved when he left office later that year. William Gifford was the full-time editor (in contrast to Scott's part-time role at the *Edinburgh Annual Register*) and had previously edited the Anti-Jacobin for Canning. This had run for 35 issues from November 1797 to July 1799. Mitchell says Gifford had a "wonderful capacity for abusing people who did not think as he thought".[325] Gifford was "keen that [Robert] Southey should himself go to Spain, to report on the war ... but for Southey the terms would have to be right, which, as it happened, they were not".[326] Southey was nevertheless to become one of the main contributors to the *Quarterly Review*, along with Scott.

## Connections between political, economic and artistic worlds

Several writers (including Anthony Sampson and Jeremy Paxman[327]) have drawn attention to two pervasive effects in current society. One is the inter-connection between apparently unrelated worlds as people who inhabit one sphere intermingle with those from others. Some of this may reflect the influence of school contacts maintained thereafter, but it also works in other ways as

---

[323] See Chapter 6 'Quarterly' in Carpenter, op cit, pp52-66

[324] Whose father John MacMurray (or sometimes McMurray), the founder of the *English Review*, had died in 1793. See Carpenter, op cit, pp5, 31 and 318. The family was moving away from its Scottish roots.

[325] Donald G. Mitchell, 'English Lands Letters and Kings: The Later Georges to Victoria', New York, Charles Scribner's Sons, 1897, p116

[326] Storey, op cit, p193

[327] See, for example, Anthony Sampson's original 'Anatomy of Britain' from 1962 and 'Who Runs This Place? The Anatomy of Britain in the 21st Century', London, John Murray, 2004. Also, Jeremy Paxman, 'Friends in High Places: Who Runs Britain?', London, Michael Joseph, 1990.

well.  This seems to happen in all societies and may reflect proximity and propinquity as much as anything else: that is to say, those who are well-known for one activity tend to live close to, or attend the same events as, those who are known for other reasons.  Inevitably, they become acquainted.  This was the case at the start of the nineteenth century as well as today - though inevitably the evolution of communications in the intervening period has increased the opportunities and propensity for interaction.

The second effect may not be restricted to British society, but its effects are certainly more obvious and more prevalent in Britain than elsewhere.  This is that prominence down the centuries in this country tends to be restricted to a limited number of families that replicate their influence across the generations.[328]  A few surnames reverberate down the years.  Again the influence of a few well-known schools should not be under-estimated.

There are a number of communities of interest and location within romanticism alone.  For example, Cambridge University Press[329] describes the book edited by Russell and Tuite (op cit) as "… [examining] modes of sociability as diverse as circles of sedition, international republicanism, Dissenting culture, Romantic lecturing, theatre and shopping …"  Similarly, Aberystwyth University offers a module on 'Romanticism: Communities of Dissent 1809-1823' involving poets such as Coleridge, Wordsworth, Keats and Shelley.[330]  "This module … investigates … the web-like structures of allegiance and shared purpose connecting politically motivated authors, including John Keats, Leigh Hunt, Percy Shelley, Charles Cowden Clarke, 'Barry Cornwall', and William Hazlitt."

Of immediate interest, however, are those instances where apparently different worlds interact and overlap - despite the limitations of mobility at the start of the nineteenth century.  In certain cases key individuals such as Walter Scott, James Mill (1773-1836) the father of JS Mill, and John Murray brought apparently disparate groups together because of their range of

---

[328] It may be assumed that this was partly, of course, what led the Stones to work on the elite and encouraged them to question its open-ness.  See Stone and Stone, 1984, op cit

[329] See http://www.cambridge.org/uk/catalogue/catalogue.asp?isbn=9780521026093

[330] See http://www.aber.ac.uk/modules/current/ENM6720.html

interests (not just as members of the nineteenth century equivalent of the chattering classes or the dinner party set). George Canning was another key node whose interests linked the political and artistic worlds. James Mill was a propagandist for Jeremy Bentham[331], providing another link between the worlds of philosophy and politics.

In other cases it was organisations and institutions that performed this role, with the Hoxton asylum providing another focal point. Charles Lamb (1775-1834) knew Coleridge and Wordsworth, spent time in Hoxton when his mental health broke down and got his sister out of Hoxton (where she had been imprisoned for killing their mother) by agreeing to look after her. James Mill was the husband of the woman who ran the Hoxton asylum.

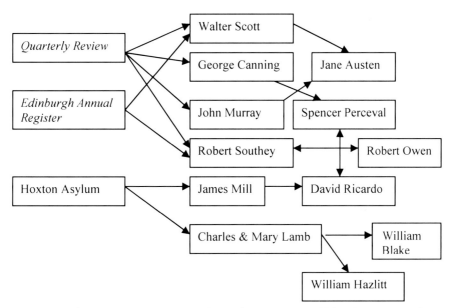

**Figure 6: Some inter-connections between political, economic and artistic worlds**

---

[331] James Mill's DNB entry says "William Hazlitt, upon learning that one of Bentham's books had been translated into French, quipped that someone should translate Bentham into English. That, in effect, is exactly what Mill did." Mill also wrote the 'History of India' without going there.

Figure 6 illustrates some of these inter-connections, though this could readily be expanded.[332] It was a smaller world of course, both in terms of geography and population. This may have gone some way to balancing the restrictions on interaction imposed by the conventions of etiquette and the difficulties of transport, movement and communication. The latter may have impacted particularly on the probability of expanding your contacts, and maintaining them once made, while the former made them more feasible within the given constraints.

## Conclusion

The political change confronting Britain in 1809 can be summarised in the following diagram:

**revolution ——————▶ reform ◀——————reaction**

Political change includes social, economic and cultural consequences in this instance. Revolutionary change was precipitate, unpredictable and ultimately uncontrolled and uncontrollable. It was uncertain who would benefit or how; the rationale and criteria for "why" were not only unclear, they were unknown. On the other hand, the status quo was unacceptable and reactionary approaches were equally unappealing.

As a consequence, the key issue was one of pace. Change had to take place on a human scale and in a timeframe that matched people's capacities and capabilities. This echoes the conclusion of Chapter 3. Expressed diagrammatically, the overall choices were:

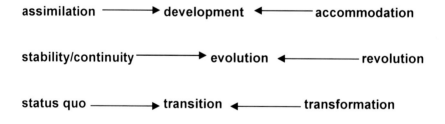

**assimilation ——————▶ development ◀—————— accommodation**

**stability/continuity ——————▶ evolution ◀—————— revolution**

**status quo ——————▶ transition ◀—————— transformation**

---

[332] For example, the inclusion of locations such as Hampshire would link Jane Austen to the political world of Parliament via the local MP William Chute, while the Lake District would link Southey to other poets.

Development, evolution and transition were the preferred outcomes. However, this implies a managed approach and it is not clear that the techniques existed, or could exist, to produce these outcomes - even in stable times, and these were far from stable times. It was all very well to express preferences for predictable, incremental, organic and sustainable results (to use modern jargon), but what actually happened would depend then, as now, on events - many of which were unforeseen and not amenable to political or social solutions. Even if the individuals were in place to exert their skills and authority, results could not be guaranteed. The key responsibility was not to be entirely at the mercy of events, but to mould these as far as possible.

## 5.    CORRUPTION, CLASH AND CELEBRATION

Two of the events that took place in 1809, helping to connect it to our own time, concerned the extremes of British weather - where continuity is in some respects as obvious an aspect as change. In the first of these Scotland experienced "a severe storm [that lasted] ... the whole month" of January and resulted in much of the country being covered in snow and ice, while parts of England experienced severe flooding in late January.[333]   The floods started near Bath, with one of Pickfords' drivers and nine of his horses being drowned at Stony Stratford in Buckinghamshire when the wagon attempted to get through the water.   The Exeter mail coach found that at Staines "... the water was so deep, that the coach floated and the horses swam".   Fortunately, the passengers and the mail came to no harm and were able to continue their journeys on other coaches. At Windsor the King was marooned and a local farmer on his way home "... was washed away into the fields, cart, horse and himself; and had it not been for the boats which went to his assistance, he and his horse must have been drowned".[334]

This was beyond what might be expected in winter, and it is clearly reminiscent of more recent disruption and disaster. The London-centred nature of the news provides another echo of modern times: "The whole country round is in the most distressing state: it is covered in water from Chertsey to Maidenhead.   In general, the water runs in torrents as high as the parlour windows."[335]   As is often the case, it was those who had the least who suffered the most.

In the second event John Rennie and Robert Stevenson continued to construct the Bell Rock lighthouse[336], building thirty feet out of solid granite on top of the foundations they had laid previously.

---

[333] 'Edinburgh Annual Register for 1809', Edinburgh, John Ballantyne & Co., 1811, volume 2, part 2, pp48-50

[334] Ibid, p50

[335] Ibid, p50

[336] Bella Bathurst, 'The Lighthouse Stevensons', London, Flamingo, 2000, pp66-105. Rennie had eventually endorsed Stevenson's view that building a lighthouse on the Bell Rock at the entrance to the Firth of Forth and the Tay would be feasible if difficult. Stevenson started lobbying the Lighthouse Commissioners in 1800, spurred on by seeing a lighthouse built on the Eddystone Rock, but agreement was only reached in December 1806. The light began operating in February 1811. See also 'Edinburgh Annual Register for 1809', op cit, volume 2, pp542-548.

Once again they had to leave the work for the winter in September 1809, but shipping in the area could now see the construction taking shape.

Scandals, notably royal and political scandals, remain familiar today. The third event was a cause celebre of its time that generated press attention and consumed public interest quite as much as any major scandal does two hundred years later. This was summarised by the *Edinburgh Annual Register* as "[The main protagonists] ... the Duke of York, Colonel Wardle (1761, or 1762,-1833) and Mrs Clarke, continue to engross the almost exclusive attention of the court, the House of Commons, and the people of Great Britain, and every tea-table party is occupied with the discussion, insomuch, that the affairs of Spain and the north of Europe seem for a time to be forgotten".[337] There were even the associated diversions involving minor players and hangers-on that have become a routine feature of such scandals more recently. For example, Mrs Clarke's brother was "arrested for a long tailor's bill, at the door of the House of Commons".[338] In other words, he was arrested for a bill that was not being paid.

Unlike scandals, the modern world is largely unfamiliar with duels. They have always been illegal in English law, categorised as affray at one extreme and murder at the other. Legally, seconds are considered as culpable as the prime movers, with their liability to prosecution intended to act as a further deterrent. Nevertheless, duels were one way of satisfying, if not settling, matters of honour. The challenge may often have been as important to restoring the self-regard, and the public esteem, of the injured party as the outcome of the duel itself. There was such a duel between two political heavyweights, Canning and Castlereagh, in 1809. If not momentous, other than for the participants who seem to have

---

[337] '*Edinburgh Annual Register* for 1809', op cit, volume 2, part 2, p65 in the entry for February 13th, shortly after the inquiry by parliament started. These were the King's second son Prince Frederick, the Duke of York, who had been made a field-marshal by George III in 1795 and then commander-in-chief of the army in 1798, one of his mistresses Mrs Clarke (with whom he had an affair from 1803 to 1806 and who he had set up in an establishment at Gloucester Place by 1804) and the MP Colonel Wardle whose accusation of corruption by the Duke of York led to the House of Commons inquiry.
[338] Ibid, p65.

escaped censure, perhaps because there was no lasting injury, it certainly proved portentous for the government and the country.[339]

The change from Portland's government to that of Perceval took place in early October 1809. This is primarily covered in Chapter 6, while the present Chapter focuses on the political, monarchical and military instability that surrounded this change and political reforms. The chronology of key events is set out in Table 7, as is the truncated timetable for the decision to celebrate the King's jubilee. Colley[340] sees this as marking both the recovery of the King's reputation and the antidote to previous events of the year. In both senses it was a patriotic apotheosis.

It might look from Table 7 as though May and June were relatively quiet months in 1809. As the following Chapter shows, however, this was far from the case. The Duke of York inquiry had consumed much of parliament's time in the first quarter of the year (a third of the session according to the *Edinburgh Annual Register* "to the grievous interruption of public business"[341]) and had raised wider issues of corruption. As well as Parliament using these months to catch up on other business, they were to prove the focus for agitation over parliamentary reform. It was also an opportunity for the politicians to focus their attention on the war, even as they continued to intrigue and manoeuvre on other matters.

## Canning, Castlereagh and the Conduct of the War: The Consequences after Cintra

After the humiliating Convention of Cintra in 1808, Canning had been at loggerheads with Castlereagh over the conduct of the war.[342] His view that Castlereagh was inefficient and inept was compounded by Moore's retreat to Corunna. Although the remnants of Moore's army avenged their retreat at Corunna, they

---

[339] For a fuller description than that provided below see Giles Hunt, 'The Duel', London, IB Tauris, 2008. James Landale, 'Duel', Edinburgh, Canongate, 2005 explores the history and laws of duels, and the changing nature of their social function and acceptability.

[340] Colley, op cit, pp217-220

[341] '*Edinburgh Annual Register* for 1809', op cit, volume 2, part 1, p227

[342] As well as her 1973 biography of George Canning already referred to, Hinde is one of those who has written a life of Castlereagh (Wendy Hinde, 'Castlereagh', London, Collins, 1981). She has therefore attempted to look at Cintra and its consequences from both sides.

were displaying the dreadful ravages of war by the time they sailed for England.[343]   Moore was killed by the French on 16th January 1809 as his troops embarked.  After Moore's death, Wellington was the senior general in the peninsula.  Wellington had impressed the inquiry into Cintra, and with Castlereagh's support had largely been exonerated.   Canning still took exception to the outcomes from Cintra and he made his reservations clear, while ostensibly supporting his colleagues, in concluding the debate on the opposition challenge to the Convention in the House of Commons in February 1809.  The following month Canning threatened to resign from the government unless Castlereagh was replaced.  He wrote to Portland on 24th March, and the King allegedly saw the letter too.[344]  Canning's view was that the war against Napoleon could not have divided leadership in the Cabinet between himself as Foreign Secretary and Castlereagh as Secretary for War.  It should be run entirely by a single person whose competence was not in question - and preferably by someone who sat in the House of Commons such as Canning himself.   Wellington's older brother Lord Wellesley would take the post of Secretary for War, but remain in the House of Lords.

The King acknowledged to Castlereagh in October that he had been aware since May 1809 of plans to replace him at the War Department.  He wrote that "The Duke of Portland stated verbally to the King in May last that difficulties had arisen from Mr Canning's representation that the duties of the Foreign & the Colonial Departments clashed, and that, unless some arrangement could be made for the removal of Lord Castlereagh, he had reason to believe that Mr Canning would resign his situation in the Government."[345] Canning had not sought to undermine Castlereagh overtly, nor had he adopted an underhand approach.  Rather he had expected that Castlereagh would be approached openly by, or on behalf of,

---

[343] Hinde, 1973, p208 says, "The rejoicing over the British victor[y] [claimed for] … Corunna was swamped in shocked dismay at the appearance of the haggard, ragged, wounded soldiers who were landed at most of the ports on the south coast from Falmouth round to Dover."

[344] Hinde, op cit, says on p218 that the letter to the Duke of Portland was not sent until 4th April.  George III's reply to Castlereagh on 3rd October stated that "The King does not recollect any communication to him of Mr Canning's letter of the 24th last …" (In 'Later Correspondence of George III', ed A Aspinall, Cambridge, Cambridge University Press, 1970, volume 5, p387)

[345] Quoted in A Aspinall (ed.), 'Later Correspondence of George III', Cambridge, Cambridge University Press, 1970, volume 5, p388

**Table 7: A chronology of 1809**

| Month | Major strands of instability/unstable circumstances* | | | | | |
|---|---|---|---|---|---|---|
| | Impact of Cintra | Scheldt expedition | Duke of York inquiry | East India Co. inquiry | Change of govt | George III jubilee |
| Jan | 16 - Moore killed at Corunna | | 27 - Wardle motion | | | |
| Feb | | | 1 - Inquiry starts | 10 - Inquiry starts | | |
| Mar | Canning resignation threat<br>24 - Canning's letter to Portland/King | | 18 - Duke of York resigns | | | |
| Apr | | | | 25 - Castlereagh accused when President of Board of Control | | |
| May | | | | | | |
| Jun | | | | | | |

**Major strands of instability/unstable circumstances***

| Month | Impact of Cintra | Scheldt expedition | Duke of York inquiry | East India Co. inquiry | Change of govt | George III jubilee |
|---|---|---|---|---|---|---|
| Jul | | Austria defeat at Wagram 28 - Troops to Walcheren | | | | Promotion of Jubilee celebrations starts |
| Aug | | | | | Portland stroke | |
| Sep | 21- Duel; Canning and Castlereagh resign | 2 - Walcheren failure becomes known; Canning demands Castlereagh's removal | | | 6 - Portland resigns as PM 30 - Perceval recommended to King | |
| Oct | 1 - Castlereagh's letter to King 3 - King's reply | | | | 2 - Perceval becomes PM | 25 - Jubilee celebrated |
| Nov | 24 - Canning's letters to Lord Camden sent to King | 4 - Evacuation from Walcheren ordered | | | | |
| Dec | | 23 - Evacuation completed | | | | |

* The events listed in each column of Table 7 provide a few of the key markers in the year. They were inter-twined across the issues (columns), as well as within them and are set out in this format only for the purposes of presentation.

Portland as Prime Minister, and that Castlereagh would then be induced to resign by taking another position in the government that he found compatible. This might avoid the necessity for resignation altogether. At this stage Canning was seen as indispensable by Portland, and by most of the Cabinet, and his view was accepted on the whole. By comparison, Castlereagh was seen as expendable.

Liverpool (then Home Secretary) wrote to George III on 11th July 1809. He said that he was motivated "by an equal feeling of fairness and justice towards both ... individuals", but concluded that "Mr Canning is under the present circumstances a more important and essential member of the Government than Lord Castlereagh".[346] However, he offered to give up the Home Office in favour of Castlereagh if this would help resolve the situation. He was not prepared to see Castlereagh moved from the War Department without an alternative being made available. Equally, though, Canning's resignation could not be contemplated either. It would lead to the entire Government falling - perhaps not immediately, but soon enough.

Nobody wished to offend Castlereagh. There were several reasons for prevaricating, given the pressure that Castlereagh was under, the King's desire to find another solution, and the indecisive characters of first Portland and then Lord Camden (Castlereagh's uncle) when he was given the task of putting the position to him. In April Castlereagh was accused of abusing his earlier position as President of the Board of Control by the Parliamentary select committee inquiring into corruption by the East India Company. He soon began planning the Scheldt expedition, but shortly after the troops landed on Walcheren island it became clear that they were in difficulty. By early September the mission was known to be a failure, giving Canning even more reason to question Castlereagh's abilities to manage the war effectively.

By the time Portland realised he would have to tell Castlereagh himself, it was August.[347] The Prime Minister then had a stroke.

---

[346] Ibid, pp310-312

[347] Camden finally made it known to Portland that he could not bring himself to tell Castlereagh at the beginning of August. Portland wrote to the King to this effect on 6th August, taking the responsibility back himself but seeking to defer this duty to another time given the Scheldt expedition. George III replied on 7th August, advising Portland to decide the best time for himself, especially given other

Potentially, this would mean Castlereagh could be moved in the reshuffle under a new Prime Minister without him being aware of earlier intentions. But by early September Castlereagh had found out. Because he had not heard through the proper channels, it now looked like Canning had been plotting to remove him. Castlereagh's equanimity and appetite for work had led many people to view him negatively, more as a workhorse than as a person. But he now showed his fury. This angry reaction proved to his benefit with the public, if not with many of his colleagues, and he improved in their estimation - if only temporarily. Ten years later Shelley wrote in 'The Mask of Anarchy' (1819):

"I met Murder on the way—
He had a mask like Castlereagh—."[348]

As a result of the treatment he believed he had received, on the 19th September Castlereagh challenged Canning to a duel. His challenge ran to three folio pages. Canning is supposed to have said that he'd rather fight him than read him.[349] "He accepted Canning's right to demand his removal, but 'not at the expense of my honour and reputation'."[350] Canning tried to explain via his second that he had been opposed to secret discussions all along. Perceval sent some of Canning's letters that demonstrated this, but it was to no avail. Castlereagh felt he had no alternative, even if this step was abhorred by many, including the King. The duel was fought on 21st September on Putney Heath and Canning was wounded slightly. His resignation followed, joining that of Portland's in early September as the grim news from the Scheldt became clear.

---

reservations about this course of action, clarifying that the King could not "become a principal" in the matter and concluding that "Whatever may be decided, HM is persuaded that every endeavour will be used to render so unpleasant a step as little distressing as possible to Lord Castlereagh." Ibid, pp320-1

[348] Shelley wrote this poem after hearing of the Peterloo Massacre in August 1819. By then Castlereagh had been Foreign Secretary since 1812, briefly in the Perceval government and then in the Liverpool government that succeeded it. The Oxford Dictionary of National Biography says that these "lines ... were some of the most vicious in the history of British political satire". They sum up Castlereagh's long-standing public reputation.

[349] 'The Complete Peerage' (edited by Vicary Gibbs), vol VIII, p112 in 1932 edition.

[350] Hinde, 1981, op cit, p166 cites this quotation from the *Annual Register* for 1809, pp562-3

Castlereagh had resigned mid-way through September. He justified himself to George III in a long letter on 1st October 1809[351] that covered the machinations over his removal from the War Department the King had been privy to and sought to defend his conduct of the war against Napoleon in the peninsula and the Scheldt. He emphasised the reasons why he had supported both Moore and Wellington in relation to Corunna and Cintra respectively. He wrote that

"If an earnest desire to protect the fame and characters of officers, exposing their reputations as well as their lives in your Majesty's service ... can be denominated *compromise*, Lord Castlereagh cannot wish to exculpate himself from the imputation. He can never cease to reflect with satisfaction ... that he never yet has abandoned one of them in a manner, of the justice of which, they felt themselves entitled to complain ..."[352]

In his view their disgrace would not have helped anyone. According to Hinde[353], Castlereagh thought that the only honourable thing for the government to do was to accept responsibility for Cintra and Corunna. Canning felt they should have distanced themselves, confronting these events head on. He complained of the Government's "spirit of compromise".

Although Castlereagh was aware that he was breaching the protocol established by Pitt that "the Prime Minister was the normal channel of communication on non-departmental business between the King and other members of the Cabinet"[354], he felt he had to respond to the earlier trampling of this convention that he believed Canning had perpetrated. Castlereagh justified his conduct in his letter to the King by writing that "...your Majesty will graciously be disposed to admit that it is impossible for Lord Castlereagh, wounded as his feelings decidedly are, to avail himself of a channel through which misrepresentations to the prejudice of his public conduct have been allowed to reach your Majesty, without any opportunity being allowed to him to meet and to refute them." With "... feelings of regret and disappointment... he now retires from your

---

[351] In A Aspinall (ed.), 'Later Correspondence of George III', op cit, pp378-381
[352] Ibid, p380
[353] Hinde, 1981, op cit, p168
[354] Aspinall, A and Smith EA (eds), 'English Historical Documents - Volume XI: 1790-1832', London, Eyre & Spottiswoode, 1969, p130

Majesty's service".[355]    George III replied on 3rd October thanking Castlereagh for the "... zeal and assiduity with which he has discharged the duties of the various situations he has filled ... [and his] exertions"[356] in supporting the King, and absolved him from any charges of neglect.    Castlereagh found this reply "... perfectly satisfactory - very full of regret, very complimentary on my services - admits how justly I was entitled to complain, and negatives all Canning's propositions".[357]

Canning took until 24th November to write to the King[358], justifying the open approach he had adopted throughout.  He referred to the assurances he had received from Portland's heir on the appropriateness of his conduct and the good character with which he had sought to conduct it.

George III prevaricated, but eventually had no option but to ask Perceval to form the next government.  (Neither Canning nor Castlereagh featured in it and, much to Canning's dismay, Castlereagh was to return to government first.    Perceval re-appointed him in spring 1812 - and as Foreign Secretary too.) Huskisson had stepped down from assisting Perceval at the Treasury when Canning resigned.  He was to remain out of office to 1814.  Perceval offered the Treasury to Palmerston (he would not have offered it in any case to Huskisson), and when Palmerston (1784-1865) refused, carried on as Chancellor of the Exchequer himself.[359]

**The Scheldt Expedition**

The Scheldt expedition was several months in the planning by Castlereagh and the War Department.  By the time 39,000 troops sailed for Walcheren island in the Scheldt on 28th July 1809, Austria had already been heavily defeated by the French at Wagram earlier

---

[355] In A Aspinall (ed.), 'Later Correspondence of George III', op cit, p381
[356] Ibid, pp387-8
[357] In a letter to his half-brother on 16th October 1809, quoted in A Aspinall (ed.), 'Later Correspondence of George III', op cit, pp388-389
[358] Ibid, pp457-9. Strictly speaking, Canning had published two letters to Lord Camden. He sent these to Lieutenant-Colonel Taylor to ensure the King saw them. The published letters are reviewed in the *Quarterly Review*, November 1809, volume 2 number 4, London, John Murray, 1811 (2nd edition), pp412-425.
[359] Fay, op cit, p76

that month. The expedition was intended as a diversion to assist Austria, but it was too late and proved to be a complete disaster.

The original plan earlier in the year had been to concentrate an attack on Flushing on Walcheren island. This had been a long-standing British ambition, and would have required a modest commitment of troops. However, even raising this limited number proved impossible given the condition of the soldiers on their return from Corunna. To the target of Flushing, Antwerp was then added as another objective as Napoleon had turned it into a centre for ship-building, with 80 gun ships being constructed. Antwerp was further up the Scheldt estuary and required a larger expedition. The British, with their navy obsession, felt bound to focus on this. However, "In the very conception of such a project there was a demonstrable absurdity ... all competition for the empire of the ocean was at an end"[360] because of Britain's naval superiority. In other words, even had Napoleon's Antwerp flotilla sailed, it would have stood little chance against the British navy (or so this jingoistic view proclaimed). Several of those consulted thought the expedition a bad idea. According to the *Edinburgh Annual Register*, they included the commander-in-chief Sir David Dundas (who had replaced the Duke of York when the latter resigned in March) and the head of his office Colonel Gordon. The Scheldt was the wrong target. Paris and the Low Countries were wide open to invasion with the French troops elsewhere, and in any case "Nothing could result from it in favour of Austria ..."[361] who hoped for an attack that would draw the French army away from Vienna. In addition, Canning and Castlereagh disagreed with each other.

To add to these errors, the military command was assigned to the Earl of Chatham (1756-1835). This took everyone aback, because his reputation for indolence and procrastination was well-known and apparently well-deserved. It made him very different from his brother William Pitt. Indeed, he was often called the *late* Lord Chatham "because his hour of rising was usually in the afternoon"[362]. He had been removed in 1794 as First Lord of the Admiralty for this reason, even though his brother was still Prime Minister at the time. Nevertheless, he was both a favourite of George III (and Canning is said to have considered him as a possible replacement for Portland as Prime Minister as a result) and

---

[360] '*Edinburgh Annual Register* for 1809', op cit, volume 2, part 1, pp661-2
[361] Ibid, p663
[362] Ibid, p660

a member of the Cabinet as Master-General of Ordnance. He was therefore on hand when the command was determined, but his Cabinet position would prove to be in conflict with this role when his dilatory and casual behaviour showed itself in the course of the expedition. His instructions were to destroy the enemy fleet in the Scheldt, its dockyards and arsenals, and, if possible, make the estuary no longer navigable for warships. Sir Richard Strachan commanded the naval contingent, including thirty-five ships of the line, but was dependent for most purposes on Chatham and his troops.

The expedition started badly when the wind prevented an early capture of Cadsand, the island across the west Scheldt from Walcheren. The French had been expecting an attack elsewhere, and this failure lost the British any element of initiative or surprise. Capturing Cadsand would have ensured Flushing could not be reinforced by this route, but this "... part of the plan which had been considered as indispensable to the accomplishment of the whole, was thus frustrated".[363] There were then a further series of errors and misunderstandings, with different parts of the force having contradictory instructions, misinterpreting them or deciding to fulfil them only partially.

The troops were eventually put ashore on 1st August, four days after they had sailed and had first anchored off Walcheren. Although they had not landed where planned, the troops soon surrounded Flushing. Chatham set up his headquarters at Middelburg in the middle of the island. Although Flushing could still be reinforced from Cadsand, other matters were very much in favour of the British: the local population detested the French as much as did the British, Flushing was mainly defended on the seaward side, with poor and old-fashioned defences against an attack from land, the enemy was not prepared to defend it in any case, and they had only 4,000 troops on the island at this point. Nor were these French troops, but Prussians, Spaniards, Dutch and Irish "all, except perhaps the latter, detesting in their hearts the usurper whom they were compelled to serve"[364]. Rather than taking advantage of their situation, however, the British decided to bombard Flushing and to do so as ineptly as possible. For example, they chose to

---

[363] Ibid, pp664-5. Chatham was later to deny that this had been part of the plan.
[364] Ibid, p670

concentrate on the town rather than on its defences, such as they were. This guaranteed that the residents would become more hostile and, even if the bombardment was effective, meant there would be less left to capture. 3000 additional troops were then sent from Cadsand to reinforce the defence of Flushing, and on 7th August a force of 2000 counter-attacked. British losses increased and it took until 15th August before Flushing surrendered. As the *Edinburgh Annual Register* says, "The plan was not more injudiciously chosen, than it was unskilfully executed".[365] The Irish force escaped to Cadsand before the town capitulated, avoiding the consequences of being treated as traitors if they had fallen into British hands.

The British forces re-assembled, but Chatham was then "undecided himself what course to pursue".[366] The navy could not attack Antwerp on its own without orders to that effect and Chatham took several days to cover the nineteen miles from Middelburg to his new headquarters in the north of Walcheren. By the time he arrived, Antwerp had been reinforced by Bernadotte as its new commander, including laying a chain across the channel to keep out the British navy. As Chatham had perhaps hoped, it was no longer possible to attack Antwerp - with the British out-numbered in any case. In addition, their remaining rations were insufficient and 3000 men were already on the sick-list.

Chatham left 17,000 troops to hold Walcheren and returned to England with the remainder on 14th September. By this stage the numbers of sick were already 8000 and increasing every day. The plan to block the Scheldt had been abandoned, and Chatham's other instructions remained equally unfulfilled. The expedition had been a failure. It now turned into a catastrophe. The sluices had been opened, and the eastern dyke cut, in early August to raise the water level on Walcheren. A thunderstorm on 10th August had made the British trenches useless and the ground impassable to heavy artillery and wagons. Walcheren was known anyway for its unhealthy climate and "marsh distempers". The mud and rising water levels compounded these, with 11,000 sick by 8th September[367]. The British began to think of evacuating Walcheren

---

[365] Ibid, p671

[366] Ibid, p678

[367] The apparent discrepancy between 11,000 sick on 8th September, and 8000 sick and increasing when Chatham left on 14th September, is not explained further

rather than holding it, but resisted an early decision given the lives that had already been lost and their alliance with Austria. In the meantime they strengthened Flushing's fortifications, only to destroy them shortly after when the final decision to evacuate Walcheren was eventually taken. The last British troops left a month later on 23rd December. The French did not intervene.[368]

The Walcheren debacle was a disaster for the troops involved, but a gift for the opposition. The Whigs continued to harass Perceval's government in early 1810 over the expedition's misguided planning and its lamentable execution.[369]

## Corruption and the Duke of York Inquiry

At first sight some writers might appear to have downplayed the significance of the House of Commons corruption inquiry into the Duke of York and the sale of army commissions by his mistress. Hilton, for instance, refers to it as the sort of trouble younger royals get into - but this is mischievous and Hilton warns elsewhere against thinking of it in this misleading way.[370] Such a view would in any case be to deny the moral and political implications of the

---

in the *Edinburgh Annual Register*. It may be that Chatham took some of the sick with him (though this seems unlikely) leaving 8000 on Walcheren, that 3000 died in the six days after 8th September (though the attrition rate was not this high at this stage), that some recovered or that the figures were confused. The latter is the most likely explanation given the chaotic nature of the expedition.

[368] Chatham's entry in the DNB says "Fortescue wrote of the expedition: 'It was dogged not merely by misfortune, but by cruel, and it may be said undeserved, adversity' (Fortescue, Brit. army, 7.96). Nevertheless, Chatham's natural laziness and mediocre military talents did not help. On his return he presented a partisan report to the King in private, instead of forwarding it to Castlereagh, the secretary of state. An inquiry into his conduct compromised his reputation, and in March 1810 he resigned as master-general of the ordnance."

[369] Thorne, op cit, volume III, p443 says that, for example, the Hampshire MP William Chute (see Chapter 4 above) "rallied to Perceval's ministry on the … Scheldt question [four times in early 1810, though Thorne identifies five divisions in volume I, p189], being listed 'against the Opposition' by the Whigs."

[370] Hilton, 2006, op cit, p217 The Duke of York was neither a younger royal, having been born in 1763 and already 40 when the affair with Mrs Clarke started in 1803, nor was he a minor royal, as the King's second son and third in line to the throne. He was a very public figure as commander-in-chief of an army at war. On p205 Hilton says that "Scandals like the Duke of York affair in 1809 made people feel that there was something rotten in the State, and affected many of the more earnest young men entering politics".

Duke's affair with Mrs Clarke, and the public values that it imperilled.[371]

**Figure 7:** '[The future] **King George IV; King George III; Frederick, Duke of York and Albany'** (probably by Charles Tomkins, hand-coloured etching, circa 1775-1800) © National Portrait Gallery, London

---

[371] Other historians have allowed it whatever space it warrants in line with their overall predilections and purpose. For example, Colley covers it succinctly in less than a page (op cit, pp217-8) and casts it primarily in relation to female emancipation, and the jubilee celebrations that she says the scandal helped generate as an antidote to public disaffection and royal disgrace.

146

Parliament certainly took this stance. The House of Commons conducted an extensive investigation, allotting it much of their time for two months. In addition to the issues that the inquiry raised directly, the circumstances surrounding it were extremely sensitive in any case. The country was reeling militarily and continued to be scandalised by the behaviour of the Prince of Wales and Princess Caroline, who had lived apart ever since their first months of marriage in 1795. The Duke of York affair raised both national issues and domestic marital ones; military corruption was accompanied by moral turpitude. In each instance the Duke might be using his civil list entitlement for purposes for which the public settlement was not intended. Furthermore, Parliament as a whole, and particularly perhaps the Whigs, had been unsettled by a publication in August 1808 that referred to the Duke of York "[along] with the queen, [as] at the head of the King's friends". This might seem unexceptionable given the close knit nature of the royal family (apart from the Prince of Wales), inevitable even given Portland's lack of decisiveness and the executive approach to monarchy adopted by George III. The allegation, however, was effectively of a private privy council that exerted undue influence and chose to ignore political advice if they preferred.

The press often blamed the Duke of York as commander-in-chief for the army's military defeats. "It cannot be denied that the Duke of York had been singularly unfortunate as a commander. This was the topic on which the hostile newspapers assailed him, and this was sufficient to make him unpopular."[372] The "foppery of the army"[373] was also laid at his door and further undermined his position. This rumbling background of unpopularity provided an opportunity to exploit the Duke of York's position and severely embarrass the government at the same time. The Whigs seemed

---

[372] '*Edinburgh Annual Register* for 1809', op cit, volume 2, part 1, p111

[373] See Colley, op cit, pp185-187 for the variety of uniforms that were designed during this period, partly to distinguish each regiment but also to distinguish each soldier and appeal to their vanity. A single uniform would have provided an appropriate display of patriotism; the separate uniforms were also about standing out as an individual and, in many cases, were fashion statements rather than practical kit. On p184 she says "Of the more than 2000 men who sat as MPs between 1790 and 1820, almost half served as militia or volunteer officers. A further fifth of all MPs, twice as many as in any pre-1790 Parliament, were officers in the regular army; one hundred more were naval officers. The supreme legislative body of GB had not just become a military headquarters ... It now looked like [one] as well."

uncertain whether this was an appropriate moment, given that the risk might backfire, but Colonel Wardle was less reluctant. As early as the second day of the new parliamentary session (20th January 1809) he said that he would bring forward a motion the following week.[374]

In late 1808 a pamphlet claimed that Brevet-Major Hogan had been offered promotion by the Duke of York himself for an inducement of £600. The pamphlet explained that "The money paid in the regular course [approximately £1000] goes into a public fund, which ... [cannot be touched] by any public officer for private purposes, while the private *douceur* [£600] is wholly applicable to such purposes."[375] Hogan said that he rejected this proposal because he felt it "unworthy ... to owe the ... commission to low intrigue or petticoat influence".[376] He resigned, but was then told by the Duke's military secretary, Colonel Gordon, that £750 of the costs of his original commission would be returned to him, but the army would retain the remaining £400. At this point Hogan made a public appeal through the newspapers to recover the full amount. He alleged in the pamphlet that the same evening "a lady left a letter at his lodgings", together with £400 "to answer for the deficit of which he complained".[377] There was no proof that these events had happened, although Cobbett and others were disposed to believe them and asked for evidence to support the accusations. It subsequently emerged that Hogan had sailed for America before the pamphlet was printed, casting further doubt on the likely truth of the allegations. Whipped up by the press, however, they added to a public climate that was predominantly hostile to the Duke of York.

On the 27th January 1809 Colonel Wardle's motion accused the Duke of York of military corruption, conniving in the sale of army promotions if not selling them himself. Wardle called "for the

---

[374] Philip Harling refers to Wardle as an obscure Welsh MP in 'The Duke of York affair (1809) and the complexities of war-time patriotism', The Historical Journal, 1996, 39(4), pp963-984. This may have been the case before the inquiry; it was not afterwards. He was one of the fifteen radical MPs who voted for Burdett's motion for parliamentary reform on 15th June 1809. He also pledged that a fully representative House of Commons would save the amount raised by the Income Tax. Cobbett reports this in his weekly *Political Register*, volume XV, no 25, for Saturday 24th June 1809, pp965-989 as "Wardle's Pledge". See Chapter 6 below.
[375] '*Edinburgh Annual Register* for 1809', op cit, volume 2, part 1, p112-3
[376] Ibid, p113
[377] Ibid, p114

148

appointment of a Committee to inquire into the conduct of the Commander in Chief, with regard to Promotions and Exchanges in the Army, &c., &c."[378] His motion was seconded by Sir Francis Burdett. Cobbett was to devote much of the available space in his weekly *Political Register* to reporting and commenting on the inquiry. While he usually found verbatim reporting undesirable, "I shall insert here the *whole* of this most interesting debate, or, rather conversation, of the honourable House".[379] He made use of the reports in the Morning Chronicle to this end, supplementing them from articles in the Courier as necessary. He justified this close attention to the inquiry's proceedings by stating that important national consequences were at stake, regardless of whether Wardle was able to substantiate his charges or not.

According to the *Edinburgh Annual Register*, "It was said that the readiest mode of obtaining promotion in the army was through one of the duke's mistresses, and that money well applied in that direction was sure of its object."[380] Wardle's opening speech identified more than six cases to illustrate his claim that money had been paid to Mrs Clarke for promotions while she was the Duke of York's mistress between 1803 and 1806. These included the case of Captain Huxley Sandon, who had paid £500 to Mrs Clarke. She had then paid the £500 to a silversmith for the plate she had ordered for the house in Gloucester Place that the Duke had installed her in. The Duke of York later paid the balance to the silversmith. Wardle claimed that Mrs Clarke had a scale of prices for different promotions and that these were the same as that of "a public office in the city for the sale of commissions ... [run by] ... agents of the present favourite mistress, Mrs Carey".[381]

The government and the Duke's friends appeared to welcome the charges, claiming this as an opportunity to bring an end to the campaign of innuendo he had experienced. They called for a parliamentary commission that could examine witnesses under oath. In their view this was the most effective way to tackle the

[378] Cobbett's *Political Register*, Volume XV, no 5, London, Hansard, Saturday 4th February 1809, p161
[379] Ibid, p162 As Ingrams, op cit, says "The affair excited a huge amount of public interest, and Cobbett devoted whole issues of the *Political Register* to ... the inquiry". (p85)
[380] '*Edinburgh Annual Register* for 1809', op cit, volume 2, part 1, p111
[381] Ibid, pp119-120

"jacobin" conspiracy and newspaper licentiousness the Duke had been subject to, clearing his name in the process. Cobbett was dismissive of this alleged jacobin conspiracy, saying it had not been mentioned previously and had only come to the fore now as a way of drawing attention away from the accusations that had been levelled at the Duke, relieving the pressure on him.[382] But he agreed that providing the publicity sought by the Duke of York and his friends was likely to prove in the wider public interest as well. A number of MPs supported the proposal of a commission, including Burdett himself. William Adam (who had taken over the Duke's affairs in 1805) warned that a select committee might quickly become a secret committee, whereas matters needed to be brought into the open in order to restore public confidence. William Wilberforce thought a commission preferable to examination by the whole House of Commons, where it would be too easy for party prejudice to intrude, but Spencer Perceval disagreed. He said that "He felt the inconvenience of a parliamentary inquiry, but that inconvenience must be encountered on so important a question".[383] For example, Wardle had accused two un-named Cabinet members in his speech of acting as agents for Government patronage. Perceval said he should be required to identify them so that they could clear their name and in order that suspicion did not fall on every member of the Cabinet. An inquiry by the whole House of Commons would force him to do so. Wardle then said that his allegations referred to the Prime Minister the Duke of Portland and the Lord Chancellor Lord Eldon. "At this the House rung with peals of laughter, so outrageously absurd the accusation was thought, and such was the surprise of all the members ..."[384]

This led MPs to agree that the inquiry should be considered by a committee. Perceval said the committee should be the whole House in order to address all the issues. Canning supported him and welcomed the widened sphere of inquiry Perceval had proposed. Castlereagh responded to the Whig objectors, such as the brewer Samuel Whitbread (1764-1815), accusing them of jacobinism (i.e., seeking to remove the monarchical branch of the constitution or, as it was conceived, one leg of the three-legged stool, thereby unbalancing the whole; later refers to any central

---

[382] Cobbett's *Political Register*, Volume XV, no 5, London, Hansard, Saturday 4th February 1809, pp179-180
[383] '*Edinburgh Annual Register* for 1809', op cit, volume 2, part 1, p123
[384] Ibid, p123

power). According to Castlereagh, "Mr Whitbread ... seemed to doubt the existence of a systematic conspiracy to traduce and calumniate the Duke of York and the royal family".[385] So, clearly, did Cobbett, who wrote in the *Political Register* that "It is an observation that can have escaped no man, that despotic governments have never tolerated free discussions on political matters. The reason is plain; that their deeds will not bear the display of reason and the light of truth."[386]

The House of Commons met for the first time as a committee of inquiry on the evening of 1st February 1809. This first day of evidence opened with Colonel Wardle seeking to substantiate the allegations of corruption. The pattern for proceedings was set at this point, with Wardle calling various witnesses, the Duke's defence counsel Spencer Perceval or his junior John Croker[387] being most prominent in cross-examining them, and Mrs Clarke then being called to explain the circumstances further.[388]

---

[385] Ibid, p125

[386] Cobbett's *Political Register*, Volume XV, no 5, London, Hansard, Saturday 4th February 1809, p191

[387] John Wilson Croker (1780-1857) had become MP for Downpatrick at the 'No popery' general election in 1807 aged 26. Perceval was to make him Secretary of the Admiralty from October 1809, an honour for someone still aged only 28 (even Samuel Pepys was 40 when he became secretary to the new Admiralty Board in 1673 and was not much younger than Croker when first made Clerk). Croker's elevation to the post, however, made the appointment a political rather than a professional one for the first time. It is said that the protests led Croker to resist the post at first, and while this may seem unlikely given the acrimony he generated later, he might be expected to look for the benefits from a superficial and political stance such as this. Eventually, he was "persuaded" to take it and was to remain there for the next 21 years to 1830. As Hilton says, he was to become one of the main contributors to the *Quarterly Review* (2007, op cit). A number of writers (e.g., Feiling, op cit; Mitchell, op cit) concur with the negative views of him held by many of his contemporaries.

[388] In some instances the Attorney-General Sir Vicary Gibbs also questioned witnesses and Mrs Clarke. However, Thorne (op cit, volume IV, p17) says that Gibbs "was reported by May 1808 to be in 'sad health and Perceval has manumitted him from long nights in the House'." Gibbs was an MP from 1804 (with the exception of 1806-1807 when he opposed the Grenville ministry and was not re-elected for Totnes). He was MP for Cambridge University from the 1807 general election to May 1812. Gibbs had assisted Perceval as Princess Caroline's legal adviser in the 'Delicate Investigation' of 1806-1807, and was to be blamed in May 1812 for rushing Bellingham's trial for murder in the week after Perceval's assassination. He had ceased to be an MP by the end of the month, becoming a judge instead.

This first day also set the pattern for incendiary claims against the Duke of York. Public interest was immediately roused; their anticipations rapidly met. Mrs Clarke's doctor Dr Thynne was the initial witness. The second was his friend Dr Knight who had asked Dr Thynne to approach Mrs Clarke on his behalf as a way of speeding up a transaction that Dr Knight's brother wished to conclude speedily because of ill-health. Mrs Clarke was then examined on their evidence, confirming Dr Thynne's claim of an exchange on behalf of Dr Knight's brother to half-pay in the infantry. Mrs Clarke said this exchange had taken place through the Duke of York and had cost £200. Dr Knight had claimed that Mrs Clarke asked him to keep her involvement secret from the Duke. Cobbett said this was absurd: why should Mrs Clarke seek to take credit for persuading the Duke on the one hand, while asking Dr Knight to make sure the Duke didn't know of her part on the other?[389] She also said that when she had recently asked the Duke for a few hundred pounds, his response had been "... if she dared speak against him, or write against him, he would put her in the pillory, or in the Bastille".[390]

The Cruikshank cartoon in Figure 8 indicates that the inquiry proceedings were so sensational that the interest generated on the other side of the Channel was almost as strong as it was among the British public. Napoleon and his generals were effected as much as anyone else, and had most to gain from the Duke's discomfiture and Britain's distraction from the war.

Mrs Clarke had previously claimed to be a widow. She now admitted under cross-examination by Sir Vicary Gibbs, the Attorney-General, that she was still married when she committed adultery with the Duke of York, a married man. When their affair ended in 1806, the Duke agreed to pay her an annuity of £400 per year but

---

[389] *Political Register*, op cit, Volume XV, no 6, 11ᵗʰ February 1809, pp213-4
[390] '*Edinburgh Annual Register* for 1809', op cit, volume 2, part 1, p129  This might appear an unusual reference were it to relate to the Paris Bastille which had been destroyed at the start of the French Revolution twenty years before. This would suggest that either Mrs Clarke did not know this, or the Duke of York didn't, or she is implying that the British monarchy was also tyrannical and required their own "Bastille" to deal with their opponents. The word "bastile" or "bastille" could be used for any prison (such as those at Spa Fields, Bristol and Manchester), and the one at Coldbath Fields was often referred to as the "English Bastille" (Spencer Walpole, 'The Life of the Right Honourable Spencer Perceval', volume 1, London, Hurst and Blackett, 1874, p99).

with the proviso that "it must rest entirely upon his word, to be performed according to her behaviour".[391]  The Duke retained the power to withdraw the annuity.

**Figure 8: 'French Generals Receiving an English Charge'**
Napoleon, Talleyrand and other French generals enjoy caricatures of the Duke of York and Mrs Clarke.  Isaac and George Cruikshank, April 1809 The Reform Club © Mary Evans Picture Library

Colonel Wardle was angered by the cross-examination to which the Attorney-General had subjected Mrs Clarke.  His irritation was shared by Cambridge University which Sir Vicary Gibbs represented as an MP.  According to Thorne, he "... was alleged to have 'incensed' the university ... by his 'very illiberal examination' of Mary Anne Clarke and to have been baffled by her evasive and

---

[391] *'Edinburgh Annual Register* for 1809', op cit, volume 2, part 1, p131. Since the Duke was aware by May 1805 at the latest that Mrs Clarke was still married, and that she was unreliable in other ways that William Adam's investigation had uncovered by then, Cobbett raises the question of why the Duke offered her an annuity at all.  (See *Political Register*, Volume XV, no 6, p222)

impertinent replies".[392]  Wardle became further infuriated at being continually questioned in the same manner himself about her evidence on dates.  "He did not feel disposed to the same sort of discipline"[393] she had been required to undergo.  Samuel Whitbread supported his position, but the Speaker and Canning demanded he respond to the questions.  Perceval explained that Wardle's veracity was not being questioned, but Mrs Clarke's evidence was being checked.  Wardle said that he had already sought to comply as far as he was able.

Colonel Gordon, the Duke's military secretary, was questioned next. He said that all commissions and exchanges went through his office.  He therefore knew about all such transactions and in this instance the record provided evidence that Dr Knight's exchange had gone through the proper channels.  It was alleged, though, that the Duke had first refused the exchange on 23rd July 1805, only to agree to it the following day.[394]  Colonel Gordon claimed this had been because further inquiries had been required.  Many MPs must have doubted this explanation of events given the evidence they had already heard.

Colonel Wardle then said that the next stage of the investigation required Captain Huxley Sandon and Colonel French to have returned from Spain and be ready to testify.  As he was not sure whether this was yet the case, he asked that they not be called until the following Tuesday (7th February).  Sturges Bourne (1769-1845) and William Adam said that such a request was unacceptable.  In their opinion Wardle should not have brought the charges against the Duke of York if they could not be substantiated: "In candour, in justice, in every principle of fair dealing, such delays should not be tolerated."[395]  Despite this protest, however, the House of Commons acceded to Wardle's request in order that all allegations were heard fully and so that they could not be accused of hurrying the business

---

[392] Thorne op cit, volume IV, p17, though "... he later defended her when she was prosecuted by Colonel Wardle".

[393] 'Edinburgh Annual Register for 1809', op cit, volume 2, part 1, p131

[394] This is at odds with Cobbett's report of Colonel Gordon's evidence.  He says in the Political Register (op cit, Volume XV, no 6, p217) that the Duke agreed the exchange on 23rd July 1805, the King counter-signed it on the 24th and the exchange was gazetted on the 30th July.

[395] 'Edinburgh Annual Register for 1809', op cit, volume 2, part 1, p134

through with undue haste. Sandon and French would be called on the Tuesday to explain their agreement for a levy of 5000 men.

This would be the third day of evidence, but in the meantime the inquiry sat for a second time on 3rd February, two days after its first hearing. This was to prove a good day for the Duke of York, and a correspondingly bad one for Colonel Wardle. It emerged that Wardle had seen Mrs Clarke more often on 31st January than his evidence on 1st February had indicated; he admitted that he had unfairly accused a Captain Maling originally, but had then been forced to proceed with the case in order to clear the Captain's name in public[396]; and he then added to the impression that he was misguided by saying that Captain Maling's brother not only served in Colonel Gordon's office, but had been promoted even though he was known not to have served with a field company as the regulations required. Wardle then bumbled over the date of the next hearing, again raising the issue of whether the charges were well-founded.

Needless to say, some Members took this opportunity to decry Colonel Wardle's approach and deflect the accusations from the Duke of York. George Canning, for example, threatened that "infamy must attach somewhere", implying, if not actually saying, that this would be to Wardle if the allegations against the Duke of York could not be substantiated.[397] Other MPs defended Wardle, with the Whigs emphasising the importance of treating him as impartially as the Duke of York. Sir Francis Burdett said Wardle should be treated fairly, protected even, or other MPs would not be encouraged "to put [themselves] forward for the detection of any great public abuses".[398] Conversely, the Whig MP and playwright Richard Brinsley Sheridan let it be known that he had previously warned Wardle that "he had lent himself to the designs of a dark conspiracy". His message had failed to reach Wardle, but he was of the view that Wardle had been "decoyed into a foul and

---

[396] This led Henry Lascelles, MP for Westbury in Wiltshire from the 1807 general election to 1812 but an MP since 1796, to say that Wardle should "weigh his accusations well before he brought them forward; [otherwise] not a single individual in the house or in the country would be safe". Ibid, p138

[397] Ibid, p141. When hearing Canning's threat, it is difficult not to be reminded of Kenneth Williams' predicament as Julius Caesar in 'Carry On Cleo' (1964) when he said "Infamy! Infamy! They've all got it in for me." Later events indicated that the government did indeed "have it in" for Wardle.

[398] Ibid, p141

unprincipled association" with Mrs Clarke.[399]  This meant that the onus was, and should be, on Wardle to prove the charges fully and not prevaricate.  With this exception, Sheridan played little part in the inquiry, being generally absent from the House as his other affairs began to unravel.  According to Thorne, Sheridan claimed to have "returned once in May 'to assure [fellow MPs] that he *was not dead*, but nobody would believe him'".[400]

In the meantime, several points were made that reflected well on the Duke.  He had changed the army's system of promotion so that it was now dependent on length of service (rather than, as previously, permitting promotions up to the rank of Lieutenant Colonel on the basis of purchase only).  According to Colonel Gordon, the Duke spent at least nine hours each day on his duties as commander-in-chief of the army.  He had been aware of the potential for abuse when the army had been augmented by 50 battalions in 1804, and had circulated a memo to all army corps reminding them of the regulations about promotions and exchanges in order to counter this.  Other matters were less clear-cut, but the *Edinburgh Annual Register* gives the Duke credit for appearing unconcerned by Mrs Clarke's angry threats to make public his letters, even though they left no doubts about the nature of their relationship.[401]  In the same vein it refers to the evidence of William Adam that one of his sons had joined the army at 14 or 15 and become a Lieutenant Colonel by the age of 21.  His rise had been entirely due to his own merits as a number of generals could testify, and had not been the result of the Duke's or other patronage as Wardle had implied.  On the other hand, Cobbett[402] says that it was totally inappropriate for someone to be a Lieutenant Colonel by 21, whatever his merits.  This would be unacceptable in a judge, and the same was true for the men asked to serve with, or under, someone of this age.

---

[399] Ibid, p142.  Sheridan was to fall out with the Prince Regent and eventually die a bankrupt.  But at one stage he had been a very prominent MP and his views were still carefully listened to.  Cobbett rubbished this allegation of conspiracy in the *Political Register*, volume XV, no 6, p223.  "Who was involved?", he asked. "Where did they meet?"

[400] Thorne, op cit, Volume V, p159

[401] '*Edinburgh Annual Register* for 1809', op cit, volume 2, part 1, pp136-7

[402] *Political Register*, op cit, Volume XV, no 7, 18th February 1809, p228

The inquiry sat again on the following Tuesday and continued to hear evidence on a further seven days over the following fortnight to February 22nd. There was a parade of witnesses, with the accusations piling up against Mrs Clarke and her influence with the Duke. In some instances this looked to extend beyond military promotions to religious and government offices.

Huxley Sandon appeared before the inquiry several times. Perceval reported to the House on 16th February that Sandon had destroyed a note from the Duke of York even though he had been asked not to. Sandon claimed he had lost the evidence rather than destroyed it. The House voted unanimously that he be taken into custody and then committed to Newgate for gross prevarication. Perceval and others were irritated that a charge of forgery could not now be proved against Mrs Clarke. General Clavering demanded to testify before the inquiry, but proved to be an old duffer with no evidence of substance. Mrs Clarke indicated he was mistaken in thinking he had spoken to her about military promotion. For a time it looked as though, like Sandon, he would be charged with prevarication and misleading the inquiry. But he voluntarily re-appeared in an attempt to clarify what he had said previously and further censure was deferred.

Mrs Clarke's sister-in-law Miss Taylor also appeared twice. On the first occasion she said that the Duke of York had been aware of the proposed levy by Colonel French of 5000 men. At one stage Mrs Clarke was to be paid £1000 and a guinea per man for securing the Duke's agreement, though the price was subsequently reduced. Spencer Perceval and Sir Vicary Gibbs attempted to discredit Miss Taylor by calling into question her father's respectability. They justified this on the grounds that "... her veracity would not be doubted on account of her poverty; but ... much of the credit due to her testimony would 'depend upon the degree of respectability which she and her connections hold'."[403] Miss Taylor stood her ground on this occasion, but was reduced to tears by Perceval when she was re-called on the last day of the inquiry. She was forced to confirm that her mother had been imprisoned for debt and her parents were not married. However, the Whigs Whitbread and Smith reminded the House that they should not confuse respectability of birth with the credibility of her evidence.

---

[403] *Edinburgh Annual Register* for 1809', op cit, volume 2, part 1, p150

Another attempt to discredit the character of witnesses also backfired. On Tuesday 3$^{rd}$ February Mr Dowler said he paid £1000 to Mrs Clarke, who had then secured the Duke's recommendation to the Treasury that Dowler be placed in the commissariat as requested. This evidence struck at Perceval's own department and also raised the question of the sale of government offices. Perceval said that "the purposes of justice required"[404] that Mrs Clarke be interviewed about this immediately, even though it was already after midnight and she had been waiting for eight hours to testify. Fortunately, the House persuaded Perceval to postpone her cross-examination so that she could not later claim not to have known what she was saying because of fatigue.

When Mrs Clarke was questioned on Dowler's evidence ten days later, she cast doubt on aspects of it - including his testimony that she had stayed with him at his hotel on the night he arrived from Portugal. Several MPs asked Croker not to pursue this salacious questioning, but Perceval pointed out that the charges against the Duke depended on the character of Mrs Clarke, and to some extent on that of Dowler too. Perceval then had Mrs Clarke identified as Dowler's "wife" by the coffee-house (i.e., hotel) keeper. The *Edinburgh Annual Register* observed that "Mr Perceval must have known little of the English people, if he supposed that the credit of these two witnesses [Mrs Clarke and Mr Dowler] could be impeached by the detection of the falsehood into which they had been driven. The effect was completely opposite."[405] It was right. The public reacted strongly in Mrs Clarke's favour as a result. There had been a clash of cultures between the overbearing and remote establishment (represented by the politician Perceval and the Duke of York and the royal family more generally) and everyday human behaviour. The public could understand and sympathise with the latter, just as they could appreciate the reasons for seeking to conceal the facts.

Sheridan asked Mrs Clarke if her influence extended to church appointments. She said that it did not, but some people applied to her as if it did nonetheless. Attention was drawn to the bishopric sought by Dr O'Meara. The Duke arranged that he preached before the King at Weymouth, with the service being reported in the

---

[404] Ibid, p144
[405] Ibid, p158 It should be remembered that these were probably Southey's words.

newspapers. Although his sermon was appreciated, the promotion was not pursued. It was said that "the King did not like the great O in his name".[406] Mrs Clarke's evidence that she had not been involved was corroborated in one of the Duke's letters.

Finally, two allegations were made on Thursday 9th February, the fourth day of evidence. They were both treated extremely seriously, though the first must have been well-known, even standard, practice.

Firstly, the evidence of Jeremiah Donovan led to a separate committee being set up the following night to look at the purchase of places in the East India Company. This is dealt with below. It was said that, while Donovan might not actually traffic in places, he certainly sought to profit from negotiating them. In other words, he clearly was a trafficker in reality. The general point about the sale of government offices was made by Perceval: "In consequence of what had been disclosed ... the House must be convinced of the necessity of ... [legislation] ... to prevent the scandalous practice carried on in the sale of commissions and places under government. Some step ought speedily to be taken to stop the evil. ... the advertising of such places ought to be made a crime; ... the money advanced, or agreed to be given, should be forfeited; ... heavy penalties should be imposed; ... all persons concerned in such traffic should be rendered guilty of a misdemeanour."[407] As Cobbett pointed out, however, this could hardly have been a revelation - even to Perceval. People advertised for government positions in the papers all the time. Such people must believe it legitimate to buy and sell positions.[408]

The second allegation was made by Mrs Clarke to indicate that the Duke of York certainly condoned and, indeed, welcomed her corrupt behaviour. This was tantamount to saying he was corrupt himself, especially as he had suggested to her the means for augmenting her income: "... after they had been acquainted some time, he told her, that if she was clever, she would never ask him for money.

---

[406] Ibid, p149  In other words George III's prejudice against Catholics extended to those who might appear so.

[407] Ibid, p151  The subsequent Perceval Bill against the sale of offices was to be put forward in mid-April as one reason why Lord Folkestone's call for a general inquiry into corruption was not needed. See below.

[408] Political Register, op cit, Volume XV, no 5, p181

This hint she profited by, and the applications made to her to exert her influence were very numerous. ... He told her which were proper, and which not; and when they were improper, she was told to say that she could not interfere." She went on, "The Duke was aware of everything which she did in obtaining money by such means... He told her that she had more interest than the queen, and that she might use it."[409] Mrs Clarke said that she was often in debt while with the Duke of York and this was why she had first approached him about money after about six months at Gloucester Place. Although he paid an annual allowance of £1000, this had to cover everything and in any case he didn't always pay it each month as promised. In the last three months before he left he didn't pay it at all.

Perceval was quick to counter the suggestion of £1000 pa for Gloucester Place by saying the Duke had spent £16,761 on it between January 1804 and May 1806. Perceval "was also authorised to state" that the Duke had given Mrs Clarke additional sums of money as well. This was a spectacular own goal. As the MP Joseph Cripps[410] said at the time, this rather supported Mrs Clarke's statement rather than disproved it. He was amazed in any case that the Duke should be prepared to admit this expenditure in public. After all he was both a married man and a public debtor.[411]

It is difficult to disagree with the conclusion that "It was the fate of the Duke of York, during this inquiry, to suffer as much injury from the efforts made by his friends to save him, as from the direct attacks of his enemies".[412] For example, the letters sent to Mrs Clarke were kept in a cupboard by Nicholls, her landlord, who used them to light the fire. When she asked for the ones that were left to

---

[409] '*Edinburgh Annual Register* for 1809', op cit, volume 2, part 1, p148

[410] MP for Cirencester from 1806-1812 and again from 1818-1841. Although the Whigs listed him on the government side, he voted against them on the Scheldt inquiry in January 1810 and abstained in March. Despite supporting Mrs Clarke on this occasion, he spoke up twice for the Duke of York - the first time drawing attention to his conduct of army business (according to Thorne, op cit, volume III, p533).

[411] The latter was one of the key issues that infuriated Cobbett. His header for Volume XV, no 6 of the *Political Register* drew attention to the loan of £54,000 the Duke had received from public funds in 1800. This had only to be repaid at £1000 per quarter starting in January 1805, even though his pensions alone were £30,000 pa. As far as Cobbett was concerned, this was immoral; the corrupt and inappropriate use of these funds added to this.

[412] '*Edinburgh Annual Register* for 1809', op cit, volume 2, part 1, p163

be returned, Nicholls demanded the money she owed him. As this was not forthcoming, Nicholls decided that the letters themselves might be worth something and sent them to the House of Commons instead. They were referred to a select committee, with the relevant ones being considered by the Duke of York inquiry. They provided further evidence of corruption.

As well as illuminating various facets of early nineteenth century life and being inherently interesting, the hearings have been reported in detail because of the wider issues the inquiry raised. Even so, much of the ten days of evidence, and the people called to give it, have been omitted. It is available elsewhere - in the *Annual Register* for 1809 (pp117-148) as well as in the *Edinburgh Annual Register* and the *Political Register* that have been cited as sources here.

On 23rd February, the day after the inquiry finished hearing evidence, the Duke of York wrote to the Speaker asserting his innocence and demanding his right to a trial if the evidence warranted it. According to Thorne, ministers were involved in "concocting" this letter.[413] It was copied to every MP. If the intention was to get the House on the Duke's side, it misfired. On the following day, Whitbread described it as "a gross violation of the privileges of the House". Perceval disagreed, claiming that the Duke was not calling into question the House's right to examine the evidence, but only requesting the same right to a trial as anybody else.[414]

The debate on the outcomes of the inquiry got under way on the 8th March. It opened with Wardle reviewing the evidence, concluding that the abuses could not have gone on for so long without the Duke's knowledge, and moving that the House should propose to the King that the Duke of York "ought to be deprived of command of the army".[415] There were some exceptional speeches, and a variety

---

[413] Thorne, op cit, volume V, p486

[414] '*Edinburgh Annual Register* for 1809', op cit, volume 2, part 1, p172. It was also on the 24th February 1809 that the Drury Lane Theatre was destroyed by fire (see the Introduction above). Sheridan was in the House of Commons at the time, about to reply to Canning on the Peninsular War. He was offered an adjournment, but preferred to carry on as the war in Spain was a national calamity rather than a personal one.

[415] Ibid, p174

of motions, including that of Perceval who "countered [Wardle] with a brilliant speech in favour of resolutions and an address acquitting the Duke of corruption but regretting his association with Mrs Clarke".[416]

Francis Burton had been a judge until his eyesight failed, becoming an MP from 1780 until his retirement in 1812. He was the MP for Oxford in 1809. Thorne says he was known as "the blind senator", though the *Edinburgh Annual Register* describes him as "the blind judge". In summarising the issues, he specifically ruled out the Duke's adultery, and church preferment, as being irrelevant to the charge before the House. On this basis, he concluded that there was "no ground for any of the charges" against the Duke. His speech was therefore very favourable to the government's case and that made by Perceval. But others reacted differently. Some of the Whigs, such as William Fremantle MP at this stage for Tain Burghs, thought it biased, omitting any evidence that did not suit his case. For an ex-judge, he considered the speech misleading and improper.[417] The reaction of people outside the House was more extreme. They were convinced that the charges against the Duke were well-founded and that the blind judge was "a stage trick" set up by the government on purpose to acquit him.[418]

Bragge Bathurst (1754-1831), MP for Bristol, said he was unable to agree with either Colonel Wardle's "total condemnation" of the Duke or Perceval's "complete acquittal". He considered that the "Duke of York [had] exposed himself to [the] *undue influence*" of Mrs Clarke. The Duke should have repelled her approaches over army promotions.[419] In his view Perceval's proposal of an address to the King was inappropriate. Rather the House should acquit the Duke, while pronouncing on his conduct in such terms that his resignation became inevitable. This would not require his father the King to dismiss him, an unreasonable expectation and therefore not one to be relied on.

This became the third motion after that of Wardle and Perceval, and several others were to follow as the debate continued over several days to the early hours of Saturday 18th March. At this point the

---

[416] Thorne, op cit, volume V, p487
[417] Thorne, op cit, volume III, pp341-3
[418] '*Edinburgh Annual Register* for 1809', op cit, volume 2, part 1, pp174-6
[419] Ibid, p182

House began to vote. The government had a majority of almost 200 (334 to 135) to reject Thomas Turton's amendment that the Duke knew of the corrupt practices. This was then reduced to 82 as Perceval's motion acquitting him of corruption was passed by 278 votes to 196. Bathurst's motion had still to be voted on.

The government's majority had been reduced substantially, with almost 200 MPs against the Duke's complete acquittal. The House of Commons had been unable to establish that the Duke of York as commander in chief of the army knew of the sale of commissions, but it was clear that his mistress Mrs Clarke had taken money and in any case knew too much of the army's business. The Duke resigned later that morning.[420] Thorne says that "Wardle basked for weeks in the glow of popular acclaim. Votes of thanks came in from nationwide meetings ..."[421]; Cobbett's *Political Register* identifying 50 such meetings that applauded Wardle's patriotism and motives in conducting the inquiry.[422]

The major issues raised by the inquiry were summarised by Cobbett in the *Political Register*. He was particularly scathing in number 7 on the 18th February 1809, adding to the concerns he had already expressed about the Duke's immoral use of public funds. In his view, this corrupt use of public money was bad enough, but it was accompanied by "robbery" that put lives at risk and increased the number of paupers. Soldiers had to serve under corrupt officers such as Donovan, Sandon and French; the public had to pay for more officers than were active; army morale was effected since it was believed that posts could be bought regardless of merit or length of service; this was taking place at a time of severe military setbacks and national risk; taxes had to be increased to pay for more unproductive people; ordinary people had increasing difficulty in paying higher taxes and they or their families might starve as a result. In Cobbett's view this was "a deep-rooted system of corruption"[423] with the taxed people paying for the upkeep of the royal family, and a mistress such as Mrs Clarke: "Every penny paid

---

[420] The Duke was not re-instated as commander in chief until the Prince Regent proposed this step in May 1811. A decent interval had now gone by and the House voted to this effect on 11th June 1811.
[421] Thorne, op cit, volume V, p487
[422] *Political Register*, op cit, Volume XV, January to June 1809
[423] *Political Register*, op cit, Volume XV, no 7, p231

to Mrs Clarke is just so much taken out of the pockets of the people."[424]

It may have been a rant, but for Cobbett it was heartfelt and based on values that were well-placed. It was a view shared by many ordinary people as well as by the radicals. Not only had they been misled, they felt betrayed. Thorne says that the Duke's acquittal "injected new life into the flagging parliamentary reform movement", and that the "scandal stimulated a cry for economical reform ..."[425] Cobbett's accusation of robbery had struck a chord.

## Corruption and the East India Company Inquiry

One of the by-products of the Duke of York inquiry was the accusation that "there was a regular, systematic, and almost avowed traffic in East India appointments", particularly in the most junior posts of writers (clerks) and cadetships.[426] Following Donovan's evidence to the main inquiry on 9th February (see above), a select committee was immediately established to examine this issue. It concluded that posts at this level were routinely trafficked and that "fraudulent agents have availed themselves of [the] belief [that the practice was widespread and accepted] to the injury of the credulous and unwary ..."[427] The report claimed that no evidence could be found to link "these corrupt or improper bargains to any Director ... or ... [the] court"[428]. Nevertheless, part of the Directors' remit was to prevent such abuses. They had singularly failed.

Cobbett wrote in the *Political Register* that such offices had been on open sale for a long time; he had seen adverts himself for eight years. "... now, all of a sudden, this horror for jobbing [has] seized them."[429]

---

[424] Ibid, p229
[425] Thorne, op cit, volume V, p487
[426] 'The *Annual Register* or a View of the History, Politics and Literature for the Year 1809', London, Otridge et al., 1811, p149
[427] Ibid, p151
[428] Ibid, p150. A summary of the committee's report is included on pp477-487 of the *Annual Register*.
[429] *Political Register*, op cit, Volume XV, no 7, p233

The select committee decided that they could only remove the "inducement to [this traffic in places] ... by making the hazard greater than the temptation".[430] In their view the only way to achieve this was to recall from India and dismiss all those in purchased posts, even if the people were innocent of corruption themselves or, in some cases, were ignorant of how their posts had been obtained. Unpopular though this action was, it was pursued to discourage any further such abuses.

The committee also stumbled across a high-profile target in Castlereagh, who had been President of the Board of Control at the East India Company from July 1802 until 1805.[431] In this capacity he had been given a writership to dispose of as appropriate. In 1805 Castlereagh had been approached by Reding "a regular dealer in contraband promotions" and "an advertising place-broker"[432] who was prepared to find him a seat in parliament in exchange for the writership. Reding would sell the writership on and pocket the proceeds. As Castlereagh did not require a seat himself, he sent Reding's letter on to his friend Lord Clancarty, who was looking for a constituency. Castlereagh offered Clancarty the writership in exchange for the place in parliament. Although the transaction never materialised for other reasons, Castlereagh's intentions were clear. On 25th April 1809 Lord Hamilton accused him of corruption on two counts, both as President of the Board of Control and as a Member of Parliament and a Privy Councillor. As well as "violating his duty and abusing his influence and authority as President", he was charged with "an attack upon the purity and constitution" of the House of Commons.[433]

Castlereagh's defence was that he had no motive for corruption and in any case this would be senseless when the matter was bound to become public. He had insisted that the writership go to someone appropriately qualified and in his view Clancarty would be a useful addition to the House and to the public's benefit. He had been motivated by friendship not gain, and the exchange never happened

---

[430] 'Edinburgh Annual Register for 1809', op cit, volume 2, part 1, p342
[431] According to the Annual Register for 1809, whereas the Encyclopaedia Britannica says January 1806 when Castlereagh left office on Pitt's death to make way for the Ministry of All the Talents.
[432] Annual Register for 1809, op cit, p152
[433] Ibid, p152

in any case.  Castlereagh then withdrew, saying "... it was an intention and not an act ..."[434]

The House's reactions were mixed.  Some had been impressed with Castlereagh's humility, expressing their concern that the "punishment proposed was greater than the offence deserved".[435] However, his attempt to differentiate the intention from the act had clearly not convinced many.  Wynn said that "Duty chalked out the line, and, however reluctantly, we must follow it".[436]  Ponsonby, the leader of the Whigs, said that Castlereagh was "guilty of a violation of the East India acts to a peculiar degree, by doing that in which it was the object of that act to prevent, in applying India patronage for purposes of parliamentary influence".[437]

In the light of views such as this, it would not have been possible for the House just to pass on to the orders of the day as if consideration of the accusation against Castlereagh had proved sufficient in itself.  A vote was needed to demonstrate the integrity of the House.  Canning then spoke in Castlereagh's favour, re-iterating that the debate had illustrated the importance of maintaining a "guard over the purity and independence of Parliament", but that the evidence did not necessitate "a criminating resolution" against Castlereagh.[438]  This sustained the principle but exonerated Castlereagh himself.  Hamilton's motion of censure was defeated by 216 votes to 167, while Canning's motion was carried by 214 to 167.  A majority of 47 was not very impressive, and Portland's government was further weakened in the process.  Canning continued to lobby Portland to move Castlereagh (with the consequences discussed above).

On 1st May, six days later, the pressure for parliamentary reform resulted in a meeting at the Crown and Anchor (see Chapter 6 below).

---

[434] Thorne, op cit, volume V, p284
[435] *Annual Register* for 1809, op cit, p153
[436] '*Edinburgh Annual Register* for 1809', op cit, volume 2, part 1, p239
[437] *Annual Register* for 1809, op cit, p154
[438] '*Edinburgh Annual Register* for 1809', op cit, volume 2, part 1, p240

# The King and the future Prince Regent: Their Continuing Clash

While the royal family generally presented a united front to the outside world, as in any large family there were tensions nevertheless. The Queen and the princesses seem to have been exempt from these on the whole, but there were jealousies and rivalries between some of the male siblings. For example, in 1810 Mrs Clarke of Duke of York notoriety published 'The Rival Princes'. This portrayed the affair "as a conspiracy organised by the Duke of Kent"[439] who sought the commander-in-chief post himself instead of his brother. Although this was never demonstrated conclusively, the Duke of Kent (Prince Edward, 1767-1820) was probably not entirely innocent either (at least in Thorne's view).

Mrs Clarke also conceded in the book that her allegations against the Duke of York were made entirely because of promises by Wardle that she would be rewarded financially. Surprisingly, this seems not to have led to charges of perjury against her. It is probable that this was because her prosecution of Wardle in December 1809 had effectively done the government's job of discrediting him. She alleged that Wardle expected the Duke of Kent to make him Secretary for War once he had become commander-in-chief in place of his brother. She accused Wardle of failing to pay her all that he had promised. The trial had undermined him, demonstrating his scheming nature, and the verdict against him called into question any remaining integrity he might otherwise have retained. Although Wardle did not disappear overnight, he was in severe financial difficulty in any case, ceased to be an MP in 1812 and fled abroad in about 1815.

The main royal dispute, however, continued to be between the King and his eldest son. The Prince of Wales had established his own power base and alliances in London and Brighton. He was a close supporter of the Whigs, whereas his father's views more readily aligned with the Tories on most issues. This was only one example of their contrasting interests, tastes and opinions. To some extent this might be expected of a son demonstrating the differences between the generations and expressing his own individuality. But it was not always easily managed, and could lead to discord and dissension if the Prince of Wales' views appeared to be prevailing

---

[439] Thorne, op cit, volume V, p489

over those of the King. While the King had the ultimate power and sanction, he had to be careful how he exercised these if they were not to be called into disrepute. In particular, George III and the Prince of Wales continued to clash over the latter's mistresses and his treatment of Princess Caroline. George III had prevented her exclusion from court, much to his son's irritation. Spencer Perceval had been involved in the earlier inquiry into her conduct (the "Delicate Investigation" referred to in Chapter 2 above), and had been her adviser at one stage. He was said not to be removed as Prime Minister during the regency because he effectively knew too much about the future George IV's behaviour. However, Ingrams says that Perceval's biographer Denis Gray dismissed the theory that Perceval was in effect blackmailing the Prince Regent as "absurd"[440].

## The Jubilee: A Nation Re-formed?

On 4th June 1809 George III celebrated his 71st birthday. As this was a Sunday, the "national festival" took place the following day.[441] Bell-ringing in the early morning was accompanied by flags flown from public buildings and churches, and there were two royal salutes in St James' Park and on Tower Wharf. The Archbishop of Canterbury gave the "oration of congratulations at the return of the day" and the birthday ode was performed in the grand council chamber at St James' Palace.[442] There were spectacular illuminations in the evening. The *Edinburgh Annual Register* highlighted the celebrations in Edinburgh as well as those in London, but said that "In every part of the united kingdom, the inhabitants testified their joy upon this occasion by suitable demonstrations of loyalty and affection to our beloved king."[443]

There was to be a second opportunity later in the year for national celebration with the start of George III's fiftieth year as monarch on 25th October. But the country had no experience of a royal jubilee, with George III's reign of 50 years being the first since Edward III over four hundred years earlier (1327-1377), and Henry III a hundred years before that. It was also the first that covered Great

---

[440] Ingrams, op cit, p121
[441] '*Edinburgh Annual Register* for 1809', op cit, volume 2, part 1, p155
[442] Ibid, p156
[443] Ibid, p158

Britain as a whole rather than just England.[444]  Colley has argued that the jubilee was a specific "patriotic initiative … [and] a remedy" generated by a Mrs Biggs to "include both festivity and beneficence".[445]  Be this as it may, the idea proved very popular and was taken up more widely.  The country was in internal turmoil as well as under external threat from the war with Napoleon.  The jubilee offered a chance for public celebration and a demonstration of unity in the country and in the royal family in the face of these adversities.  This was precisely the release that was called for.

The country responded very favourably to this opportunity and participated as fully as possible despite, or perhaps because of, the difficulties they continued to face.  Prochaska says that George III was very popular among the general public, with the jubilee being seen as an "expression of political reconciliation and social harmony"[446].  In his memoirs in 1840 Samuel Romilly says that the King was by 1809 "one of the most popular [of princes]; and yet in nothing is the character or spirit of his government altered."  Colley cites this, going on to say that "After huge unpopularity when [losing the] American empire, Romilly attributes his growth in popularity to [his] standing with the people and against [the] Fox-North coalition in 1783, attempt on his life, behaviour of Prince of Wales, madness and particularly 'the horrors of the French Revolution'".[447]

The jubilee celebrations are described in the *Annual Register*[448], but only briefly, with the introduction to this Whig publication focussing on Britain's isolation in the face of Napoleon's ambitions, with Austria no longer providing a counter-weight in mainland Europe after its defeat at Wagram.  Cobbett goes even further in the *Political Register*[449].  He wrote that as a country "We appear to have lost all shame … [firing] cannonades of joy" instead of directing them against Napoleon's advance.  He saw this as an inappropriate time to hold a national jubilee; people had been forced to participate or be charged with disloyalty; it was "bread and circuses" to amuse

---

[444] Subsequently, Victoria (1837-1901) was to reign Great Britain for longer than George III.  Elizabeth II has also exceeded 50 years as queen since 1952, but of the United Kingdom (i.e., excluding Ireland).

[445] Colley, op cit, pp217-220

[446] Prochaska, 2000, op cit, p35

[447] Colley, op cit, p208

[448] *Annual Register* for 1809, op cit, pp395-399 for events at Windsor, the fete at Frogmore and in London, and pp703-707 for celebrations in Bombay.

[449] *Political Register*, op cit, Volume XVI, no 17, pp635-639

people and distract them from "their real situation". Even the relief provided to the poor he described as hypocrisy when it took place on this day only. He asked whether the jubilee made up "for a life of starvation" over the previous 49 years.

Cobbett's points are no less relevant for being politically motivated. The *Edinburgh Annual Register* as a Tory publication describes the celebrations much more fully, as it does the pardons bestowed by the King on deserters, debtors and foreign prisoners other than the French.[450] It claims that "Without any order or suggestion from authority, preparations were made to celebrate the day in a manner worthy of the cause." Regardless of whether the celebrations were in any way forced or cynical, it is clear that they did provide the opportunity the country required after the earlier traumas. If only for a day, current circumstances were forgotten and unity was more apparent than division. The nation was re-formed as a united kingdom, but only superficially and on the surface. The underlying fissures of economic and political reform had yet to be properly addressed.

A year later, on his fiftieth anniversary as King, George III made his last public appearance.

---

[450] '*Edinburgh Annual Register* for 1809', op cit, volume 2, part 2, pp276-283 and p287 for the address at Heligoland and the celebration by troops still on Walcheren.

## 6.    POLITICS AND THE PRESSURES FOR REFORM

*"Many join in the cry of Reform from ignorance, many from folly, many from fanaticism.  Some are incited by the vilest passions, and some from more pure, but not less dangerous principles. Numerous are the knaves and numerous the dupes desirous of change."*
William Windham, House of Commons debate, 26th May 1809

*"Wolves will not allow certain animals to herd with them; and yet they [MPs] could sit there and associate with Ministers and others who had practised corruption, and had even the effrontery to acknowledge it!"*
Francis Burdett, House of Commons debate, 26th May 1809

These quotations demonstrate the very strong views held by opponents and proponents of political reform.  While they represented two extremes in the debate, Windham and Burdett were not alone in expressing opinions that were deeply entrenched and of long standing.  Even allowing for the effects of parliamentary "performance", the emotive language used left no doubts about the strength of feeling, though it risked generating more heat than light.

It might appear from the above that Windham was a staunch Tory defender of the status quo, but he was in fact a Whig who had served as secretary at war under Pitt and was secretary for war and the colonies in the Ministry of All the Talents.  He had resigned along with Pitt in 1801 over the failure to push through Catholic emancipation in the face of the King's opposition.  Yet he had long been an opponent of parliamentary reform.  To his mind "no one would begin repairing a house during the hurricane season"[451], as he said in a speech as early as 4 March 1790.  His initial support for the French Revolution changed to horror at the increasing bloodshed, and by December 1792 he had become the leader of the alarmists.  In parting company with Fox and adopting the views of Burke, Windham "argued that there was real danger of revolution at home and also that Britain would be right to interfere in French

---

[451] See Windham's Oxford DNB entry.  This argument was adopted by others in 1809, while to some minds the best time at which to reform was at moments of greatest risk such as this.

affairs in order to protect European stability".[452]   In the May 1809 debate on the Curwen Bill Windham expressed the view that corruption arises from people selling their votes rather than from the people prepared to buy them.   This might appear tortured, not to say back-to-front, logic to some, but Cobbett took the proposition at face value, as he often did in order to tackle an issue at source on his opponent's ground.   He said that this was in any case another argument for political reform, as it would remove the market for votes.   If people couldn't sell them, nobody would be able to buy them.[453]

Sir Francis Burdett[454] was the most prominent radical member in the House of Commons and had been seeking both parliamentary and economic reform for some time.   As early as May 1797 he had chaired a meeting at the Crown and Anchor tavern[455] calling for

---

[452] Ibid   In this respect his views were similar to Burdett's, who had refused to be presented to Napoleon for patriotic reasons - see Chapter 4 above.

[453] And vice versa. *Political Register*, op cit, volume XV, no 22, p836

[454] He was MP for Boroughbridge from 1796 to 1802 and then for Middlesex from 1802 to July 1804.  The 1802 election was declared void at this point and he lost the re-run.  He regained the seat in March 1805 only to lose it again in February 1806.  He became MP for Westminster in the 'No popery' election of 1807 and was to hold the seat until 1837.  He was then MP for Wiltshire North from 1837 until his death in January 1844.  As Thorne, op cit, Volume III, pp313-314 says "Burdett's career is of central importance in the history of radicalism in the early 19th century and the movement which he inspired ... was one of considerable strength and scale."

[455] The Crown and Anchor tavern stood in Arundel Street, Strand and, as one of the principal venues in central London, has several historical connections.  See 'The Strand (southern tributaries)', Old and New London: Volume 3 (1878), pp. 63-84 at http://www.british-history.ac.uk/report.aspx?compid=45134  This says "At the upper end of [Arundel] street, on the site of the Temple Club, formerly stood the noted 'Crown and Anchor' Tavern - so named, no doubt, from the anchor of St. Clement ... - the head-quarters of the Westminster Reformers in the days of Fox and 'Old Glory', Sir Francis Burdett.  Here, too, were held many of the meetings of the Catholic Association before the passing of the Roman Catholic Relief Act in 1829. The tavern stood as nearly as possible on the site of the buildings in which the Academy of Ancient Music was first instituted in the reign of Queen Anne.  The premises extended a considerable way down the street, and at the back of them was a large and spacious room, upwards of eighty feet long, which was used as a banqueting apartment.  Upon the occasion of Fox's birthday, in 1798, a great banquet was given here, at which 2,000 Reformers sat down to drink the toast of 'The People the Source of Power'.
"Here the portly form of Dr. Johnson, in company with his friend Boswell, might often be seen; and during the Westminster elections in the last century [i.e., primarily the 18th] it became one of the principal houses where the candidates of both sides were wont to address the constituents.  It was at the 'Crown and

---

parliamentary reform, going on to support Grey's reform motion in parliament later that month just as Pitt sought to negotiate peace with France.

Hard on the heels of the Duke of York affair, Burdett uncovered another scandal in which the Duke's military secretary Colonel Gordon was involved.[456] The government had acquired 4.25 acres of land along the Thames that had previously belonged to the Chelsea Hospital. The government had paid £5000 for this plot, but had then assigned 4 acres (i.e., nearly all of it) to Colonel Gordon at £52pa. After Burdett had carried out a site inspection, he concluded in Parliament that the building Colonel Gordon planned for the site would have interfered with the existing infirmary, reducing the light and air for the sick soldiers, as well as restricting access to the river and outside space for those recuperating, and precluded the future expansion of the infirmary. Huskisson then undertook a site inspection on behalf of the Treasury and came to the same conclusions as Burdett. The House of Commons was incensed. They were even more furious when it emerged that the land had only recently been given back to the Hospital specifically so that the infirmary could be expanded. Despite this, the government had then passed the land on to Colonel Gordon for another building.

Burdett described this transaction as the epitome of government corruption. In his view it was "the job", and "the jobometer" against which other abuses should be measured. The transaction was "exceedingly improper, and not less imprudent" given Colonel Gordon's role in the Duke of York inquiry.[457] It was also somewhat amazing given the parlous state of the war with Napoleon. Colonel Gordon was forced to give up the land and it reverted to the Chelsea Hospital. The government escaped wider sanction, but the affair contributed to a growing sense of corruption and rot.

Public opinion had turned against the House of Commons when the Duke of York had been acquitted despite the evidence against him.

---

Anchor' that Daniel O'Connell first assailed that 'venerable champion of civil and religious liberty', Henry Brougham; and it was here, too, that Cobbett fell foul of Sir Francis Burdett, who, we are told, at once angrily responded by stating that Cobbett owed him a thousand pounds. Cobbett acknowledged receiving the money, but stated that it was a gift, and consequently not a debt."
[456] '*Edinburgh Annual Register* for 1809', op cit, volume 2, part 1, pp231-234
[457] Ibid

The public saw this as the establishment closing ranks, protecting their own. While the Duke's resignation had become inevitable, and Wardle was applauded for the stand he had taken against corruption, the argument for reform had been strengthened. It was now about economic as well as political reform. The case Cobbett had made in the *Political Register* against "robbery" was endorsed by the *Edinburgh Annual Register* when it said that "Government was a combination of the rich to raise money from the people, and divide it among themselves and their dependants".[458] The Chelsea Hospital affair added to this view. According to the *Edinburgh Annual Register*, "This was a new triumph for the radical reformers: the discovery of any abuse strengthened their arguments, and increased the popularity which Colonel Wardle had acquired for the party".[459] Or, to paraphrase Burdett, "jobbery" had been added to "robbery". Either the government had lost sight of its objectives and principles, or it was prepared to peddle these to the highest bidder, overlooking them if it got a better offer. At the very least it appeared out of control.

Concepts such as transparency, governance and accountability are very modern. But even today they depend on a press able to report freely and fully. These were alien concepts in 1809, with the press only recently being allowed to report parliamentary proceedings after long battles by Wilkes and others in the 1770s. Even then the House of Commons could readily exclude "strangers" if they did not wish a debate to be reported (indeed they were about to exercise this power early in 1810 in relation to the Walcheren inquiry to which the government had been forced eventually to agree). In these circumstances, the quality of government depended on the principles of individuals and whether the leadership could ensure these were adhered to. But even in 1809 the public was becoming better informed and the influence of Cobbett and others (such as Cartwright and Clifford) outside the House mirrored the call for reform from within it. The government was slow to accept the implications and frequently sought to resist them.

---

[458] '*Edinburgh Annual Register* for 1809', op cit, volume 2, part 1, p229
[459] Ibid, p234

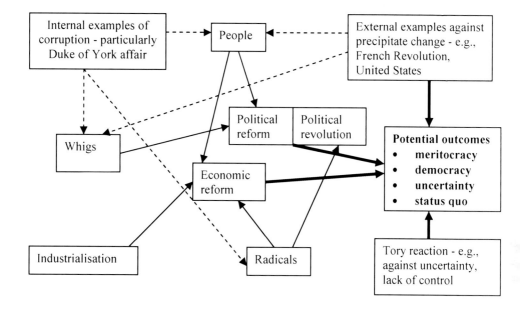

**Figure 9: Essentials of reform in 1809**

Figure 9 attempts to summarise the overall position. Some of the pressures were recent, but others were well-known and had been around for some time. For example, in contrast to Windham's long-standing opposition, Cobbett quotes William Pitt advising the House of Commons in 1782 that "The defect of representation is the national disease ... No honest man can, according to the present system, continue Minister."[460]

Figure 9 necessarily relies on generalities, but another way of putting this is to say that it is about the *essentials*. It does not attempt to capture all the nuances. Some Whigs sought economic reform, some industrialists will have thought that political reform was a requirement, if not a pre-condition, for economic reform, and some people certainly wanted to bring about a political revolution (perhaps the weavers among them, as Chapter 4 above suggests). Ireland remained a significant issue, but one where the outcome was not necessarily clear. Catholic emancipation was an

---

[460] This features in the header to the *Political Register* on 24th June 1809, but Cobbett had also cited it in the 3rd June issue. See *Political Register*, op cit, volume XV, no 25 and volume XV, no 22, p833. However, in Chapter 3 above the question is raised of whether Pitt's commitment was more apparent than real.

opportunity for some, but for others the relief of poverty entailed land reform that threatened entrenched protestant positions.[461] As such, they considered it too great a risk. What Figure 9 emphatically does not mean, of course, is that radicals such as Burdett and Cobbett sought political revolution for its own sake[462]; only that their calls for reform went further and deeper than those of their more timid colleagues. They were seen as revolutionary by their opponents and by those who were prepared to settle for more moderate change. Whigs in general may have wanted political reform, but for some this just meant a change of government, while for others such as Windham any reform was anathema.

The pressures for and against political and economic change in Figure 9 came together in 1809 in a series of House of Commons motions and debates. The corruption inquiries in the previous Chapter were a key part of the imperative for change, but not the whole story. The House of Commons mounted other extensive examinations in 1809 that were overtly political and brought wider reforms in their wake. These are set out in Table 8.

## Table 8: Chronology of reform in 1809

| 1809 month | Date | Details |
|---|---|---|
| April | 17th | Lord Folkestone calls for general inquiry into corruption. His motion receives 30 votes in support. |
| | 20th | Second reading of Perceval's Bill for prevention of sale of offices |
| | 25th | Debate on East India Company inquiry and Castlereagh accused of corruption (See above) |
| May | 1st | Meeting at Crown and Anchor tavern off the Strand |
| | 4th | Curwen Bill introduced |
| | 5th | Madocks charge of corruption against both Perceval and Castlereagh. Madocks asked to re-frame the charge to |

---

[461] At this stage only Protestants could hold land in Ireland. For Catholics to own land they had either to conceal their religion or to renounce it and convert.
[462] This might not have bothered them though, despite their preference for legal and constitutional solutions. Rather it would have been a badge of honour, identifying them as concerned with principles rather than perceptions. According to the 'Edinburgh Annual Register for 1809', op cit, volume 2, part 1, p234, Burdett thought 'Jacobin' had become too stale a term, but said that he "... would wear any name that goes along with the reformation of abuses".

| 1809 month | Date | Details |
|---|---|---|
|  |  | conform to House of Commons regulations/conventions. |
|  | 11<sup>th</sup> | Madocks' regularisation of this charge and reasoning against borough-mongering. 310 votes against the motion proposing an inquiry and 85 for, a majority of 225. But only 395 MPs voted. |
|  | 26<sup>th</sup> | Debate on Curwen Bill (see Windham and Burdett quotes above). |
| June | 1<sup>st</sup> | Speaker's views on Curwen Bill in committee of the whole House: "To do nothing is to do everything." In other words, to take no action would be to allow seats to carry on being sold, and in effect to approve this. |
|  | 1<sup>st</sup> | Perceval amendments to Curwen Bill in committee; his views against the oath shared by Burdett (and by Cobbett in *Political Register* 13<sup>th</sup> May) |
|  | 8<sup>th</sup> | Henry Martin[463] (and Whitbread) motion against placemen and pensioners. |
|  | 12<sup>th</sup> | Revised Curwen Bill passed. 97 votes for; 85 against. Folkestone proposes revised title to demonstrate Perceval emasculation on behalf of the Treasury. Folkestone and 28 others voted for the proposed revision. |
|  | 15<sup>th</sup> | Burdett's address on parliamentary reform. 15 votes in favour |
|  | 19<sup>th</sup> | Colonel Wardle repeats savings pledge |

## Positions on Reform

The events listed in Table 8 are addressed in detail below. But it may be helpful first to take stock of some of the prevailing positions on reform (other than, or rather between, those of Windham and Burdett).[464] These cover both general issues, as well as the resistance of specific Tories such as Perceval and Canning.

### General issues

It is worth remembering that political parties were not yet rigidly demarcated; differences not always delineated let alone enforced. Allegiance was more obvious during elections, but otherwise a spectrum of opinion was apparent. For example, after the 'no

---

[463] MP for Kinsale April 1806-1818. See Thorne, op cit, volume IV, pp556-557

[464] Some of these are referred to in the matrix in the Introduction above.

popery' election both the Treasury and the opposition found it of assistance to try and calculate the supporters each might usually anticipate. Some earlier governments, such as those of Pitt and Grenville, had set out to blur, if not transcend, the distinction of party affiliation. For most MPs "Membership of Parliament was commonly regarded, not as a means of promoting party objectives, but as one of the duties of rank; and the higher the rank, the more pressing the duty."[465] While those such as Chute might see themselves as amateurs rather than professional politicians, they did not take their responsibility any less lightly, but this did mean that Parliament had to find its place alongside their other interests. For instance, attendance should not interfere with their summer pursuits. As John Cannon points out, Parliament was in recess from June 1809 to January 1810.[466] This no doubt suited a government under pressure as well as these MPs.

"Land and a country seat ... did not merely mean a secure if small economic return. It also signified power and status."[467] This was both a consequence of the property franchise, and a justification for withholding the vote from those with insufficient or no property. As Stone and Stone say "The forty-shilling freeholder franchise in the countryside was defended on the grounds that a stake in the land was a necessary qualification for political rights." For those with wealth, there was a danger that "... reform ... would substitute merit for influence and thus might erode one basis of their family fortunes ..."[468] According to Colley, "Peers and MPs regularly disagreed over the executive's influence in the House of Commons, or over the frequency of general elections, or over the conduct of an individual minister. But these conflicts stemmed from real or assumed anxiety that the beauty of the system was being adulterated, not from doubt about the validity of the system as a whole."[469] For some the key issue was the pace of change. It had

---

[465] Harvey, op cit, p17

[466] John Cannon, 'Parliamentary Reform 1640-1832', Cambridge, Cambridge University Press, 1972, p164. This was the case in 1810-1811 as well, but in most years from 1804 to 1820 the recess lasted from July to January. See Thorne, op cit, volume I, p388.

[467] Stone and Stone, op cit, p13

[468] Ibid, p422

[469] Colley, op cit, p50   In this respect it is interesting to note that electoral reform has gone through several stages from 1809 to our own time. These have included the property franchise, gender, age as well as constituency boundaries and devolution. In one view these changes were incremental; in another they were

to be at a speed which they could accept and to which they could adjust. The difficulty was that such an argument could equally lend itself to excessive caution and holding back as to pressing forward. This was not straightforward as the Marquess of Ely found when he wrote to Perceval on 7th January 1810:

"I have this day for the first time learned ... that [there] is to be a total neglect of parliamentary influence in his ecclesiastical arrangements ... I have at an expense of many thousand pounds returned two members to support you in Parliament ... and I cannot help saying it would have been but fair to have informed me at first that the only object I had in view was not to be obtained ..."

Perceval's reply on 11th January makes it clear that he would not interfere on behalf of the Marquess' brother, the Bishop of Killaloe, who was seeking to move to another bishopric:

"... With respect to the determination of Government not to advance to the bench, either of the law or of the church, any persons on the mere ground of parliamentary interest, I do not now perfectly recollect at what period I first heard of it ... [but] nothing could be more acceptable than such a determination ..."

As Aspinall and Smith observe, "in 1809 it was no longer possible to purchase a bishopric, even in Ireland, with parliamentary votes".[470]

**Tory resistance**

There were similarities as well as differences in the views of senior Tories such as Perceval and Canning. Both were comfortable with, and were used to, the established order – perhaps because they had grown up with it and it had lasted for some time. But the expectation that the conservative party would automatically seek to "preserve" only went so far. Rather "They were not prepared to see [the existing system] replaced by something that might produce unforeseen consequences."[471]

---

piecemeal. It was only from the general election of 1950 that the Representation of the People Act 1948 removed separate representation for Cambridge and Oxford Universities, among others, as well as plural voting and the business vote.

[470] Aspinall and Smith, op cit, p649

[471] On p11 of my article 'Spencer Perceval: Private values and public virtues', The Historian, Number 98, Summer 2008, pp6-12. Or, for Edmund Burke "... it can

For Canning there were two additional objections. Firstly, he was concerned that a uniform system of electing MPs would reduce the breadth of the views represented in Parliament: "... he stuck doggedly to Burke's view of ... a 'deliberative' assembly, the members of which represented the interests of the whole nation and not just of their own constituents (if they had any)."[472] Secondly, "... he feared that if one part [of the current electoral system] were tampered with the whole would be deranged and ultimately destroyed. This was the basis of his stubborn opposition to even the most moderate and tentative proposals for parliamentary reform."[473] The latter is a specific version of Colley's general argument above. It is usually the accusation levelled at Perceval, though it is then put in noticeably cruder terms as if this was all that was required to discredit his views. The *Times Literary Supplement* review in 1964[474] refers to him as "a Victorian born out of time". This is assumed to refer to the influence of the Anglican Evangelicals who "...offered what has been called a 'new moral economy' of sobriety, self-control, sexual restraint and respectability; a challenge both to the hedonism of the aristocracy and to the levelling and violence of the Revolution, it inaugurated that 'Victorianism' which appeared decades before the accession of Queen Victoria herself."[475]

There can be little doubt that Perceval held a number of repugnant views, not least against the Catholic church and emancipation. He is described as "a complete reactionary" who resisted all reforms. He was also perhaps too open and forthright for his own good as far as posterity is concerned, though this was one of the aspects that his contemporaries most valued. He also had a duty to perform and a role to play as Chancellor and later as Prime Minister that, with his legal background, conditioned some of his views. But these covered various shades nevertheless and he clearly was influenced by evidence.

---

seldom be right ... to sacrifice a present benefit for a doubtful advantage in the future ... the state of affairs which we seek to promote should be ... sufficiently better to make up for the evils of transition." John Maynard Keynes, 'The Political Doctrines of Edmund Burke', 1904

[472] Hinde, op cit, p283
[473] Ibid, p284
[474] See Chapter 2 above
[475] Obelkevich, op cit, p326

**Towards Reform**

Alongside these personal and political perspectives on reform, there was a philosophical underpinning as well. This came together with the wider intellectual and activist arguments, and the recent examples of corruption, to further generate, and reinforce, the impetus for reform in 1809. It would be later that summer before Jeremy Bentham was in a position to circulate a text of his 'Parliamentary Reform Catechism' (and even then he would have to do so privately before it was eventually published in 1817), but his views were already becoming clear. These proposed that the good of all is bound up with parliamentary reform in line with the central tenet of utilitarianism (i.e., the greatest happiness of the greatest number). Some of Bentham's proposals echoed those put forward previously by John Wilkes and William Cobbett (e.g., reports of parliamentary speeches). Others, such as household franchise and equal electoral districts, were under consideration again at the time of the 1832 Reform Act, as was Burdett's preference for fixed three year parliaments. Bentham also wanted to see compulsory attendance at parliament by MPs in order to deliver more enhanced representation and improved democracy.

As the examples of corruption increased, Lord Folkestone sought a general inquiry on 17th April 1809. Perceval argued against this, saying that not only had he just introduced an omnibus bill against the sale of offices, but an inquiry at this time would add inappropriately to the "public ferment". Samuel Whitbread and others on the Whig benches disagreed, saying this was more likely to be the outcome of "stifling" such an inquiry.[476] Canning supported Perceval against a general inquiry, arguing that "It held out no hope of immediate advantage to the people, but it held out the whole cast and class of public men to suspicion."[477] Only thirty MPs voted for Folkestone's motion.

Three days later Perceval's bill received its second reading. This was allegedly to "prevent" the sale of offices, but Folkestone and others thought it unlikely to have this effect. Rather it would just make detection more difficult by driving practices underground. In addition, the bill exempted law offices and parliamentary seats

---

[476] 'Edinburgh Annual Register for 1809', op cit, volume 2, part 1, p234
[477] Ibid, p236

(despite the findings of the East India Company inquiry), so this was hardly the general measure claimed. Nevertheless, the bill was passed. The *Edinburgh Annual Register* concludes that this was "... most humorous. By making the brokerage of offices penal, it empowered every suspected person ... to decline answering, lest he should criminate himself, and thus completely precluded the discovery of the practices which it professed to punish."[478] To underline the point that the effects would be opposite to those intended, the example given in Parliament was of a churchyard that had a 12 foot wall built round it to prevent the corpses being dug up. In practice, however, this made it easier for the resurrection men to remove the bodies unseen. This analogy turned out to be unusually apposite in more senses than one.

The debate on the East India Company inquiry followed on the 25th April.

## Crown and Anchor meeting

On 1st May a meeting took place at the Crown and Anchor calling for parliamentary reform. John Cartwright was chairman of the organising committee while Burdett presided over the meeting itself. Cobbett reports 1100 to 1200 diners, with thousands of people in the surrounding streets.[479]

Cartwright had approached the Earl of Selkirk to act as one of the stewards at the meeting. Despite his family's traditional support for reform, the Earl's response was to refuse. He explained his reasons at length and the letter, dated 25th April, was published.[480] He started off by saying that he had an "abhorrence and contempt for corruption and venality", but now doubted that changes in representation would make sufficient difference on their own. The example from America was that "universal suffrage and frequency of election prove no bar to the misconduct of representatives". As a result, respect for political integrity had declined and yet the American constitution was now the one sought by the reformers in Britain. Meanwhile, the lessons from the French Revolution were

---

[478] Ibid, p238

[479] *Political Register*, op cit, volume XV, no 18, pp685-692

[480] Earl of Selkirk, 'A Letter Addressed to John Cartwright, Esq. Chairman of the Committee at the Crown & Anchor on the Subject of Parliamentary Reform', London, Constable et al., 1809

that the mob did not respect authority, freedom was attacked and despots came to the fore. "Though I do not suppose that the English reformers would imitate the mad fury of the French Revolutionaries ..." their principles were similar and, in Selkirk's view, so might be the effects. The reforms required in Britain were economic as well as constitutional so that personal liberty increased, justice was more equitably distributed and people had the security to enjoy "the fruit of [their] industry". He concluded that constitutional changes alone might "kill rather than cure", saying "... I firmly believe, that amidst violent changes, there is more probability of making our government worse than better ..." Cartwright, Burdett and the other radicals were not discouraged by this reply. It was a recipe for doing nothing, whereas they were determined to do something. This might well prove not to be sufficient, but it was certainly necessary in their view, a starting-point, and possibly a pre-requisite, for further change.

As well as Cobbett's full report in the *Political Register*, and that in the *Edinburgh Annual Register*, Maccoby[481] briefly lists the fourteen resolutions passed at the meeting. These included:

"1.     That it is the grand principle of the Constitution, that the People shall have a share in the Government, by a just representation in Parliament.

"4.     That this Meeting believes that individual patronage in Boroughs has increased since 1793 ...

"9.     That in every department of the State, into which inquiry has been made, scandalous corruptions and abuses have been detected.

"11.    That so long as the People shall not be fairly represented, corruption will increase; our debts and taxes will accumulate; our resources will be dissipated; the native energy of the People will be depressed; and the country deprived of its best defence against foreign foes.

"13.    That the remedy is to be found, and to be found only, in a full and fair Representation of the People in the Commons House of Parliament ...

---

[481] S. Maccoby (ed.), 'The English Radical Tradition 1763-1914', London, A&C Black, 1955 (2nd edition 1966), pp71-73. In addition to those listed here, Resolutions 5 and 6 were specifically directed at sinecures and are covered below in relation to Martin's motion on 8th June.

"14.  That we therefore recommend to every town, city, and county, to take the state of the Representation into consideration, and urgently, but temperately, to apply to Parliament ..."

Two things in particular stand out from these resolutions. Firstly, the modest call in the final resolution for temperate, and democratic, action is far from being a battle cry for revolution. Change was to result from the people making their voices heard, from petitions; "revolutions" don't come much more genteel than this. Burdett and the other radicals were aware of the importance of remaining within accepted conventions, and within the law, if change was to be supported and sustained, but this was in any case their preference. Cobbett reported that a journalist from *The Courier* asked him whether George III should turn MPs out of Parliament as Cromwell had done. Cobbett's reply was that he would wish the House of Commons to be reformed through Act(s)[482] - in other words, legally and democratically. Secondly, the shrewd way in which political reform was linked to patriotism. At the meeting Burdett had proposed a toast to the King and his people who were equally affected by corruption. In his view "The borough-mongering faction, for I will not dignify them with the name of government, have involved our country in perpetual misfortune, by degrading all the wise provisions of our old laws."[483] The result in his view was that the people were oppressed and the King controlled.

Cobbett reported that *The Courier* thought reform was desirable, but had fallen back on the Windham argument that "a time of war is not the proper time".[484] Cobbett disputed this position and countered with a number of alternative arguments, including that constitutional reform through Unions with both Scotland and then Ireland had taken place during wars. Most tellingly, though, he stated that people's faith in reform would make them even more prepared to fight Napoleon in order to safeguard the country's independence. In his opinion, "... we go on ... adopting any thing rather than that, which, by making us *sound at home* [Cobbett's emphasis], would enable us to set the world at defiance."[485]

---

[482] *Political Register*, op cit, volume XV, no 18, p688
[483] '*Edinburgh Annual Register* for 1809', op cit, volume 2, part 1, p242
[484] *Political Register*, op cit, volume XV, no 18, p689
[485] Ibid, p691

## Madocks and the Cashel corruption charge

Four days later on 5<sup>th</sup> May William Madocks (1773-1828)[486], who had been at the Crown and Anchor meeting, accused both Perceval and Castlereagh of corruption. Madocks was of the view that Quintin Dick had been pressurised, primarily by Castlereagh but with Perceval's endorsement, either to vote with the government in the Duke of York affair or resign his seat. Dick had purchased his seat at Cashel through the Treasury and was therefore open to this leverage. (Cashel was to be sold on again to Robert Peel after Dick ceased to be an MP in 1809.) Perceval was furious and stormed out of the House of Commons. It was not necessarily the charge itself to which he objected, so much as the fact that Madocks had given him no prior notice and he had been denied the customary right of immediate reply. Madocks apologised to the House of Commons for disregarding its conventions and the motion was removed at the Speaker's request.

Madocks re-introduced it on 11<sup>th</sup> May in a form that Parliament found acceptable. He argued against borough-mongering, citing four constituency examples of Cambridge, Rye, Hastings and Queenborough (Kent) "each of which places the actual power of returning members ... in the hands of an individual holding sinecures as the reward of borough services to government".[487] These examples were not chosen at random, with Liverpool having been MP for Rye until 1803, while Hastings provided a lengthy list of Treasury figures including William Sturges Bourne and Nicholas Vansittart (1766-1851) as MPs to 1802. George Canning was the MP in 1809, while Vansittart had moved to the notorious Old Sarum, remaining as MP there to 1812. Not only was the practice of borough-mongering immoral, it cost the taxpayer money. In addition, Madocks argued that Castlereagh had threatened Dick that his seat could be removed as rapidly as it had arrived if he did not support the government against Wardle.

Lyttelton, another of the few MPs who had attended the Crown and Anchor meeting, supported Madocks' motion against ministerial corruption. Perceval rejected the imputation of borough-mongering and the accusation that he had connived with Castlereagh in

---

[486] MP for Boston 1802-1820 and subsequently for Chippenham
[487] '*Edinburgh Annual Register* for 1809', op cit, volume 2, part 1, p245

exerting pressure on Dick. Windham's view was that the sale of seats, or borough-mongering, was an integral and indivisible part of the current arrangements. Seeking to change this aspect might unwittingly remove more valuable elements of the constitution as well. The Whig leader Ponsonby also spoke against Madocks' motion (since the sale of seats was common practice on the Whig side of the House too). He thought Castlereagh's behaviour in Ireland at the start of the century had been lamentable, but Quintin Dick had been treated no differently to many others who had been sold their seats. "It could not be justice to select him to be the victim."[488] Madocks' motion was rejected by a majority of 225, with only 395 MPs voting.

In a letter a few days later Quintin Dick wrote to say that Castlereagh had not persuaded him to resign, but that he had decided to do so as a matter of honour. Meanwhile, borough-mongering and the sale of seats were already under scrutiny as a result of the Curwen Bill that had been introduced a week earlier on 4th May. This was more carefully judged than Madocks rash charge of corruption.

## Curwen Bill

Curwen[489] was concerned that a time of war might not be the best time to introduce such a Bill. He also recognised that it might make public agitation worse. Nevertheless, the House of Commons had to respond given that "To them were imputed the corruption, the prodigality, and the waste of public money: the defects in the representation were pointed out as the source of all these evils, and they were called upon to reform it."[490] In Curwen's view Parliament either had to show that the charges were false and refute them, or reform. This would re-establish public confidence in the House.

---

[488] Ibid, p249

[489] John Curwen (1756-1828) had been John Christian until he married his cousin in 1790. He was MP for Carlisle from 1786 to 1790, from 1791 to 1812 and from 1816 to 1820. He then became MP for Cumberland until his death in 1828. He had been defeated at Carlisle in 1812 as a result of his unpopularity after he had seduced the Bishop of Llandaff's daughter. He was out of Parliament for four years before he regained the seat.

[490] 'Edinburgh Annual Register for 1809', op cit, volume 2, part 1, p249

Curwen's aims for the Bill were "for better securing the independence and purity of Parliament, by preventing the procuring or obtaining seats by corrupt practices, and likewise more effectually to prevent bribery."[491] In order to achieve these objectives the main measures were to be oaths against bribery by those elected as MPs, penalties against the sale of seats, and extension of the bribery laws to cover agents with respect to votes and all voters. When the Bill was first introduced, Windham left no doubt about his position, saying that "We have the benefit of the French revolution fresh in our memory: Parliamentary reform is of the same cast and character; it is blindness, infatuation, and madness in the people to think of relieving themselves by pulling the government to pieces".[492] In addition, in his view the Bill could not produce unanimity, but was bound to antagonise one party or the other. He was to amplify the strong views he held against reform in the debate later in the month (see quotation at the head of this Chapter).

Perceval said he was against the Bill because it was bound to increase administration and the associated costs - a canny, if perhaps expected, response from a Chancellor of the Exchequer. However, while he was prepared to see the Bill debated, he went on to say that nobody should be in any doubt that resolutions passed by meetings such as that at the Crown and Anchor did not represent, let alone equate to, wider public opinion. By implication, Curwen's point about public confidence was misplaced.

Another MP George Johnstone (1764-1813)[493] spoke against the Bill on the basis that he thought Parliament was less corrupt than previously. This might be the case, but did not justify further inaction. An equally curious view was the argument put forward in some quarters that it was better to enter the House through corrupt means, but behave honestly when there, to entering without blemish but then to be bought through the influence of the party system thereafter. This appeared to value the independence of MPs ahead of that of electors and elections, but ignored the evidence of seats purchased in the expectation of support in Parliament (as in the case of Quintin Dick).

---

[491] Ibid
[492] Ibid, p251
[493] MP for Aldeburgh 1800-1802 and for Hedon in Yorkshire 1802-1813

When the Bill was debated by the House on 26<sup>th</sup> May, William Smith (1756-1835), MP for Norwich (and another of those who had attended the Crown and Anchor meeting[494]) put forward the proposition that the purchase of seats had certain advantages. While boroughs continued to be bought the government had to compete with others for influence, but if this depended entirely on patronage the government would have the market to themselves. In his view any oath, therefore, "should exclude promises of this kind as well as money".[495] This would provide a further check on Ministers.

Burdett was against the Bill, saying that the House of Commons was not "the Commons of England in Parliament assembled"[496] as it should be, but a much narrower body. The Speaker called him to order, but he was not prepared to be deterred. He followed up his accusation of corruption (see quotation at the head of this Chapter) by saying that the House of Commons could only perform its proper functions of keeping the government in check if it was "properly constituted". It should not comprise lawyers and other adventurers nor be "made a kind of theatre for the exercise of debating powers and political talents".[497] It should provide the "bolts and bars" if it was to ensure the security of the country, not "ornaments". Burdett was also against the proposed oath, as was Cobbett. As far as Cobbett was concerned, any purchase of a seat represented a breach of the existing oath of office.[498] Property as the basis for representation remained the sticking-point, in that "those who have interests to manage ..." are bound to choose the managers that suit them. A fairer system would require the electoral franchise to be greatly extended to ensure much wider representation (but not necessarily, it should be noted, as far as universal suffrage).

From 1<sup>st</sup> June the House of Commons moved into committee to consider Curwen's Bill in detail. The Bill was supported by Charles Abbot, the Speaker of the House of Commons who made his support clear at the start of the sitting (see Table 8). A number of other MPs praised Abbot's views in their speeches. Nevertheless,

---

[494] Though perhaps as much out of curiosity and a sense of duty as a Whig MP, or to urge restraint, than necessarily because he was in sympathy with the objectives.
[495] 'Edinburgh Annual Register for 1809', op cit, volume 2, part 1, p257
[496] Ibid
[497] Ibid, p258
[498] Political Register, op cit, volume XV, no 19, pp721-723

Perceval made sure that [the Bill] was heavily amended. In particular, he insisted that the words 'or implied' were removed from the phrase prohibiting contracts for money 'express or implied'. This ensured that government patronage through payments in kind, rather than cash, could continue. Perceval recognised that the time for change was fast approaching and that his role was to ensure, as far as possible, that this was planned and coherent. It might be argued that he was prepared for reform, but not for revolution.[499] Despite Wilberforce's cautious support for the oath, Perceval ensured that it was removed. He said that it could not be defined well enough what it referred to.[500]

According to Cannon, Perceval's objections were 'not unreasonable'[501], while Harvey says that the handling of the Bill was a tactical victory for the government and Perceval: "... [it] underwent extensive surgery at the hands of Perceval, who, according to Ponsonby, left only three and a half lines of the original draft."[502] Effectively, the Bill had been neutered by the time of its third reading on 12th June; "nugatory"[503] in Burdett's words. That only 182 MPs voted no doubt reflects this. As Thorne says elsewhere, "... [the Bill] was admitted to be a dead letter".[504] Folkestone proposed an amended title to recognise this: "A bill for more effectively preventing the sale of seats in Parliament for money, and for promoting a monopoly thereof to the Treasury by means of patronage."[505] He was supported by 28 other MPs when this was put to the vote.

Liverpool supported the revised form of the Bill when it reached the Lords, describing "... parliamentary reform ... as a dangerous tendency".[506] He had in mind that radical reform could only be promoted by undermining the House of Commons through scandal. By contrast the reformers might argue that Parliament was achieving this end without any help from them; indeed the recurrent scandals demonstrated the necessity for reform. As an illustration

---

[499] As in my article 'Spencer Perceval: Private values and public virtues', The Historian, Number 98, Summer 2008, pp6-12
[500] 'Edinburgh Annual Register for 1809', op cit, volume 2, part 1, p276
[501] Cannon, op cit, p155
[502] Harvey, op cit, p249
[503] Thorne, op cit, volume III, p551
[504] Thorne, op cit, volume I, p355
[505] 'Edinburgh Annual Register for 1809', op cit, volume 2, part 1, p280
[506] Ibid, p281

of the Act's consequences, Thorne says that it drove Treasury activity underground, but did not remove Rye and the other boroughs from Treasury control.[507]  In other words, this outcome was very far from, if not directly opposite to, Curwen's original modest and moderate intentions.

Some people thought the Curwen Bill valuable nevertheless.  In Madocks' view it had not only raised the profile and generated debate on the issues, but had demonstrated that a stand had to be made.  He distinguished the position whereby someone who sold their vote, or stole a goose from the common, could be hung, but it was thought acceptable to buy a vote, sell your seat or steal the common from the goose.[508]  As he might have said, this was a nonsense.  Cobbett devoted eleven pages in number 23 of the *Political Register* to setting out his objections to the Bill[509], but had already come to the conclusion that "... it is valuable as having drawn forth a confession from a majority of the House ... that *something* ought to be done".[510]

## Sinecures

As well as these measures designed to promote political reform, there were onslaughts on the necessity for economic reform. Resolutions 5 and 6 at the Crown and Anchor meeting were directed specifically at this:

"5.    That in the Act (commonly called the Act of Settlement) ... it was asserted, and recognised as a Constitutional principle, that no person who 'has an offer of place or profit under the King, or receives a pension from the Crown, shall be capable of serving as a Member of the House of Commons'.

---

[507] Thorne, op cit, volume II, pp464-480   Although the population of Rye was 2187 in 1801, it had less than 20 freemen eligible as voters.  Treasury control was exercised through offering posts in the customs service to voters.  Similarly, Thorne quotes from Canning's letter of 6th October 1809 (after Canning's resignation from the government as well as after the Curwen Act) wondering whether the agent Milward (the agent at Hastings) could be persuaded to support him at the next election.  In the event Canning was invited and successfully contested Liverpool in 1812.

[508] *Political Register*, op cit, volume XV, no 22, p843

[509] *Political Register*, op cit, volume XV, no 23, pp872-883

[510] *Political Register*, op cit, volume XV, no 22, p842

"6.	That it appears by a Report laid on the table of the House of Commons in June last [i.e., 1808], that 78 of its Members are in the regular receipt under the Crown of £178,994 a year."[511]

The requirements for economic and political reform were bound together for radicals such as Burdett, but it was recognised that tackling some of the worst excesses of patronage, such as sinecures, might have to be addressed on their own.

The slogan of "no corruption" adopted by the Whigs in the 1807 general election had led to a parliamentary committee looking at sinecures.	Henry Bankes (1756-1834), an independent MP[512], chaired the committee. He had hoped to restrict the scope of the inquiry, but had been outmanoeuvred by Perceval who extended it to all places and pensions, perhaps to delay the outcome.	This slowed up the select committee's work and it did not report until the start of 1809.	The report "...revealed that 76 members of parliament at that time were holding offices of some sort costing £150,000."[513]	Bankes' preface to the report identified savings of more than £80,000 per year and a supplement indicated that, of these 76 MP office-holders, 28 held sinecures.[514]

This patronage by the King and government has been described as 'Old Corruption'.	Rubinstein says[515] that the Supplementary Report of the Committee of Public Expenditure in 1809 found that the main sinecures alone came to £356,000 per annum.	While the economic reforms of Burke and Pitt had begun to reduce sinecures and influence, this reduction was to continue to 1830 and did not disappear altogether.	As an illustration that this process was to

---

[511] As listed by Maccoby, op cit, p72
[512] MP for Corfe Castle 1780-January 1826 and for Dorset February 1826-1831
[513] J Steven Watson, op cit, p447
[514] Thorne, op cit, volume III, p131	Colley op cit, p188 says that "In 1809, the House of Commons would establish that well over one million pounds of public money was still being distributed every year, of which only 8 per cent went to reward conspicuous public service.	A year later, it revealed that, despite administrative reform, 250 men and women were still in receipt of sinecures.	To this extent, accusations that the British aristocracy and their relations were, in William Cobbett's words, 'a prodigious band of spongers' had some truth to them."
[515] W.D. Rubinstein, 'The end of "Old Corruption" in Britain 1780-1860', Past and Present, 101 (1983), pp55-86

continue for some time, Rubinstein refers to the Black Book published in 1816 and its 83-page list of Government placemen.[516]

Bankes decided not to press the case at this stage and opted out of the committee for the 1809 parliamentary session. This undoubtedly reduced the momentum. Thorne suggests that Bankes may have been dissatisfied that the report was not more incisive, but it could also have been that he wished to engage as an individual MP with the other corruption inquiries, starting with the Duke of York affair from the start of the session in January 1809. Chairing a select committee might have hampered him in this. Removing sinecures and unnecessary public pensions was a long-standing objective of the MP Henry Martin (1763-1839) to reduce public expenditure and bring about economic reform. Martin took the opportunity provided by the Bankes Committee report to bring forward a motion in April 1809 asking for the government to respond by reducing sinecures. However, the Whigs Grenville and Grey ensured that the motion was watered down. On 8th June Martin moved for legal sinecures to be abolished and, with Whitbread, to limit the number of placemen and pensioners, while Bankes sought for "every superfluous office"[517] to be abolished. The motions were defeated.

Bankes was re-elected to the finance committee from the start of the next parliamentary session in January 1810 and became chairman once again. Reducing government patronage and removing sinecures became the over-riding objective. There were thirteen divisions on the issue by 1812. Martin was added to the committee and Bankes continued to chair it for some time to come.

## Wardle's savings pledge

Wardle had first claimed that he could make savings in public expenditure at the Crown and Anchor meeting on 1st May[518]. He

---

[516] Ibid, p60   He also says that Lord Arden (Perceval's brother and Registrar of the Court of Admiralty) left £700,000 when he died in 1840.  This is a substantial amount today (the equivalent of nearly £31m) and a huge sum of money at the time.
[517] Thorne, op cit, volume III, p306
[518] This was not reported in Cobbett's account of the meeting in the *Political Register*, op cit, volume XV, no 18, but is included in the later version in the 'Edinburgh Annual Register for 1809', op cit, volume 2, part 1, p273

was alleged to have added that these reductions would be so significant that the income tax would no longer be necessary. Ponsonby challenged him to repeat this in the House of Commons. Wardle denied saying that the income tax would no longer be required, but he did re-iterate that his plan would save millions. When he produced his Plan of Public Economy on the 19th June Wardle proposed swingeing cuts in expenditure, particularly by the gambits of granting Catholic relief and cutting a third of the navy budget. The latter was unrealistic and unachievable at a time of war, particularly when Britain's navy was the only edge the country had on Napoleon at this time. Catholic relief was never going to be agreed by a government who had refused this previously. Nevertheless, Wardle was allowed access to the accounts that he asked for. The government did so knowing that his proposed figures would not stack up. They were sure of their ground as Huskisson, in replying to Wardle's speech on the 19th June, had already "… demolished Mr Wardle in a learned survey …"[519] Thorne says that Huskisson had exposed Wardle's plan as "half-baked nonsense".[520] Wardle was "discovered to be no wizard"[521], much to the relief of several Whigs as well as the Tories.

Far from convincing the government to adopt his plan, Wardle continued to be discredited (as the government had hoped) as the year went on. However, the pressure building on the economy could not be so readily ignored. As Chancellor of the Exchequer, Perceval was well aware of both the impact of Napoleon's economic warfare on trade and Britain's national debt, and the resulting impetus for reform that this strain gave rise to. Fortunately, the blockade was having a similar effect on France and her Empire. For example, French customs receipts declined in one year to one-sixth of 1808 levels, her exports fell by 25% in the three years to 1809 and French manufacturers were no longer obtaining the raw materials they required from the colonies. Napoleon changed the system so that French exports had to exceed imports, but allowing this exchange of goods rapidly weakened the system as a whole.

---

[519] Fay, op cit, p75
[520] Thorne, op cit, volume V, p487
[521] Ibid

## Burdett's plan of reform

Burdett brought forward a motion for political reform in the House of Commons on 15th June 1809. The plan he had agreed with other leading radicals previously (including Cobbett, Cartwright, Madocks and Wardle) combined the Crown and Anchor discussions with some of the other electoral proposals they had been pressing. It included extending the franchise to tax-payers, equalising the size of electoral constituencies and bringing all elections to an end on the same day. In addition, it proposed that the length of parliaments should return to a 'constitutional duration'. This form of words had been agreed because, while Burdett had a long-standing preference for three-year parliaments, Cartwright sought annual elections. In presenting the proposals to the House of Commons, Burdett adopted the moderate tone that Curwen had taken when introducing his Bill and that Cobbett had chosen in explaining the Crown and Anchor resolutions to *The Courier*. The reform plan might be radical, but the approach was anything but. Thorne says that Burdett's speech "stressed the conservative and restorative nature of the reformers' objects".[522]

When the House divided, Burdett's motion was defeated by 74 votes to 15. These low figures might appear to indicate that reform was a non-issue for the House of Commons or that ignoring it might be the best way to make it go away. However, even senior Tories had been left in no doubt that the call for reform was growing rather than diminishing. In part the voting figures demonstrate that the Whigs mistrusted Burdett and the firebrand nature of his colleagues such as Cobbett, and failed to support the plan as a result. While the Whig Whitbread might be expected to vote in favour of reform, he was absent on this occasion[523] and, as Briggs says, "... Grey and the Grenvilles were cautious and aloof ..."[524] In addition, Whigs such as Lyttelton paired in favour even though "he had said that he could not go so far as Burdett on the question of reform".[525] Furthermore, fifteen MPs in support of the motion was more than twice the number who had attended the Crown and Anchor

---

[522] Thorne, op cit, volume III, p307
[523] According to Thorne, op cit, volume III, p307, Burdett distrusted Whitbread and saw him as a potential rival. Burdett may even have chosen this date for the debate because he knew Whitbread could not attend.
[524] Briggs, 2000, op cit, p157
[525] Thorne, op cit, volume IV, p481

meeting. This must have been encouraging progress for Burdett and his colleagues, who no doubt felt justified in keeping reform on the parliamentary agenda.

This was mirrored in the attention it continued to receive nationally. Having detailed his objections to the Curwen Bill in one *Political Register*, Cobbett set out the reforms he thought required in the next. Once again he presented these in the form of a letter to the "independent people of Hampshire". This was published on 17th June 1809 and refreshed the proposals Burdett had presented to parliament earlier in the week.[526]

## From Portland to Perceval

As Table 7 and Chapter 5 demonstrate, there was no respite for the government even after the parliamentary recess started in June. Attention shifted away from reform to the war and the government's handling of it. Then in August Portland suffered a stroke and, despite initial signs of recovery, resigned on 6th September. On 21st September Lord Folkestone wrote to Thomas Creevey "Old Portland is going both out of the Ministry and out of the world - both very soon, and it is doubtful which first; but the doubt arises from the difficulty of finding a new Premier, though both Perceval and Canning have offered themselves."[527] Canning soon put himself out of the running after his duel with Castlereagh and subsequent resignation.

George III considered Perceval "the most straightforward man he had almost ever known".[528] Nevertheless, he became Prime Minister primarily because the Whigs Grey and Grenville had turned it down. Boyd Hilton says that Perceval's "administration ... was probably unparalleled for mediocrity and inexperience"[529] with only two Cabinet members in the House of Commons (Richard Ryder and Perceval himself). According to J Steven Watson, if "...any other administration could have been invented, that of Perceval would not have existed".[530] From this unpromising start, however, things rapidly improved – particularly in comparison with the

---

[526] *Political Register*, op cit, volume XV, no 24
[527] Quoted in Gore, op cit, p71
[528] Gray, op cit, p463
[529] Hilton, 2006, op cit, p218
[530] Watson, op cit, p485

preceding government. Perceval's cabinet worked collectively as a team, perhaps because their initial unpopularity brought them together and because Perceval provided co-ordination and skill in continuing to lead the House of Commons.

Perceval appears from the records to have been less sanctimonious in Parliament than some of his contemporaries and he comes across as less priggish than some colleagues who have fared more positively since. Robert Southey is said to have described him as "the best minister we ever had".[531] While it is difficult not to be influenced by this, Perceval did say that a man was less guilty of adultery than a woman. It might be argued that this was in line with the tenor of the times, particularly for Evangelicals, but this does not necessarily make it acceptable. More positively, his wife was one of the few women who contributed to charities in her own name, indicating that Perceval could take an enlightened view of female emancipation in some areas (possibly a natural, even necessary, stance as the father of six daughters?).[532] Perceval was aware of his own deficiencies in talent and was a reluctant Prime Minister. This does not seem to have been false modesty, but reflected his natural humility and a self-deprecating style. He intended to compensate for his deficits through energy and hard work, and was sustained by his evangelical beliefs.

Encouragingly, and perhaps most importantly, the balance had begun to shift in the Peninsular War. The Portland government had made some progress and Liverpool at the War Office now built on this success. Perceval's government was determined to defeat Napoleon, and to bear the costs of doing so.

---

[531] Dick Leonard, 'Nineteenth-Century British Premiers: Pitt to Rosebery', Basingstoke, Palgrave Macmillan, 2008 ranks the twenty Prime Ministers of the nineteenth century, putting Peel and Gladstone first equal and Rosebery last. He ranks Spencer Perceval 12th, ahead of Melbourne, Derby and Wellington.
[532] Lucille Iremonger takes a different view of Perceval in 'The Fiery Chariot: A Study of British Prime Ministers and the Search for Love', London, Secker and Warburg, 1970. But, it has to be said, she appears to reach her conclusions largely on the basis of a psychodynamic and judgemental stance. She takes a similar approach with other premiers.

## 7.    SOCIAL AND ECONOMIC CHANGE AFTER 1809

### To 1812 and Liverpool

The years at the start of the nineteenth century are often thought of mainly, if not solely, in terms of their military impact.  This is not surprising, given that, in the ten years between 1805 and 1815, Trafalgar was followed by the Peninsula campaign, by Napoleon's march on Moscow, by war with America and eventually by Waterloo.  And this is just to take a European and north Atlantic perspective (the sort of historical blinkers that EH Carr[533] warned against fifty years ago).  The southern hemisphere was not exempt from military ambitions and interventions in this period either.  Simon Bolivar is one example, the Peruvian revolution in 1809 another.  In the fifty years after 1776, of course, this was even more marked with the American war of independence, the French Revolution, Napoleon's territorial ambitions beyond France and Britain's colonial exploration and exploits in India, Australia, South America and Africa.

Despite this turmoil, however, military events were accompanied, and in the longer view dwarfed, by the economic, social and political transformations that took place at this time.  The previous Chapters focussed on those of 1809.  The pace generated then was to quicken in subsequent years.  Not all the changes would necessarily have been apparent at the time - but several of them were, not least because military debacle or corruption frequently had implications beyond the conduct of the war and hastened and strengthened calls for reform.  The world did not begin after Waterloo, even for Britain and even though one can accept that historians writing in the first half of the twentieth century might be most struck by, and often give primacy to, the military parallels.  However, Hilton is surely right when he says that 1815 was of purely military significance.[534]  This is more understandable from an early 21st century viewpoint where shifts in historical perspective since 1950 have included the "cold war", the demise of totalitarian regimes in eastern Europe at the end of the 1980s and the dismantling of apartheid in South Africa.  These have then been followed by globalisation, climate change and the rise of third world

---

[533] Carr, 1961, op cit
[534] Hilton, 2006, op cit, p670

economies, with India and China exerting their potential for growth and threatening western hegemony. The military perspective has necessarily been subordinated to the social, cultural and economic ones.

This is not to downplay the military threat posed by France and her empire at the end of 1809. Two (almost) contemporary quotations vividly illustrate this. The first is taken from the Edinburgh Review and the second from a short story by Balzac, one of the most prominent novelists of any time and a leading French observer and chronicler in the first half of the nineteenth century.

"The diadem of Bonaparte has dimmed the lustre of all the ancient crowns of Europe; and her nobles have been outshone and out-generalled, and out-negotiated, by men raised by their own exertions from the common level of the populace."[535]

"The events ... took place about the end of November, 1809, a time when Napoleon's ephemeral Empire had reached the height of its splendour. The fanfares of the victory of Wagram were still resounding in the heart of the Austrian monarchy. Peace was being signed between France and the Coalition. So kings and princes came, like stars, to perform their revolutions around Napoleon, who gave himself the pleasure of dragging all Europe in his train, a magnificent first exercise of the power which he later displayed at Dresden."[536]

The threat was real and of pressing concern, therefore, but should be seen in a wider perspective.

### Portugal and the peninsula

In the Peninsular War Britain had offered an armistice to Junot and his French troops following the battle of Vimeiro in August 1808. The Convention of Cintra seemed to have thrown away any of the advantage gained by victory. Although it had benefits in removing the French army from Portugal for the moment, the humiliating

---

[535] Colley, op cit, p150 follows John Cannon, 'Aristocratic Century: The peerage of eighteenth-century England', Cambridge, Cambridge University Press, 1984 in including this quotation from the *Edinburgh Review* of 1809.
[536] Honore de Balzac, "Domestic Peace" in 'Selected Short Stories', London, Penguin, 1977, p26 (p1 of this story)

terms allowed the defeated French forces and their loot to be repatriated with British help, able to rejoin the war if they chose.[537]

After the Cintra inquiry, and then Corunna and Moore's death in January 1809, Wellington had become the senior general in the Peninsula. Although the government still intended to pursue the same policies as before, Wellington was no longer expected to liberate Spain and Portugal and remove French troops from the Peninsula. Rather his 1809 letter of service put the emphasis on defending Portugal. His arrival in Lisbon in April 1809 was seen as indicating "that England was to make a long and determined effort to establish herself in Europe". By May 1809 Wellington had integrated Portuguese troops with British ones and had a first victory at Oporto. The battle of Talavera was fought in July and the French retreated after two days of fighting. However, Wellington's army had also absorbed heavy casualties and was unable to pursue them. Talavera is said to have "yielded a measure of political, if not military, profit", that gave the cabinet and public in Britain "a success in Spain ... [to] ... avenge Corunna", and gave Spain some hard "evidence of British readiness to give them support".[538] Wellington was made a peer. There was no fighting for the army between August 1809 and February 1810, while Napoleon's defeat of Austria at Wagram enabled him to focus his attention on Spain. In December 1809 he announced that he would lead 140,000 veterans in order to drive Britain from the Peninsula. In the event Napoleon's divorce and re-marriage led him to put Massena in command instead.

Meanwhile, the political crisis in Britain had seen the resignation of Castlereagh, the minister with whom Wellington had most affinity. Perceval's cabinet had replaced Portland's. Perhaps fortuitously, and certainly fortunately, the new Secretary for War, Lord Liverpool, continued to seek Wellington's views on strategic and other issues in Spain and Portugal and to support them as Castlereagh had done.

Although it would be 1812 before the war was over in Portugal, and

---

[537] Charles Esdaile, 'Napoleon's Wars: An International History, 1803-1815', London, Allen Lane, 2007 and 'The Peninsular War: A New History', London, Allen Lane, 2002 provide extensive detail.
[538] Norman Gash article on Wellington in the Oxford Dictionary of National Biography

1814 before it was concluded in Spain, the seeds of Wellington's success had already been sown in these early months. As well as his skills as a general, and support from ministers when he most needed it, other significant factors included his cultivation of the local population by ensuring they were treated properly, with the army paying for supplies rather than taking them, as did the French. In addition, Wellington encouraged and benefited from local information on French deployments to add to the intelligence gathered by his staff, and developed effective mapping of the terrain so that the best routes were identified and advance planning was possible. This should not imply that victory was inevitable. Wellington also depended on luck, as well as on his leadership skills and logistical initiatives. For example, he was under no illusion that Napoleon would have pursued his advantage in ways that Massena did not. A month after Almeida Wellington wrote, "If Bony had been there we should have been beaten".[539] He was perhaps also fortunate that Napoleon invaded Russia in 1812 just before Wellington decided to enter Madrid. The march on Moscow diverted forces that might otherwise have been deployed against the British.

## Perceval and politics in Britain

Perceval had effectively been Prime Minister for some time as both Leader of the House of Commons (while the Duke of Portland, the nominal Prime Minister, was in the House of Lords) and Chancellor of the Exchequer. In addition, his previous roles as Solicitor General and then Attorney General meant that he was well-placed to take the government lead in dealing with the inquiries and corruption scandals of 1809. The records of parliament demonstrate that it was often Perceval who responded first for the government, with Canning then supporting his position. This might mean that Canning's was considered the more authoritative voice, but it is noticeable that he never eclipsed Perceval and rarely supplanted his arguments with more telling ones of his own. The impression generated is that Canning reinforced the government position already set out by Perceval.

---

[539] Maxwell, 1899 quoted in Wellington's DNB entry

Perceval formally became Prime Minister at the start of October 1809[540] on Portland's demise. "Canning and Castlereagh were out of the running after the duel that had led to their resignations, and in addition Canning had alienated the King. Perceval became Prime Minister mainly because George III thought him principled, their views on Catholic emancipation were the same, and, most importantly, he was neither Canning nor a Whig."[541] Perceval continued as Chancellor of the Exchequer since the post would have remained empty otherwise.

Perceval's government was to become solid if unspectacular, but at this stage it was not expected to last. Perceval soon had to deal with the aftermath of the Walcheren debacle, and ultimately with George III's loss of sanity and the Prince Regent. That the future George IV chose not to replace him as Prime Minister as expected says much for his powers and skills.

The government had eventually been forced to concede an inquiry into Walcheren. This began on 2nd February 1810 with the whole House of Commons sitting as a Committee - as it had for the Duke of York inquiry. "Strangers", in other words journalists, were cleared from the galleries, allegedly so that the inquiry was not reported ahead of the official minutes. It fell to Perceval as Prime Minister to attempt to justify the affair. There were three votes in February and March as the inquiry proceeded. Although the opposition were successful in condemning Chatham's reports of the expedition in the first two divisions, the censure motion on 30th March was defeated by 275 votes to 227. This was a government victory, but not as decisive a one as they might have hoped. Walcheren was a high profile issue, and the government had put in substantial effort to mobilise its supporters, but in addition the Canning and Castlereagh factions maximised their importance by changing sides during the votes, only returning to the government lobby en masse in the final division.[542]

---

[540] Perceval replied to George III accepting the post on 2nd October 1809, but other sources date the start of his premiership to 3rd or 4th October. Gray, op cit, p255 says Perceval kissed the King's hands on the latter date.
[541] Gault, 2008, op cit, p8
[542] Thorne, op cit, volume I, p198

John Gale Jones[543] (1769-1838) was one of those who objected to the vote excluding strangers from the Walcheren inquiry and ensured that a debate at the British Forum condemned it. When he then paraded the outcome of the debate (literally on a placard outside parliament), he was found guilty of contempt by the House of Commons and sent to Newgate for four months until the House rose for the summer on 21st June. Burdett sought Gale Jones' release in early March but received only 14 votes in support. Burdett followed up by condemning the House for accusing Gale Jones of breach of privilege, and repeated the charge in Cobbett's *Political Register* on 24th March. Burdett was then accused of breach of privilege himself on 27th March and found guilty on 5th April. The House voted 190 to 152 in favour of sending him to the Tower of London. Both Thorne and Cannon are agreed that this proved a diversion that served to get the Perceval government off the hook of Walcheren.[544]

Speaker Abbot issued a warrant for Burdett's committal to the Tower on Friday 6th April 1810. When Parliament's Sergeant-at-Arms attempted to serve this warrant, Burdett initially indicated that he would submit to it voluntarily. However, he then disputed the legality of the action and said that he would have to be taken into custody by force. Burdett barricaded his house over the weekend "and serious disturbances occurred when troops clashed with the crowds which had assembled".[545] The Sergeant-at-Arms' Hansard report of his attempts to arrest Burdett before he was eventually taken into custody on Monday 9th April 1810 is included in King-Hall and Dewar[546].

The City of London could be relied upon to adopt the reformist line if this matched the interests of the Whigs. It petitioned the House of Commons on 4th May 1810 against the imprisonment of Gale Jones and Burdett, and for "an immediate and radical Reform in the Commons ... and ... a full, fair and substantial Representation [of

---

[543] Gale Jones was not an MP but politically active in the Westminster constituency with Burdett, Francis Place and others, in the London Corresponding Society and in the British Forum, a radical debating society. He had escaped imprisonment for libel in 1797, but was to be jailed again, this time for twelve months, at the end of 1810 for libelling Castlereagh. He was then bound over to keep the peace for three years.

[544] Thorne, op cit, volume III, p307 and Cannon, 1972, op cit, p158

[545] Thorne, ibid

[546] King-Hall and Dewar, op cit, p27

the people]".[547]  However, Burdett's defiance, and the riots over that April weekend, had alarmed many politicians who might otherwise have supported the case for reform.  It set the cause back in parliament, but not in the public mind where Burdett's imprisonment was a cause celebre.  By making him an example, the government had served to martyr him.  It strengthened the public's sense of oppression at the hands of an improper, and unfairly elected, political class.  Burdett remained in the Tower until the summer recess on 21st June, choosing to leave unobtrusively rather than greet the large crowd that had gathered to celebrate his release.  It seems that Burdett chose this course in order to avoid further riots rather than because he did not appreciate the popular support.[548]  Certainly, he had no wish to appear aloof and he was passionate about the need for change.

As had been the case a year earlier, spring was a difficult time for the government.  In 1809 the fall-out from Cintra and corruption inquiries[549] had undermined the establishment and resulted in calls for reform[550], while in 1810 the Walcheren inquiry had destabilised the government, adding to the view that it could not last long, and that it had reacted harshly, probably over-reacted, in the case of Burdett.  In April 1810 Perceval said that sinecures and place-holders were less significant than they had been: "I don't believe there ever was a period in the history of this country, when the enlightened knowledge, the wealth, the strength, the character of the people more directly and powerfully influenced and controlled

---

[547] Included in Maccoby, op cit, pp73-75 from *Blagdon's Political Register*, 9th May 1810
[548] The support for Burdett's position extended beyond London, echoing the national movement for reform that had become apparent during 1809.  For example, Bohstedt, op cit, p158 refers to a congratulatory address from Manchester to Burdett over this imprisonment.  Burdett's background in London and Middlesex, the House of Commons action and the mob's reaction all echoed the Wilkes experience more than thirty years before and the Gordon Riots of 1780. The attacks on parliamentary privilege led to the establishment of a reform society in 1811 and the Hampden Club in 1812.
According to Cannon, 1972, op cit, p161 the latter followed the principle that those who paid taxation were entitled to representation, though with the proviso that they were worth at least £300 pa in landed property.  Cannon says that the general population showed no interest at all.  Many were wary of clubs, associations and reform politics; in his view they preferred the early trades unions, Luddism and even conspiratorial political activity.
[549] See Table 7 above
[550] See Table 8 above

the measures and opinions of the Government."[551]  It was the case that people were better and more speedily informed on political topics and events, but this did not necessarily enhance their influence.  His argument was essentially government propaganda, the "special pleading" that goes with the territory, and an attempt to deny and deflect the impetus for reform.  In May 1810 "... Brand had argued that to reject reform would court military government to hold down the people, [while] Canning retorted that to grant it would promote military government by way of democracy and anarchy.  Either way the future looked bleak."[552]  Canning, in addition to the other arguments with which the Tories justified their resistance to reform, claimed that the balanced constitution (of monarchy, House of Lords and House of Commons) might not survive the extension of democratic representation.  In this view the lower House would become so identified with the people and under their control that it would become all-powerful.  This was an outcome to be resisted as far as he was concerned.

The interests of the reformers and those who feared a loss of control were in conflict.  The resulting stalemate has been summed up by Dickens in his portrait of 'The Parlour Orator':

"'Mr Snobee,' said Mr Wilson, "is a fit and proper person to represent the borough in Parliament."  "Prove it," says I.  "He is a friend to Reform," says Mr Wilson.  "Prove it," says I.  "The abolitionist of the national debt, the unflinching opponent of pensions, the uncompromising advocate of the negro, the reducer of sinecures and the duration of Parliaments; the extender of nothing but the suffrages of the people," says Mr Wilson.  "Prove it," says I.  "His acts prove it," says he.  "Prove *them*," says I.'[553]

In most cases inequalities (including those already identified) had still to be tackled.  While they persisted, the effects were insidious and pernicious - for neighbourhoods and communities as much as for individuals and their families.  For example, "in 1810 nearly a quarter of parish livings were worth less than £100 a year.  The

---

[551] Gray, op cit, p36

[552] Cannon, 1972, op cit, p160

[553] Although Dickens was writing about reform in the 1830s, this also reflects the situation in 1809.  See Charles Dickens, 'The Parlour Orator'.  First published as 'The Parlour' in *Bell's Life in London*, 13th December 1835.  Collected in 'Sketches by Boz', February 1836, London, Penguin, 1995, p274

result was rampant pluralism, absenteeism and careerism, seriously reducing the church's effectiveness at the parish level."[554]   The Lancashire spinners formed a union and went out on strike for "three or four months"[555] in 1810 for improved piece-rates (aligned so that unscrupulous owners could not profit at the expense of mills with higher rates of pay).   The strike covered all the spinners in the region so that those in Manchester could not be undercut by spinning firms in the more rural areas.   It was largely non-violent in Manchester, with many prosecutions under the Combination Acts being thrown out for technical reasons, whereas riot and assault were more common in other areas and led several spinners to be imprisoned.   "The union had planned to conduct a rolling strike, calling out a few mills at a time and supporting them [with strike pay] from the contributions of employed spinners.   But the masters out-maneuvred [sic] them by locking out whole districts, so as to break the unions' [sic] funds."[556]   Despite the hardship, there were strikes again in 1811, and it was claimed by one poor law inspector that "Lancashire Luddism had its roots"[557] in the 1810 strike.

Tilly examined contentious gatherings in the south-east and London in thirteen sample years between 1758 and 1820.   In his comparator years there were more gatherings in 1807 and 1819 than in 1811.   He accepted that his approach was not ideal, especially as it ignored "...the chronology of parliamentary reform as a major issue.   To be sure, our scattered years miss the grand reform debates of ... 1809-1810 ..."[558]   He explained the low figure for 1811 in terms of his focus on the south-east, whereas "in the northern industrial districts, machine-breaking reached a new height" and would peak in 1812.   Arrests increased during the period, whereas deaths reduced.

In December 1810 Perceval re-introduced Pitt's Regency Bill.   This was initially for one year only from February 1811 on a restricted basis.   The Prince Regent had been expected to replace Perceval immediately, but he chose not to do so.   Initially, this may have been in case George III recovered.   Like others, Thomas Creevey looked to the Prince Regent to ask the Whigs to form the

---

[554] Obelkevich, op cit, p313
[555] Bohstedt, op cit, p130 (and mentioned in Chapter 4 above)
[556] Ibid
[557] Ibid, p131
[558] Tilly, 1995, op cit, p102

government from 1811. When this did not happen immediately, Creevey explained in a letter to his wife on 2$^{nd}$ February 1811 that all was not yet lost: "The Prince has written to Perceval ... stating to him his intention ... *not* to change the Government at the present, and at the same time expressing the regret he feels at thus being compelled to continue a Government not possessing his confidence, and his determination of changing it should there be no speedy prospect of his Majesty's recovery after a certain time."[559] But by July delay had turned to disappointment: "... Prinny's attachment to the present Ministers, his supporting their Bank Note Bill, and his dining with them, must give them all hopes of being continued, as I have no doubt they will ..."[560] By the time full Regency powers were introduced in February 1812 Perceval was "confirmed as Prime Minister".[561] Perceval had won the full support of the Prince Regent, with the latter increasingly opposed to Catholic emancipation as well.

The Prince Regent's altered view of the government is understandable, given that it stood firm in the face of disorder at home and Britain's prospects in the Peninsular War continued to improve. In addition, "In the course of the session of 1811 Perceval went from strength to strength". He promoted the plan to build churches in new industrial towns and helped defeat the East India Company's intention in 1808 to restrict missionary work within its territory. Perceval "... was also one of the earliest and keenest supporters of the claims of the Church of England to control popular education, playing a decisive role in founding the church's National

---

[559] Quoted in Gore, op cit, p80

[560] Ibid, p87

[561] Briggs, 2000, op cit, p137   Cannon, 1972, op cit, p162 says that the Whigs stayed aloof from radical politics during 1811 and 1812 because they expected that the Prince Regent would return them to power. He also refers to Ward's speech against reform in the debate on 8$^{th}$ May 1812. Ward (1781-1833) was at this stage the Whig MP for Wareham (his fourth constituency of six), but he was to desert the Whigs when they failed to take office in June that year, moving to join Canning (in whose government he was Foreign Secretary in 1827). Ward opposed reform on the grounds that it would be irreversible and people had already enjoyed 100 years of prosperity under the existing system, with the previous twenty years being particularly good for economic improvement. According to Thorne, op cit, volume V, p480, Ward's attack on democracy was "a greater shock to some ... than Perceval's death" (three days later). Cannon concludes that Perceval was happy to support the Whig and Ward point of view. The reform vote dropped to 88 (53 less than when Pitt had first proposed it thirty years before). It had been 174 (against 248) for Pitt's reform motion of 1785.

Society in opposition to the Lancastrian Society."[562]  The First Lord of the Admiralty Lord Mulgrave is said to have commented that "he only wanted 'something more of the Devil to be a very good premier'."[563]  Grattan identified this resilience and adherence to principles when he said of Perceval that "He is not a ship of the line, but he carries many guns, is tight-built, and is out in all weathers".[564]

The trade crisis of 1811 came on top of, and added to, the monetary difficulties brought about by the war.  Whereas the latter had initially led to increased demand and expansion of the economic system, there was now significant contraction.  According to Asa Briggs "... the boom collapsed, customs receipts and prices fell sharply ... bankruptcies increased, and ... there was large-scale unemployment".[565]  The harvest was also poor, compounding difficulties in previous years.  Boyd Hilton says that "... during the [crisis] as a whole, there was a surge in suicides, which more than balanced the decline in deaths from duelling".[566]

David Ricardo's criticisms of inflation were supported by a House of Commons committee report in 1811.  The run on Britain's gold reserves, and pressures from French wheat farmers, led Napoleon to tighten the embargo by requiring the British to exchange gold for wheat.  He expected that this would increase inflation and reduce the country's will to carry on fighting.  It proved to be a misplaced hope.  Things began to resolve themselves when the Government took out more loans, though not with this purpose.  Trade was completely freed up in 1812 when Liverpool rescinded Grenville's

---

[562] Gray, op cit, p25   Gray says that, following Joseph Lancaster's visit to Northampton in winter 1810, Perceval as the local MP would not support setting up a school based on the Lancaster or monitorial system.  Perceval then helped the Bishop of Durham draft a circular to all clergy advocating that the Church set up a National Society, and persuaded the Prince Regent to withdraw his patronage from Lancaster.  "It was Perceval's most important and least happy intervention in educational problems."  Prochaska, op cit, p51 refers to the support of George III and the royal family for the Lancaster Association so this represented a significant shift.  Dickens mentions a national school in his 'The Beadle' sketch (op cit, p21). The accompanying note says this was an "Anglican day school.  The National Society for Promoting the Education of the Poor in the Principles of the Established Church was founded in 1809, and by 1831 there were 13,000 national schools. The British and Foreign Society administered schools for nonconformists."
[563] Thorne, op cit, volume IV, p772
[564] Cited by Gray, op cit, p468
[565] Briggs, 2000, op cit, p144
[566] Hilton, 2006, op cit, p23

Orders in Council and Napoleon brought the "Continental System" to a close. In the meantime, however, Manchester firms had gone bankrupt in 1810 and a three-day week was being worked in Lancashire by May 1811. Other consequences included increasing costs of provisions, declining wages, changes from paternalism to laissez faire capitalism, and the introduction of inventions that reduced the status of some crafts and craftsmen. As J Steven Watson says, "The remedy of the working man was machine smashing".[567] This was the start of the Luddite riots that peaked in 1812 but went on to 1817.

Perceval then moved to strengthen the government in early 1812 by obtaining Lord Wellesley's resignation as Foreign Secretary and replacing him with Castlereagh. He also added Lord Sidmouth to the Cabinet. Perceval was demonstrating well-developed political skills by this stage and his administration now looked "impregnable". The previous summer Liverpool had praised the authority he had shown in the House of Commons, comparing him to Pitt in this respect.

The government at first resisted an inquiry into the Orders in Council, but finally agreed when confronted by petitions reflecting their unpopularity with British merchants and in order to avoid war with America.[568] The City of London could not miss the opportunity afforded by this crisis and, true to form, on the 28th April 1812 they petitioned the Prince Regent, asking him to dismiss the government and "call to the ... government men ... whose public spirit would stimulate them to effect those reforms ... which at this perilous crisis are absolutely necessary to the restoration of national prosperity ..."[569]

A fortnight later on 11 May 1812 Perceval was assassinated at the House of Commons by an aggrieved merchant John Bellingham[570]. Perceval may not have been the intended target, but he was certainly a symbolic, as well as convenient, one. This was at the height of the Luddite riots and the police were ordered on to the

---

[567] J Steven Watson, op cit, p469

[568] Thorne, op cit, volume IV, p772

[569] Maccoby, op cit, pp75-77

[570] Bellingham was aggrieved by his long imprisonment in Russia, the resulting failure of his business and the lack of support from the British authorities rather than by the Orders in Council.

streets to keep the peace in case Bellingham had not acted alone. "Perceval's death was much mourned by his colleagues at the time. This contrasts with the popular reaction. His murder is said to have led to 'savage rejoicing' among those outside Parliament. (Some people thought the Prince Regent would be next.) This alarmed Robert Southey and others who had welcomed Perceval's strong and dogged war leadership."[571] Perceval had a strong sense of principle[572], doing things out of duty rather than ambition, and recent assessments of him have become as positive about his time in office as they were of him as a person and a parliamentarian at his death.

He was replaced as Prime Minister by Lord Liverpool. The Whigs once again failed to exploit his early defeat in the House of Commons to form their own ministry, with Thomas Creevey[573] referring sarcastically to a continuation of Perceval's government "... such is the worthy *new* Administration" of Liverpool. Liverpool remained in this role for the next 15 years. J Steven Watson says he was a mix of firm decision on the Napoleonic wars and drift at home, while Ingrams is very scathing, claiming that he sought to avoid anything that might have led to change. This is a similar view to that of Feiling[574], who says that Liverpool's motto was "do nothing rather than do harm". In Feiling's opinion, "wait and see" and "laissez faire" might have been coined for Liverpool as articles of faith.

### Robert Owen: A case in point

Two of the five busts on the Leicester Secular Society building are of Tom Paine and Robert Owen. This reflects their contribution to

---

[571] Gault, op cit, p11

[572] For example, Perceval did not accept the Chancellor of the Exchequer's salary when he was also Prime Minister, even though he was entitled to it. Leaving this aside, one issue that remains to be resolved is Perceval's financial health. He is said not to have been well-off, frequently depending on support from his wealthy brother. This is not entirely consonant, however, with the large size of his family, their Elm Grove home in Ealing from 1808 or Perceval's donations to charities and people in need.

[573] In Gore, op cit, p103 Creevey's note is dated 10th June 1812, two days after the Prince Regent had appointed Liverpool Prime Minister. This was almost a month after Perceval's assassination and gives a flavour of how tortuous the negotiations were.

[574] Feiling, op cit, pp19-31

human rights and humanism, and to the politics of change. Owen not only saw the importance of environment and education if individuals were to fulfil their potential, but was ahead of his time in understanding the significance of cooperative societies and rational self-interest to the wider welfare of communities. After taking over New Lanark from David Dale from 1800, Owen was in a position to test out his ideas there. Subsequently, he developed new communities isolated from the outside world to assess his notion that cooperation was preferable to competition. He believed that labour was the source of all value, which led in turn to the trade union movement.

The living conditions of children and apprentices at New Lanark had been improved in 1809 when Owen added Nursery Buildings to the village. He had also planned new schools by this point, but objections from his partners at that stage prevented them being built until 1813. With more sympathetic partners, he opened the Institute for the Formation of Character in 1816. This building was used as a school during the day and by the workers in the evenings. It was effectively the first attempt at adult education.

He has been described as autocratic[575], as a benevolent despot[576] and as a "model paternalist mill-owner and self-made man"[577]. These are not necessarily contradictory, and may have been vital facets of his character in order to put his ideas into practice. His developments at New Lanark put him in the vanguard of changes that were subsequently carried on by Titus Salt at Saltaire, Joseph Rowntree in York and George Cadbury at Bournville. They each included the well-being of their employees in assessing the prosperity of their businesses. These were not just philanthropic changes. They were implemented by businessmen who may have had enlightened principles, but who still had to show a profit. The changes turned out to be in everybody's interests. This seems obvious now, but was not necessarily the case in Owen's day. For example, it was not generally expected that reduced hours would lead to increased productivity, and, while some employers sought to improve their employees' conditions, Robert Owen was unique at this time for understanding that the improved welfare of employees would benefit employers as well.

---

[575] Briggs, 2000, op cit, p249
[576] J Steven Watson, op cit, p553
[577] EP Thompson, op cit, p858

According to GDH Cole's biography[578], Owen regarded "... it as the duty of society to provide useful employment for its members, and set out to devise a plan of social organisation which will achieve this end". In time this became known as Socialism. Jones says that "By the turn of the century [William] Godwin was living in London keeping a bookshop at 41 Skinner Street which became a mecca for free thinkers and a power house of political thought. One visitor was Robert Owen [in 1813] ... Owen and Godwin shared a belief in social reform but differed about the means. Godwin believed that men would see the virtue of acting for the common good of their own volition. Owen felt that there had to be an external authority, such as he was providing at New Lanark, to create the circumstances for improvement: proper schooling, good housing and rules of behaviour."[579] This might help explain why Owen could be seen as autocratic, while he would have said that there was legitimate purpose in this.

Lord Sidmouth and Owen jointly circulated the latter's 'A New View of Society' to governments in 1814 and went through the comments together.[580] At Sidmouth's suggestion it was then sent to bishops, and John Quincy Adams[581] the American ambassador asked for copies for all Union governors. Napoleon is said to have read a copy on Elba. However, William Hazlitt saw this as "old" rather than "new" thinking, harking back to ideas of twenty years before. For example, Hazlitt said that it may have been true but it was not new.[582] William Cobbett was as scathing about Owen's proposals in 1817 for village communities to provide productive work for the

---

[578] G.D.H. Cole, 'Robert Owen', London: Ernest Benn Ltd., 1925

[579] Jones, op cit, p15 He goes on to say that "Another engaged in the debate that characterised 41 Skinner Street was William Hazlitt ... whose mother, as Godwin's did, hailed from Wisbech. In 'On Genius and Common Sense', Hazlitt refuted the idea that man, in all his important activities, is motivated by 'hasty, dogmatic, self-satisfied reason'." He saw feelings as paramount with reason as "the interpreter of nature and genius, not their law-giver and judge." Education should be about sensibilities and emotions as well as intellect; Gradgrind's facts could not be enough (to anticipate Dickens 'Hard Times').

[580] Cole, op cit, pp115ff

[581] He was subsequently the sixth President of the USA 1825-1829. He lived in Ealing from 1815-1817 after Spencer Perceval's death and tried, but failed, to meet Perceval's widow who had re-married after her first husband's death (less than three years later in January 1815).

[582] In an essay on Robert Owen's 'A New View of Society'. See Duncan Wu, (ed.), 'The Selected Writings of William Hazlitt volume 4 - Political Essays', London, Pickering & Chatto, 1998

unemployed as he had been, and was to remain, about Malthus' proposals for population control.   When Owen's proposals were also rejected by authorities still wrestling with the impact of post-war recession and increasing expenditure under the Poor Laws, he sought to develop new communities in the United States.

Robert Owen and Robert Southey had much in common, exchanging ideas when visiting each other in 1816 and 1819. Although their views of politics and political reform were different by this stage, Southey agreed with Owen that education and co-operation were critical routes to economic reform.  Southey wrote of Owen's benevolence in his colloquy on Thomas More.[583]   The Factory Act of 1819 fell short of the proposals Owen had made to parliament, but it began to improve conditions with children restricted to twelve hours work a day.   There was a division in parliament on "Robert Owen's social experiment" [584] a week after the Cotton Factories Act had been put before the House on 7th December 1819 by Robert Peel (senior) who had been seeking to improve conditions for children and apprentices since 1802.  In his 'Address to the Working Classes' in 1819 Owen set out plans for an agricultural village.[585]   In due course this was to become the New Harmony community in America which Owen initiated from 1825. John Quincy Adams was by now the President of the USA and heard Owen speak to a Washington audience shortly after his arrival in America.

Owen attracted many admirers, not least in the Fens where James and Caroline Hill (the parents of Octavia Hill, the social reformer and housing pioneer) "had become fired with enthusiasm for [his] ideas".[586]   Jones goes on to say that "...the unhappy social and environmental effects of the industrial revolution could be countered by the creation of manufacturing and farming self-governing communities providing welfare and education as well as employment.  Because of James and Caroline's efforts Wisbech must have been one of Robert Owen's most important centres.

---

[583] Storey, op cit, pp316-317

[584] Thorne, op cit, volume I

[585] See pp8-9 of
http://www.ibe.unesco.org/fileadmin/user_upload/archive/publications/ThinkersPdf/ owene This article was originally published in UNESCO's *Prospects* journal in 1994.

[586] Jones, op cit, p29

When he came to the town in June 1838 500 people came to hear him."[587] After this visit, "William Hodson, a Methodist preacher and farmer of Brimstone Farm, Upwell ... purchased 200 acres of land on Manea Fen and offered it to the Central Board of Owenites. They pronounced the scheme too small and lacking capital but Hodson was not to be dissuaded and went ahead on his own. In July 1839, possibly with James Hill at their head, a hundred idealists drawn to the project from all over the country marched through Wisbech and on to Manea to take ownership of the land and establish a community according to Owenite principles."[588] Unfortunately, the project soon disintegrated as those who preferred to idle took advantage of those keen to work.

After the collapse of the societies in America, Owen returned to Britain. His leadership of the cooperative and trade union movements was being sought and he found himself at the head of the working class movement by 1834. This Grand National Consolidated Trades Union never fulfilled its promise, partly because some of the main trades stayed separate from it, and Owen sought refuge in the safer co-operative groups. Owen's subtlety had always fallen short of his enthusiasm, and his later years became mired in increasing irrationality. This made, and makes, it easier to ignore his significant contributions, including to education, improvements in factory conditions and working lives, cooperative societies and socialism as a whole.

### After 1812: From Perceval to Peterloo and public expectations of the future[589]

Liverpool's government from 1812 proved to be very stable at home – so stable in fact that it looked to some observers like the absence of policy rather than its implementation. Briggs describes it as "safe". Overseas it continued to prosecute the war vigorously, ensuring that any remaining threat from Napoleon and France was removed at Waterloo. In the years up to 1820 one characteristic that appears most striking is the contrast between a government almost divorced from day to day events at home until forced to

---

[587] Ibid

[588] Ibid, p31

[589] An alternative title for this section might be "Industrialisation and the survival of the fittest". This would be appropriate in view of subsequent developments and apposite given that Charles Darwin was one of those born in 1809.

213

react, and the extreme nature of many of those events themselves as the inexorable progress towards reform gathered pace. It was almost as if popular passions were accompanied by political indifference. This may be what Feiling had in mind when he took such a dim view of Liverpool's inaction. Relaxed might be one description of his administration, comatose another.[590]

Some examples[591] of the popular mood help illustrate the chronology of this time and the government's dilatory, but ultimately harsh, response:

"Southey was unfortunate in coming to the laureate's office [in 1813] at a time of acute social disruption, when political conflicts were savage and apocalyptic hopes and fears all too plausible."[592]

Riots in Littleport, Cambridgeshire took place in 1816 before being suppressed by the Royal Dragoons and the Cambridgeshire Militia. Despite Cambridgeshire being recognised for traditions of dispute that can be traced back to Cromwell at least, and of non-conformity and dissent, the Littleport riots are remembered locally as a major upheaval.[593]

---

[590] This is clearly to belittle Liverpool's considerable political skills. See Boyd Hilton, 'The Political Arts of Lord Liverpool', Transactions of the Royal Historical Society, 1988 (38), pp147-170

[591] Gregory and Stevenson, op cit, pp222-224 provide a considerably longer list of disturbances in Britain over these years.

[592] See Southey's entry in the Oxford DNB

[593] See Muskett, op cit, where they are a significant component of his book and http://www.cambridgeshirehistory.com/cambridgeshire/timeline/index.htm The latter includes

"This general dissatisfaction hotted up and eventually boiled over in Littleport on 22nd May 1816 in the Globe Inn (since removed) where the would-be rioters were angry and inflamed with drink. This situation inevitably led to a riot. They broke into houses and shops in the Main Street, marched on the vicarage and generally caused mayhem. They then decided to march on to Ely where they caused more disruption before returning to Littleport. News reached them that the Militia had been called from Bury St Edmunds and so they decided to barricade themselves in the George and Dragon public house."

Hinde, 1973, op cit, p279 says "To the problems of economic and social adjustment arising out of the industrial revolution were now added the strains created by the difficult transition from war to peace. When the government stopped its wartime spending, there was a sudden and drastic drop in the demand for British manufactures. At the same time, the soldiers and sailors returning from the war were demobilised as quickly as possible and thrown on to the labour market. Less work was to be had and more men were looking for it [in agriculture as well] ... In 1816 barns were burnt, agricultural machinery was smashed and

"... a huge meeting of political reformers was held at the Crown and Anchor tavern in London. ... Burdett thought it prudent to stay away, but Cartwright, Cobbett and [Orator] Hunt were there. ... when Parliament reassembled on January 28, 1817, Hunt ... arrived in Old Palace Yard with a petition in favour of parliamentary reform. On the same day, as the Regent was driving home after making his Speech from the Throne, a stone or a bullet (it was never decided which) pierced the window of his coach. Rightly or wrongly, it was assumed that the 'Pop-gun Plot' was an attempt on the Regent's life. A few days later secret committees of both Houses of Parliament were set up to examine the mass of evidence of supposedly seditious activities collected by government spies and informers all over the kingdom. The committees' reports were alarming, not to say blood-curdling, and the government reacted with shocked severity. It asked Parliament to suspend *habeas corpus*, and by the end of March a bill to prevent seditious meetings had also become law."[594]

For Prochaska this incident "... was reminiscent of the attack on George III's coach in 1795; and the government, as earlier, used it as an excuse to introduce repressive legislation. The Prince Regent ... shared the government's view that the radical leaders sought revolution rather than reform."[595]

The Luddite riots continued to 1817, with the difficult employment conditions resulting in strikes and marches as well. They were to be followed by the Peterloo massacre, demonstrating the anxiety of vested interests at continued agitation for reform. Hansard refers to unrest in the country on 5th February 1818.[596] The election of 1818 was contested that June against a background of reduced civil liberties and reviving interest in reform. Prochaska[597] contrasts the Prince Regent's lifestyle with that of most people: monarchical munificence against humility, piety and poverty. The Peterloo massacre occurred in November 1819 when the local magistrates over-reacted. This was then compounded by the repressive

---

there were bread riots at many places in East Anglia. There was an outbreak of machine-smashing at Nottingham, serious rioting by the unemployed at Birmingham and plundering of food shops at Dundee."
[594] Hinde, 1973, op cit, p280
[595] Prochaska, op cit, p39
[596] King-Hall and Dewar, op cit, p37
[597] Prochaska, op cit, p41

legislation known as "the Six Acts". These were introduced in December 1819 after they had been thrashed out at a dinner hosted by Castlereagh on 22<sup>nd</sup> November. The call for an inquiry into industrial areas was resisted as the seditious meetings bill was debated. "Liverpool's government and most of the middle and upper classes ... feared ... the imminent approach of civil war and revolution."[598] Prochaska says the Prince Regent described the action of the troops as "forbearance".[599]

In February 1820 the Cato Street conspirators planned to murder the Cabinet as they sat down to dinner in Dudley Ryder's house. This was intended to be the first action in a revolution that would result in a republic. The plot was discovered and the five leading conspirators executed.[600]

These uprisings go beyond the ritualised forms of protest that Briggs allows for in rural areas and it is difficult not to raise the same concern as Garside that "The problem ... is to account for the failure of [the] 'revolutionary moment' to materialise."[601] Garside's answer is to endorse the view of Tilly and Schweitzer that "the riots and demonstrations typical of the 1760s and 1770s [in London] came to be replaced over the next fifty years by scheduled meetings and symbolic public assemblies ...".[602] He appears to agree with Hone's opinion that doubted "... the revolutionary commitment of radical leaders, emphasising instead their preference for 'keeping their political options open' and their

---

[598] Hinde, 1973, op cit, p293

[599] Prochaska, op cit, p39

[600] Sir Henry Carr and his wife Lady Jane Carr (Spencer Perceval's widow) were two of the contributors to the reward fund for those officers who discovered the Cato Street conspirators. See the report in *The Times* on 7<sup>th</sup> February 1820.

[601] Garside in FML Thompson, op cit, pp486-487   Garside is writing about London but the same points apply elsewhere. He says, "The nature and scale of political agitation in London between 1750 and 1820 has led many observers to think that London's 'repertoire of contention' came close to revolution. They point to the frequency of industrial disputes, the size of demonstrations, the Gordon Riots (1780), the high degree of political organisation displayed by the London Corresponding Society and the insurrection of 1820 planned by the Cato Street conspirators."

[602] Tilly, C. & Schweitzer, R.A., "How London and its conflicts changed shape: 1758-1834", 'Historical Methods', 1982, volume 15, pp67-78

involvement in a wide range of activities – philanthropic, scientific and educational – in the pursuit of social change."[603]

The lax attitude of Liverpool's government may have encouraged the boundaries to be tested, but they did still exist as the ultimately repressive responses showed. Radical leaders such as Cobbett and Burdett (his 1810 resistance to arrest notwithstanding) had already shown their commitment to the democratic approach. Owen was not alone in preferring cooperation (indeed, Bohstedt traces the evolution from riots to collective bargaining in the nineteenth century[604]) and, once the Combination Acts had been repealed in 1824 and 1825, trade union forms of organisation and collective bargaining became feasible. As the response became more temperate and proportionate, less repressive, non-violent strikes had benefits for the participants as well as for those they were protesting against.

Wages began to recover after 1810 for those whose skills were in demand, but the standard of living for others remained variable and comparable to 1790 levels. The point was not reached when all groups were in a position to test de Tocqueville's theory that revolution comes about as circumstances improve. Meanwhile, the general population continued to be made aware of their limited influence and restricted importance compared to the wealthy and privileged.[605] Although education was beginning to develop, it

---

[603] J. Ann Hone, 'For the Cause of Truth: Radicalism in London 1796-1821', Oxford, Oxford University Press, 1982

[604] Bohstedt, op cit, p209ff

[605] For example, Colley, op cit, p152 states that "Compilations such as THB Oldfield's *Representative History of GB and Ireland* (1816) revealed the extent to which landowners, and particularly members of the peerage, interfered in the electoral process; while the *Extraordinary Red Book* (1816) or John Wade's *Black Book: or corruption unmasked* (1819) spelt out in relentless detail exactly why they bothered to do so. [Wade] ... proved, or seemed to prove, that everyone in the British Establishment had his hand in the till, advanced his own male and female relations and was closely related by blood or marriage to everyone else in high office ..."
Cannon, 1984, op cit, p179 says that "...the discernment of the aristocracy, not as part of the natural and inevitable order of things, but as a separate group, pursuing its own interests, and the dawning recognition that the influence of that group was, if anything, increasing. The author of the 'Black book' in 1820 complained that the aristocracy had 'swallowed up, not only the rights of the people and the prerogatives of the crown, but also the immunities of the church. At no former period was the power of the aristocracy more absolute.' The chronology is

would be some time before this was more than a panacea. A general education system began to be implemented from 1810, with adult education taking place through clubs, Corresponding Societies and Sunday schools. Ragged schools started in 1818 when John Pounds (1766-1839) began teaching poor children without charging fees.[606] Watson says that "All such organisations were ladders to climb out of the state of crowded but isolated savagery"[607], but the ladders were not yet long enough to lead to much social mobility, let alone equality, and it would be many years before they were.

On May 26th 1820 Edward Law (1790-1871), later Earl Ellenborough and Governor General of India, wrote that "The system of the poor law is so execrable that I am convinced that if we do not destroy it, it will destroy us. It demoralises the whole country."[608] But he recognised that this would be no easy task since the Poor Law benefited both rich and poor, the former by the sensation of doling out charity, the latter by receiving it. Ellenborough is said to have been a liberal Tory who, though he supported Castlereagh at this stage, held similar views to Canning. The difficulty was to come up with an alternative welfare system. In the meantime, stability required the current order to be maintained even if the result was "keeping people in their place". Both push and pull forces had their adherents and both were significant factors in the diversion from general disorder. As late as 1827, Canning saw it as his duty as Prime Minister "to hold a middle course between extremes". Hinde says "... to most of his countrymen, who saw the signs of economic and social change all around them but had not forgotten the excesses of the French Revolution, it was what they wanted to hear."[609]

This was a preference for gradual and graduated change, for reform rather than for revolution.

---

doubtful, the case exaggerated and the language melodramatic, but it would be a mistake to dismiss it as no more than radical rhetoric."
[606] Prochaska, op cit, pp364-365
[607] J Steven Watson, op cit, p525
[608] Cited in King-Hall and Dewar, op cit, p40
[609] Hinde, op cit, p466

## Conclusion

Figure 9 on page 175 above includes the potential outcomes from political reform of

> - **meritocracy**
> - **democracy**
> - **uncertainty**
> - **status quo**

It would not be correct to say that the impetus for reform (in 1809, or in the period 1806-1812, or even in the fifty years after 1776) resulted in Britain moving predictably from the status quo to democracy. The shift from a society based on privilege and the influence of wealth did not happen in short order, and the transition was often more crab-like than linear. But this was undoubtedly the direction of travel. The events of 1809 created further pressure and uncertainty in a world that was already unstable, economically and socially, as well as politically and militarily. What had previously appeared as givens and cultural certainties were being overturned. 1809 was a critical year in this transformation.

Britain did not go down the path of revolution and rebellion. The impact for individual people and the unforeseen consequences for society were all too apparent. But the country did move towards political and economic reform - though perhaps more gradually than some might have wished at the time. The populace was often pitted directly against the establishment, traditions of dispute and dissent might result in riot, and there was always the risk of an over-reaction - particularly if people felt themselves or their property to be threatened. On the whole, though, there was a preference for predictable change at a pace which many could accept. In this context the year was **between hope and history**.

A fundamental connection, if not an illustration of these points, lies in Seamus Heaney's re-working of the play 'Cure at Troy'.[610] The quotation from Heaney's Chorus is

---

[610] Referred to in R.F. Foster, 'Luck and the Irish', London, Penguin, 2008, p188

"It means once in a lifetime
That justice can rise up
And **hope and history rhyme**."

Foster describes this as a cliché. It may be today, but it was not in 1809.

# APPENDIX: STABILITY AND INSTABILITY - THE GOVERNMENTS OF 1776 TO 1807

There were eight governments over this period from the concluding years of Lord North's to the brief administration led by William Grenville and known as the 'Ministry of All the Talents'. North was followed rapidly by Rockingham, Shelburne and Portland before Pitt's first administration lasted from 1783 to 1801. The Table below shows that Pitt's two administrations accounted for nineteen years and were only briefly interrupted by the Addington administration from February 1801 to May 1804 after Pitt resigned over George III's failure to endorse his Emancipation of Catholics Bill.

**Table: List of Cabinets from 1776 to March 1807**

| Dates | PM/First Lord of the Treasury | Party | Reason for End of Cabinet/Change of Government |
|-------|-------------------------------|-------|-----------------------------------------------|
| Jan 1770 – March 1782 | Lord North | Tory | North resigned after a vote of no confidence |
| March 1782 – July 1782 | Marquis of Rockingham | Whig | Rockingham's death |
| July 1782 – March 1783 | Earl of Shelburne | Whig | Shelburne resigned after two Commons defeats over American failure to compensate British loyalists |
| April 1783 – Dec 1783 | Duke of Portland | Whig | Portland dismissed over George III opposition to Fox's India Bill regarding the East India Company |
| Dec 1783 – Feb 1801 | William Pitt | "Tory" | Pitt resigned following George III failure to endorse Emancipation of Catholics Bill |
| Feb 1801 – May 1804 | Henry Addington | Tory | Addington resigned due to breakdown of Treaty of Amiens, threat of Napoleonic invasion and lack of support from Pitt. |

| Dates | PM/First Lord of the Treasury | Party | Reason for End of Cabinet/Change of Government |
|---|---|---|---|
| May 1804 – Jan 1806 | William Pitt | Tory | Pitt's death |
| Feb 1806 – March 1807 | William Grenville | "Whig" | Dismissed by George III after disagreement over army commissions for Roman Catholics |

Although most of the administrations after North's were in power only long enough to be faced with, and often destabilised by, one aspect of foreign policy, it was Pitt's first government that had to tackle all of them. By doing so with firmness and certainty, stability in Britain was heightened and his administration continued to expand its support. Pitt did whatever he considered necessary at the time, for example entering into coalition government with the Portland Whigs in July 1794 to ensure national success in response to the declaration of war by revolutionary France. Significantly, this was also the only Cabinet that sustained a clear mandate from George III to govern and was not at odds with his views until the end of its term of office.

Although the Table includes the party to which the leader of the administration belonged, this was not as significant a factor as it became after the deaths of Pitt and Fox in 1806. It was from this date that two-party government began to become a reality. Prior to this, the distinction had been pertinent at disputed elections, but other interests and connections became more relevant in parliament. For example, the cause of Catholic emancipation was something that united many Whigs and Tories (or, at least, members of both parties could see that the potential political benefits outweighed any scruples over principle). George III was against it. Governments that went against the King's view did not survive for long, regardless of their political colour on other matters. Catholic emancipation frequently, but not always, proved to be the defining issue that saw the end of governments during this period. This was the case for Pitt's first administration and the 'Ministry of All the Talents'.

The stability provided by Pitt contrasts sharply with the change around him. For Pitt the foreign challenges came particularly from

France and Ireland, but American support for the French revolution was significant. Similarly, the Irish were dependent on support from France. It had been America that had proved most difficult for his predecessors. It was as if each rebellion was building on previous experience.[611] North's government (see Chapter 1) was followed by three very brief Whig administrations of Rockingham, Shelburne and Portland that lasted less than two years in total.

## Aristocratic Interludes: Rockingham, Shelburne and Portland

Rockingham had previously been Prime Minister for a year from July 1765 to July 1766, but his relationship with George III had rapidly deteriorated and the King had then turned to Pitt the Elder. By 1782 Rockingham represented both the reversal of British policy on America and an aristocratic approach that ensured his re-appointment was anathema to George III. This view was understandable given aspects of what Rockingham stood for. These included linking developments in America, India and Ireland to the excessive influence of the monarchy (in early 1780), making speeches from time to time on the parlous state of the nation, and periodic campaigns against the civil list and the public expenditure it represented. Shelburne and Pitt also supported economic and parliamentary reform, but put forward their proposals in ways that stressed the administrative benefits, and, unlike the approaches taken by Rockingham and Fox, did not antagonise George III.

Rockingham over-played his hand badly in 1780 when North invited him to join the administration. There was no chance that his excessive demands (including for American independence) would be granted and he was taken aback when an early general election was called. When North's resignation was accepted by George III in 1782, it was the Earl of Shelburne who led discussions on the new government, but Rockingham who became Prime Minister. George III had made it clear that he would not negotiate directly with Rockingham, while Shelburne recognised that Rockingham was a stronger candidate than himself. Fox became foreign secretary and continued to favour American independence;

---

[611] Foster, op cit, 1988 refers to the United Irishmen seeing this as an almost linear development. But he points out on p265 that Presbyterian radicalism long pre-dated the American war and events took place in Ireland in the early 1790s that occurred before the implications of the French Revolution could have been understood or assimilated.

Shelburne had responsibility for the colonies and saw independence discussions as a vital part of later negotiations. Inevitably, the two disagreed. Rockingham was ill when he took office and was in no condition to reconcile their views. Critically, little attempt was made to regain George III's trust and confidence. He was already seeking to replace Rockingham when the latter died four months after taking office.

Shelburne then became Prime Minister and, in protest, Fox returned to his accustomed position in opposition – a position, it has to be said, with which he felt more comfortable. Shelburne took personal responsibility for negotiating the peace settlement with America, but it would appear that he was either outmanoeuvred or gave up his position too readily. In particular, it is questionable whether the outcomes adequately safeguarded the interests of British loyalists. He gave way to the American negotiators in their insistence on independence, and on their refusal that America should compensate the loyalists, leaving this up to individual colonies.

American independence was formally recognised by Britain when the Treaty of Paris was signed on September $3^{rd}$ 1783. By this stage Portland was Prime Minister. However, the preliminaries had been agreed by both sides the previous November under Shelburne's premiership and they were sustained thereafter. When these were reported to parliament in December 1782, Shelburne and William Pitt (his Chancellor of the Exchequer) gave opposing accounts to the Lords and Commons respectively on whether American independence was conditional. Needless to say, Fox exploited their differences, especially when evasion seemed to be Shelburne's preferred tactic in the face of further questioning and Pitt was not keen to recant. George III began to doubt his reliance on Shelburne. When North allied himself publicly with Fox from February 1783, with Shelburne's government disintegrating around him, it could only be a matter of time before his resignation was inevitable. Although Shelburne won a vote in the Lords over compensation to British loyalists being decided by individual states (rather than America nationally), the government was narrowly defeated in the Commons. In a second vote in the Commons, Shelburne was defeated more heavily and forced to resign. He remained Prime Minister for a further month until March 1783 to enable the Duke of Portland to form the next administration. It took until April for George III to be convinced that that there was no alternative at this stage and for the tortuous negotiations with Portland to take place. Although they were to develop a good working relationship later (when Portland became Home Secretary in Pitt's coalition government from July 1794), this was not the case at this point. Portland had been closely associated with Rockingham and had been preferred to Fox as the group's leader in opposition to Shelburne. Fox had shown himself to be an opponent of the King's on several fronts over the years, not least in disagreeing over American independence. By allying himself with Fox, North was no longer on the side of the angels as far as George III was concerned.

The King eventually had little choice but to acquiesce in Portland becoming Prime Minister (with the Cabinet including Fox and North), but George III was determined that his government should last as briefly as possible and that William Pitt should be ready and prepared for succession thereafter. He did not have long to wait. The India Bill to reform the East India Company was introduced in the autumn. Although it was supported in the House of Commons, George III let it be known that he would consider anyone voting for it in the Lords as an enemy who had slighted him personally. The Bill was becoming increasingly unpopular in any case. The supervisory board it would create was viewed as a new form of patronage by parliament and specifically by the government (since Portland adhered to the principle that the Board could not be appointed by the monarchy as this would increase royal power). When the Bill was defeated in December, Portland was dismissed.

### Pitt: A Politician for the Time

If the title of the preceding section makes it sound as though the country was waiting for a strong Prime Minister, while the gap was filled by three Whig incumbents, that is correct. More pertinently, however, George III was waiting for a Prime Minister with whom he had a positive relationship, whose views he respected and who could be trusted to deal with the business of the country appropriately. That he should turn out to be a Tory proved to be a bonus for George III.[612] That he should turn out to be William Pitt

---

[612] Ehrman argues that Pitt would not have seen himself in these terms. He would have identified pragmatism and competence as more significant than party allegiance. It should also be noted that Pitt and George III were not personally friendly. Their relationship was based on mutual respect and national interests.

proved to be a bonus for the country as well as the King. Except that George III was not waiting, of course, but actively pursuing Pitt and exercising his prerogative to appoint ministers with whom he could do business.

Much has been written on William Pitt and particularly on the seventeen years of his first administration from December 1783. There is no necessity to attempt to repeat that here.[613] Suffice it to say that his years as Prime Minister up to February 1801 encompassed several factors that would leave their legacy for those who came after. As well as tackling events at home, such as the first Regency crisis, his administration's foreign policy had to address the after-effects of American independence, revolutions in France and Ireland, the rise of Napoleon, and the role of the East India Company. This period also saw Australia being colonised by Britain (in 1788 with convicts being sent to Botany Bay for the first time, a British governor being appointed, and Sydney being founded) and in 1795 the seizure of Cape Colony in South Africa from the Netherlands. Spain had designs on parts of Canada, Russia on the mediterranean area. Military ambition and diplomatic objectives for many countries often accompanied their trade and commercial aspirations. Britain was no different. The challenges, therefore, came from much of the known globe.[614]

Shortly before becoming Prime Minister, William Pitt told the House of Commons in November 1783 with regard to Fox's India Bill that "Necessity is the plea for every infringement of human freedom. It is the argument of tyrants; it is the creed of slaves." This reflected their enmity, but Pitt was also alive to examples of tyranny closer to home – e.g., in rotten boroughs and bribery, and the necessity for parliamentary reform as a result, or the position of Catholics in Ireland. His character was principled, determined and "unbending". Importantly, he maintained his independence from George III in order to maximise his room for manoeuvre. An early example of this, which the King to his credit applauded, was his refusal to become Prime Minister on Shelburne's resignation. At this stage he would have had to rely on Lord North not opposing him. This was

---

[613] See, for example, William Hague, 'William Pitt the Younger', London, HarperCollins, 2004 or in more detail J. Ehrman, 'The younger Pitt', (3 volumes), London, Constable, 1969, 1983 and 1996

[614] For example, there were trade and diplomatic missions to China (e.g., by Lord Macartney in the 1790s), one of the few cultures admired in Europe.

an impractical option that he rejected, taking the view that the associated risks would have outweighed any short-term benefit.

Pitt did not seek out new friendships as Prime Minister, but assiduously cultivated the few close relationships he had already developed.  He was politically aware and adept at all times.  For example, he sought to take advantage of the divisions between the opposition Whigs Fox and Portland in 1792 by offering "individual rewards and vague hints of a wider coalition".  Inevitably, this led his opponents to see him as duplicitous.  He entered a coalition with Portland and the conservative Whigs from July 1794 as the threat of war with France grew.  By this stage Portland had decisively broken with Fox over his attempts to export reform and radicalism from France.

Two of the major issues Pitt and his government had to address were revolutionary France's declaration of war on Britain in 1793 and events in Ireland.[615]  They were to resonate with his successors and have an impact in 1809.  They are addressed in Chapter 1.

## Addington: The "Doctor" and a Remedy but no Cure[616]

It appears that the King never sought, nor approached, anyone other than Addington as a replacement for Pitt as Prime Minister.  Similarly, Pitt never contemplated joining the Whigs in opposition nor moving into opposition himself.  Nor did he expect others to resign with him.  On the contrary, Pitt's view was that Addington's government would require their assistance as the war continued – and especially if it continued to deteriorate.  Canning resigned because his mentor Pitt had (despite the latter's attempts to persuade him against this action).  This was significantly different to

---

[615] Other events of Pitt's time, such as the behaviour of the Prince Regent if not always a full-blown "Regency crisis", or the consideration by parliament each year of the abolition of transatlantic slavery, also had an effect for his successors.  The latter was resolved in 1807 when Grenville made it a government issue and Parliament voted in support as a result.  Pitt had always resisted pleas to make it a government issue in the 1790s.

[616] Henry Addington was the son of William Pitt the Elder's doctor and was often called "the doctor" as a result.  He had been an MP since 1784 and speaker of the House of Commons since 1789.  He was put forward for this post as a loyal member of the younger Pitt's party rather than because of any speaking talents he may have had.

other influential members of the Cabinet (such as Grenville and Dundas), who had chosen to resign because they agreed with Pitt over the principle of Catholic emancipation. The resignations had left vacancies in the government that Addington found difficult to fill. Pitt was also aware that the issue of Catholic emancipation was a matter of deep concern to the King, even affecting his health. Out of respect and admiration (if not affection), Pitt promised not to raise it again while George III was monarch. In theory, this left the way open for him to be re-instated as Prime Minister, or at least to serve under Addington. This did not happen, although their relations remained cordial, with Pitt's brother in his Cabinet initially as Lord President of the Council and then as master general of the ordnance. Addington continued to draw from time to time on Pitt's experience.

'Pitt is to Addington as London is to Paddington' was George Canning's assessment of Addington's regime.[617] Though the government may have been enfeebled by the resignations, it was not as feeble as Canning's views might suggest. It had, on the whole, an effective and hard-working Cabinet, including the future Lord Liverpool as foreign secretary and, from 1802, Castlereagh. Like Pitt's administration, it remained hostile to Napoleon's intentions in Europe, and recognised that peace might be necessary because of Britain's political isolation and domestic problems. Unlike Pitt and unsurprisingly, not least given the resignations, it saw Catholic emancipation as a less pressing issue.

The peace terms were agreed with France by October 1801. Addington had taken personal responsibility for the policy, though checking with Pitt that the economic situation was such that the public finances would not allow for any other outcome. As time went by, the peace treaty seemed to become a goal in itself regardless of the terms that were struck. In the event Britain was required to relinquish all the overseas territories it had acquired (apart from Ceylon and Trinidad), while the French made very limited concessions in mainland Europe. Whatever he thought about it privately, Pitt's public support for the treaty was critical. This was especially the case as others thought it went too far, with Grenville particularly opposed. Nevertheless, the Treaty of Amiens in 1802 was seen as a personal triumph for Addington, as was the

---

[617] Hinde, op cit, p98

accord he struck with Russia, removing their hostility to Britain and opening the way for a future alliance. These events ensured that he was thought of as being independent from Pitt.

Addington followed up in 1802 by reducing the tax burden and improving home defences by removing the use of volunteers. Early in March 1803 he sought to strengthen his position, approaching Pitt and Dundas to join the government, while increasing his distance from the opposition of Grenville. However, Pitt was opposed to this approach and a second attempt by Addington fared even worse.

War with France was re-opened in May 1803. Pitt returned to Parliament and spoke strongly in favour of both the war and Britain's prospects. However, he said nothing about the government. This was taken to imply his disapproval and Canning would have introduced a censure vote at that stage. However, Pitt "said he could not vote for it"[618] and the motion was dropped. It may be that Pitt did not wish to alienate the King, and he considered that support for Addington at this stage would not preclude his being invited to return as Prime Minister later on. Addington was thought at the time to have had little choice but war. It was considered that the administration's strategy and continuing discussions with Russia were entirely appropriate. Britain's declaration of war had ensured that Napoleon was not ready to invade. However, British defences remained an issue.

Pitt continued to avoid outright opposition to Addington in the new parliamentary session from autumn 1803, and maintained that each issue would be considered on its merits. He had not been persuaded by Grenville to confront Addington directly, though Fox and Grenville agreed to cooperate. By late April 1804 Pitt had reacted to Fox's motion on national defence by speaking against Addington's approach. He demanded the government's resignation and obtained it by the end of April as they saw their support slipping away. From a high point at the end of 1802 the government's standing had plummeted. Credibility, competence and capability were again seen to lie with Pitt. The national defences against Napoleon and the influence of Pitt's supporters would remain issues into 1809 and beyond.

---

[618] Ibid, p117

## Pitt's Second Administration

Pitt recognised that he was now dependent on George III. One illustration of this was that the King held out against Fox joining Pitt's second administration, but readily conceded he could join the Grenville government immediately afterwards. Grenville and his supporters were excluded as well. Pitt was left with a weakened administration and Canning was dismayed at the poor quality government Pitt formed. Rather than moving into opposition, Addington adopted Pitt's approach of treating each issue on its merits.

It is worth noting that the new foreign secretary was Dudley Ryder (1st Earl of Harrowby from 1809). He had been a friend of Pitt's for some time, having been in the government (if not yet the Cabinet) since 1789. With the exception of a short break while Grenville and Portland were Prime Ministers from 1806 to 1809, he was to remain in the Cabinet until Canning's death in 1827. In total, therefore, he was closely involved in government for nearly 40 years and was a witness to many events.[619] Addington had joined the government in January 1805, replacing Portland as lord president, while Harrowby had to give up the foreign office at the same time because of ill-health. Both he and Portland remained in the Cabinet as ministers without portfolio.

Pitt developed Addington's links with Russia to form an alliance from July 1805. The third continental coalition that came together later that summer also included Austria and Sweden. Since Britain was at war with Spain, having attacked ships bringing bullion from South America a year earlier, only Prussia stood outside the conflict. Victory at Trafalgar was confirmed in November.

On the debit side, however, there were significant domestic difficulties and several further Cabinet reshuffles in 1805 as a result.

---

[619] Born 22nd December 1762 and died at the age of 84 in 1847. He was aged 46 when created 1st Earl of Harrowby in July 1809. He was Pitt's second in his 1798 duel with Tierney, a privy councillor from 1790, and owned the house in Grosvenor Square where the Cato Street conspirators planned to murder the Cabinet in 1820. He appears in four portraits held by the National Portrait Gallery (including Pitt addressing the House of Commons on the French declaration of war, 1793 and Trial of Queen Caroline, 1820).

Pitt came under scrutiny over Melville's alleged speculation with public funding for the navy. The King prevented Pitt from strengthening the government as he wished in September. In addition, Napoleon decisively defeated the Austrians and Russians at Austerlitz in December 1805. Alongside Pitt's already poor health, this news proved to be the final straw. He died in January 1806 aged forty-six.

# A NOTE ON THE TITLE

In concluding the draft of this book in September 2008, I decided to look up "between hope and history" on the internet for the first time. I was somewhat surprised and taken aback to find that there were already a few books with these words in the title. One was a 1996 book by Bill Clinton (then soon to start his second term as President of the USA) entitled 'Between hope and history: Meeting America's challenges for the 21st century'. A second was 'Divided Ireland: Between hope and history' in the "Understanding Global Issues" series from 2001 and a third was 'Hope and history' by Gerry Adams from 2003. I hadn't read any of these, or was even aware of them as far as I knew, but the title for this book was clearly not as novel as intended.

However, given the significant impact and influence of both America and Ireland on developments in Britain at the start of the nineteenth century, these books seemed apposite. As far as I was concerned, the title had been chosen independently but the symmetry made sense.

Finding a precursor in French, of course, would complete the metaphor. "Between hope and history" translates as "entre l'espoir et l'histoire", but I failed to find any such entries - though "between hope and fear" featured quite frequently. Even the French search engines francite and voila.fr drew a blank.

Bill Clinton spent much of his childhood in a town called Hope, Arkansas. This of course puts a different complexion on his choice of title. I found this out through Matt Frei's 2008 book 'Only in America', since it was not something I was likely to check for myself given that "hope" had a completely different meaning in the context of this book.

# BIBLIOGRAPHY

'The Annual Register or a View of the History, Politics and Literature for the Year 1809', London, Otridge et al., 1811

Aspinall, A. (ed.), 'Later Correspondence of George III', 5 volumes, Cambridge, Cambridge University Press, 1970

Aspinall, A. & Smith, E.A. (eds.), 'English Historical Documents - Volume XI: 1790-1832', London, Eyre & Spottiswoode, 1969

Baker, Kenneth, 'George III', London, Thames & Hudson, 2007

Balzac, Honore de, 'Selected Short Stories', London, Penguin, 1977

Bartlett, C.J., 'Castlereagh', London, Macmillan, 1966

Bathurst, Bella, 'The Lighthouse Stevensons', London, Flamingo, 2000

Bohstedt, J., 'Riots and Community Politics in England and Wales 1790-1810', London, Harvard University Press, 1983

Briggs, Asa, 'A Social History of England', London, Weidenfield & Nicholson, 1983

Briggs, Asa, 'The Age of Improvement: 1783-1867', 2nd edition, Harlow, Longman, 2000

Brown, R., 'Society and Economy in Modern Britain 1700-1850', London, Routledge, 1991

Burnett, John, 'Idle Hands: The Experience of Unemployment 1790-1990', London, Routledge, 1994

Burton, Anthony, 'Canal Mania', London, Aurum Press, 1993

Butler, Marilyn, 'Jane Austen and the War of Ideas', Oxford, Clarendon Press, 1975

Butler, Marilyn, 'Maria Edgeworth: A Literary Biography', Oxford, Clarendon Press, 1972

Cannadine, David (ed.), 'What Is History Now?', Basingstoke, Palgrave Macmillan, 2002

Cannon, John, 'Parliamentary Reform 1640-1832', Cambridge, Cambridge University Press, 1972

Cannon, John, 'Aristocratic Century: The peerage of eighteenth-century England', Cambridge, Cambridge University Press, 1984

Carpenter, Humphrey, 'The Seven Lives of John Murray: The Story of a Publishing Dynasty, 1768-2002', London, John Murray, 2008

Carr, E.H., 'What Is History?', London, Macmillan, 1961

Cash, Arthur H., 'John Wilkes: The Scandalous Father of Civil Liberty', London, Yale University Press, 2006

Castlereagh's Correspondence, volume 6, 26 September 1808

Clarke, John, 'The Price of Progress: Cobbett's England 1780-1835', London, Granada Publishing, 1977

Clayton, Tim (ed.), 'Caricatures of the People of the British Isles', London, British Museum, 2007

Cobbett, William, *Political Register*, London, Hansard,
        Volume XI, 4th April 1807
        Volume XV, January to June 1809
        Volume XVI, July to December 1809

Cobbett, William, 'Rural Rides', London, Penguin, 2001

Cole, G.D.H., 'Robert Owen', London: Ernest Benn Ltd., 1925

Colley, Linda, 'Britons – Forging the Nation 1707-1837', Yale, Yale University Press, 1992

Colquhoun, Patrick, 'Treatise on Indigence', London, Hatchard, 1806

Cookson, J.E., 'The British Armed Nation 1793-1815', Oxford, Clarendon Press, 1997

Craig, David, 'Republicanism becoming conservative: Robert Southey and political argument in Britain, 1789-1817', University of Cambridge, 2000

Curry, Kenneth, 'Sir Walter Scott's *Edinburgh Annual Register*', Knoxville, University of Tennessee Press, 1977

Cutmore, Jonathan, 'Contributors to the *Quarterly Review: A History 1809-1825*', London, Pickering & Chatto, 2008

Deane, P. & Cole, W.A, 'British Economic Growth, 1688-1959', Cambridge, Cambridge University Press, 1969

Derry, John, 'Castlereagh', London, Allen Lane, 1976

Diamond, Jared, 'Collapse: How Societies Choose to Fail or Survive', London, Allen Lane, 2005

Dickens, Charles, 'The Parlour Orator'. First published as 'The Parlour' in *Bell's Life in London*, 13th December 1835. Collected in 'Sketches by Boz', February 1836, London, Penguin, 1995

Earl of Selkirk, 'A Letter Addressed to John Cartwright, Esq. Chairman of the Committee at the Crown & Anchor on the Subject of Parliamentary Reform', London, Constable et al., 1809

FM Eden, 'The State of the Poor', 3 volumes, London, White, 1797

*Edinburgh Annual Register* for 1809, Edinburgh, John Ballantyne & Co., 1811, volume 2, parts 1 & 2

Ehrman, J., 'The younger Pitt', (3 volumes), London, Constable, 1969, 1983 and 1996

Etc., Etc., Esquire, 'Sir Frantic the Reformer; or the Humours of the Crown & Anchor: A Poem in Two Cantos', London, Stockdale, 1809

Fay, C.R., 'Huskisson and His Age', London, Longman Green & Co, 1951

Feiling, Keith, 'Sketches in Nineteenth Century Biography', London, Longmans, Green & Co., 1930

Fitzwilliam Museum, 'Vive la différence! The English and French stereotype in satirical prints, 1720-1815', Cambridge, Fitzwilliam Museum, 2008

Fitzwilliam Museum, 'The field calls me to labour', Cambridge, Fitzwilliam Museum, 2008

Foster, R.F., 'Modern Ireland: 1600-1972', London, Allen Lane, 1988

Foster, R.F., 'The Irish Story: Telling Tales and Making It Up in Ireland', London, Allen Lane, 2001

Foster, R.F., 'Luck and the Irish', London, Penguin, 2008

Gatrell, Vic, 'City of Laughter: Sex and Satire in Eighteenth-Century London', London, Atlantic Books, 2006

Gault, Hugh, 'John Wilkes: A man of principle at a time of change', unpublished, 2005

Gault, Hugh, 'Spencer Perceval: Private values and public virtues', *The Historian*, Number 98, Summer 2008, pp6-12

George, M Dorothy, 'English Political Caricature to 1792', Oxford, Clarendon Press, 1959

George, M Dorothy, 'English Political Caricature 1793-1832', Oxford, Clarendon Press, 1959

Gore, John (ed.), 'The Creevey Papers', London, The Folio Society, 1970 (from Batsford 1963)

Gray, Denis, 'Spencer Perceval – The Evangelical Prime Minister. 1762-1812', Manchester, Manchester University Press, 1963

Gregory, J. & Stevenson, J., 'Britain in the Eighteenth Century, 1688-1820', London, Longman, 2000

Hague, William, 'William Pitt the Younger', London, HarperCollins, 2004

Harling, Philip, 'The Duke of York affair (1809) and the complexities of war-time patriotism', *Historical Journal*, 1996, 39(4), pp963-984

Harvey, A.D., 'Britain in the Early Nineteenth Century', London, Batsford, 1978

Hill, B.W., 'Executive monarchy and the challenge of parties 1689-1832', *Historical Journal*, 1970, 13, pp379-401

Hilton, Boyd, 'The Political Arts of Lord Liverpool', Transactions of the Royal Historical Society, 1988 (38), pp147-170

Hilton, Boyd, 'A Mad, Bad and Dangerous People?: England 1783-1846', Oxford, Clarendon Press, 2006

Hilton, Boyd, "Sardonic grins and paranoid politics: Religion, economics and public policy in the *Quarterly Review*" in Cutmore, J. (ed.), 'Conservatism and the *Quarterly Review*', London, Pickering & Chatto, 2007

Hinde, Wendy, 'George Canning', London, Collins, 1973

Hinde, Wendy, 'Castlereagh', London, Collins, 1981

Hone, J. Ann, 'For the Cause of Truth: Radicalism in London 1796-1821', Oxford, Oxford University Press, 1982

Hunt, Giles, 'The Duel', London, IB Tauris, 2008

Ingrams, Richard, 'The Life and Adventures of William Cobbett', London, HarperCollins, 2005

Iremonger, Lucille, 'The Fiery Chariot: A Study of British Prime Ministers and the Search for Love', London, Secker and Warburg, 1970

Jenkins, Elizabeth, 'Jane Austen: A Biography', London, Gollancz, 1948

Jones, Harry, 'Free-thinkers and Trouble-makers: Fenland Dissenters', Wisbech, Wisbech Society and Preservation Trust, 2004

King-Hall, S. & Dewar, A. (eds), 'History in Hansard 1803-1900', London, Constable, 1952

Landale, James, 'Duel', Edinburgh, Canongate, 2005

Leigh, Ione, 'Castlereagh', London, Collins, 1951

Leonard, Dick, 'Nineteenth-Century British Premiers: Pitt to Rosebery', Basingstoke, Palgrave Macmillan, 2008

Maccoby, S., 'English Radicalism 1786-1832', London, Allen & Unwin, 1955

Maccoby, S. (ed.), 'The English Radical Tradition 1763-1914', London, A&C Black, 1955 (2nd edition 1966)

Macleod, Christine, 'Heroes of Invention', Cambridge, Cambridge University Press, 2007

Madden, Lionel (ed.), 'Robert Southey: The Critical Heritage', London, Routledge, 1972

McCalman, Iain, Mee, Jon, Russell, Gillian & Tuite, Clara, 'An Oxford Companion to the Romantic Age: British Culture, 1776-1832', Oxford, Oxford University Press, 1999

Mitchell, Donald G., 'English Lands Letters and Kings: The Later Georges to Victoria', New York, Charles Scribner's Sons, 1897

Muskett, Paul, 'Riotous Assemblies: Popular Disturbances in East Anglia 1740-1822', East Anglia Records Offices, undated

O'Brien, Conor Cruise, 'The Long Affair: Thomas Jefferson and the French Revolution', Chicago, University of Chicago Press, 1996

O'Connell, Maurice R., 'Daniel O'Connell: The Man and His Politics', Dublin, Irish Academic Press, 1990

O'Toole, Fintan, 'A Traitor's Kiss: The Life of Richard Brinsley Sheridan, 1751-1816', New York, Farrar, Strauss & Giroux, 1998

Owen, Robert, 'A New View of Society and Report to the County of Lanark', edited and with an introduction by Vic Gatrell, London, Pelican, 1970

Pakenham, Thomas, 'Year of Liberty', London, Abacus, 2000

Paxman, Jeremy, 'Friends in High Places: Who Runs Britain?', London, Michael Joseph, 1990

Pearce, Edward, 'Reform! The Fight for the 1832 Reform Act', London, Jonathan Cape, 2004

Polanyi, Karl, 'Origins of Our Time: The Great Transformation', London, Gollancz, 1945

Prochaska, Frank, 'The Republic of Britain 1760-2000', Allen Lane, 2000

Quarterly Review, November 1809, volume 2 number 4, London, John Murray, 1811 (2nd edition)

Riello, Giorgio & O'Brien, Patrick, 'Reconstructing the industrial revolution: analyses, perceptions and conceptions of Britain's precocious transition to Europe's first industrial society', LSE Working Papers in Economic History, 1, 2004

Rounding, Virginia, Review in Guardian June 2007 of Ben Wilson, 'Decency and Disorder: The Age of Cant 1789-1837', London, Faber, 2007

Roy, Donald (ed), 'Romantic and Revolutionary Theatre, 1789-1860', Cambridge, Cambridge University Press, 2003

Rubinstein, W.D., 'The end of "Old Corruption" in Britain 1780-1860', *Past and Present*, 101 (1983), pp55-86

Russell, Gillian & Tuite, Clara (eds), 'Romantic Sociability: Social Networks and Literary Culture in Britain, 1770-1840', Cambridge, Cambridge University Press, 2002

Sampson, Anthony, 'Anatomy of Britain', London, Hodder & Stoughton, 1962

Sampson, Anthony 'Who Runs This Place?  The Anatomy of Britain in the 21$^{st}$ Century', London, John Murray, 2004

Smart, William, 'Economic Annals of the Nineteenth Century, Volume 1 (1801-1820)', London, Macmillan, 1910

Speck, W.A., "Robert Southey's contribution to the *Quarterly Review*" in Cutmore, J. (ed.), 'Conservatism and the *Quarterly Review*', London, Pickering & Chatto, 2007

Spence, Peter, 'The Birth of Romantic Radicalism: War, popular politics and English radical reformism 1800-1815', Aldershot, Scolar Press, 1996

Stein, Richard L., 'Victoria's Year: English Literature and Culture 1837-1838', Oxford, Oxford University Press, 1987

Stevenson, J. (ed.), 'London in the Age of Reform', Oxford, Blackwell, 1977

Stevenson, J., 'Popular Disturbances in England 1700-1832', London, Longman, 1979 (2$^{nd}$ edition 1992)

Stone, Lawrence & Stone, Jeanne C Fawtier, 'An Open Elite? England 1540-1880', Oxford, Clarendon Press, 1984

Storey, Mark, 'Robert Southey: A Life', Oxford, Oxford University Press, 1997

Dennis Taaffe, 'Impartial History of Ireland', Dublin, J Christie, 1809

Thompson, E.P., 'The Making of the English Working Class', London, Penguin, 1980

Thompson, F.M.L. (ed.), 'Cambridge Social History of Britain 1750-1950: Volume 1 Regions and Communities', Cambridge, Cambridge University Press, 1990

Thompson, F.M.L. (ed), 'Cambridge Social History of Britain 1750-1950: Volume 2 People and their Environment', Cambridge, Cambridge University Press, 1990

Thompson, F.M.L. (ed.), 'Cambridge Social History of Britain 1750-1950: Volume 3 Social Agencies and Institutions', Cambridge, Cambridge University Press, 1990

Thorne, R.G. (ed.), 'The House of Commons, 1790-1820', 5 volumes, History of Parliament Trust, Secker & Warburg, 1986

Tilly, Charles, "Misreading, then rereading nineteenth century social change" in Wellman, B. and Berkowitz, S.D., (eds), 'Social Structures: A Network Approach', Cambridge, Cambridge University Press, 1988

Tilly, Charles, 'Popular Contention in Great Britain 1758-1834', London, Harvard University Press, 1995

Tilly, C. & Schweitzer, R.A., "How London and its conflicts changed shape: 1758-1834", *Historical Methods*, 1982, volume 15, pp67-78

*Times Literary Supplement* review of Denis Gray, 'Spencer Perceval – The Evangelical Prime Minister. 1762-1812' 9th January 1964

Tomalin, Claire, 'Jane Austen: A Life', London, Penguin, 1998

Tone, Wolfe, 'Memorandums', 1796

Trevelyan, G.M., 'English Social History: A Survey of Six Centuries Chaucer to Queen Victoria', London, Longmans Green and Co., 1944

Turner, Michael, 'The Age of Unease: Government and Reform in Britain, 1782 - 1832', Stroud, Gloucs., Sutton Publishing, 2000

Tyerman, Christopher, 'A History of Harrow School 1324-1991', OUP, 2000

Walker, Eric C., 'Marriage and the End of War', in Shaw, Philip (ed.), 'Romantic Wars: Studies in Culture and Conflict, 1793-1822', Aldershot, Ashgate, 2000

Walpole, Spencer, 'The Life of the Right Honourable Spencer Perceval', 2 volumes, London, Hurst and Blackett, 1874

Watson, J. Steven, 'The Reign of George III 1760-1815', Oxford, Oxford University Press, 1960

Watts, Michael, 'The Dissenters, Volume ii: The Expansion of Evangelical Nonconformity', Oxford, Clarendon Press, 1995

Weightman, Gavin, 'Industrial Revolutionaries', London, Atlantic Books, 2007

Winborn, Colin, 'The Literary Economy of Jane Austen and George Crabbe', Aldershot, Ashgate, 2004

Winch, Donald, 'Riches and Poverty: An Intellectual History of Political Economy in Britain 1750-1834', Cambridge, Cambridge University Press, 1996

Winn, Christopher, 'I Never Knew That About Ireland', London, Ebury Press, 2006

Wolmar, Christian, 'Fire and Steam: A New History of the Railways in Britain', London, Atlantic Books, 2007

Wrigley, E & Schofield, R., 'The Population History of England 1541-1871: A Reconstruction', Cambridge, Cambridge University Press, 1981

Wu, Duncan (ed.), 'The Selected Writings of William Hazlitt volume 4 - Political Essays', London, Pickering & Chatto, 1998

# WEBSITES

Bank of England
http://www.bankofengland.co.uk/about/history/major_developments4.htm

William Blake
http://www.poetseers.org/the_poetseers/blake

British Prime Ministers
http://www.number10.gov.uk/history-and-tour/prime-ministers-in-history

Calderdale weavers
http://www.calderdale.gov.uk/wtw/timeline/1800_1810/1800_1810_1.html

Cambridgeshire archives
http://www.cambridgeshirehistory.com/cambridgeshire/timeline/index.htm

Cruikshank cartoon at Harvard University
http://oasis.lib.harvard.edu/oasis/deliver/~hou01640

Dartmoor prison
http://www.dartmoor-prison.co.uk/history_of_dartmoor_prison.html

Fencible regiments
http://www.regiments.org/regiments/uk/lists/fen1793.htm,

Gillray cartoons and pictures at the National Portrait Gallery
http://www.npg.org.uk/live/search/person.asp?LinkID=mp01777&role=art

Law Society
http://www.lawsociety.org.uk/aboutlawsociety/whoweare/abouthistory.law

Library Ireland
http://www.libraryireland.com/

Liverpool port
http://www.mersey-gateway.org

London Stock Exchange
http://www.londonstockexchange.com/en-gb/about/cooverview/history.htm

Malthus - Economist article, May 2008
http://www.economist.com/research/articlesBySubject/displayStory.cfm?story_id=11374623&subjectID=348918&fsrc=nwl

Martello Towers
http://www.ecastles.co.uk/martello2.html

Minimum wage in Scotland cotton industry
http://gdl.cdlr.strath.ac.uk/haynin/haynin1005.htm

National Portrait Gallery
http://www.npg.org.uk/

Orders in Council
http://www.napoleon-
series.org/research/government/diplomatic/c_continental.html

Robert Owen
http://www.ibe.unesco.org/fileadmin/user_upload/archive/publications/Thin
kersPdf/owene

Oxford Dictionary of National Biography
http://www.oxforddnb.com/

Quarterly Review
http://www.quarterly-review.org/id1.html

Religious dissent/nonconformity
http://www.buildinghistory.org/Church/Nonconform.htm

Romanticism networks/communities
http://www.cambridge.org/uk/catalogue/catalogue.asp?isbn=97805210260
93
http://www.aber.ac.uk/modules/current/ENM6720.html

Romney Marsh in 19th century
http://www.liv.ac.uk/geography/RomneyMarsh/RM%20Hum%20and%20N
at/19th.htm

Royal Military Canal
http://www.royalmilitarycanal.com/pages/facts.asp

Speenhamland system of poor relief
http://www.workhouses.org.uk/index.html

Strand, London and Crown & Anchor
http://www.british-history.ac.uk/report.aspx?compid=45134

JMW Turner
http://www.tate.org.uk/britain/turner/biog_reputation.htm

Vision of Britain re population density
http://www.visionofbritain.org.uk

Weedon Royal Ordnance depot
http://www.daventrydc.gov.uk/common/includes/filedownload.asp?type=pdf&id=1706

John Wilkes and free press
http://www.south-central-media.co.uk/tuppenny_press.htm

# INDEX

Principal references are in **bold** type. Most entries refer to Britain and Ireland; some minor references are not indexed. Sub-entries are in alphabetical order. n preface refers to the notes; it is followed by the note (rather than page) number.